THEORIES
IN
SOCIAL
PSYCHOLOGY

BASIC TOPICS IN PSYCHOLOGY

Edwin G. Boring, EDITOR

SOCIAL PSYCHOLOGY

LEONARD BERKOWITZ
The Development of Motives and Values in the Child

ARTHUR R. COHEN
Attitude Change and Social Influence

MORTON DEUTSCH AND ROBERT M. KRAUSS
Theories in Social Psychology

BERTRAM H. RAVEN
Interpersonal Relations and Behavior in Groups

THEORIES
IN
SOCIAL
PSYCHOLOGY

❧❧❧❧❧

Morton Deutsch

AND

Robert M. Krauss

Basic Books, Inc.

PUBLISHERS

NEW YORK : LONDON

Ninth Printing

1965 ©︎ by Basic Books, Inc.
Library of Congress Catalog Card Number 65–25230
Manufactured in the United States of America

DESIGNED BY VINCENT TORRE

EDITOR'S FOREWORD

THE ENORMOUS GROWTH of scientific research and activity since World War II has included psychology as one of the recognized life sciences. Psychology now makes no small contribution to the rapid change in Western culture and civilization, a contribution that consists of a stream of new discoveries. There is also to be remembered, however, psychology's contribution to its own maintenance. That lies in teaching, for every academic generation must train the next. The roots of psychology must grow if the branches are to spread and the seeds of new growth germinate in the classroom. Research would ultimately exhaust itself were adequate prior training of the scientists deficient. That fact is now well recognized in principle, if not always in practice.

These short books are designed, in the first place, to make instruction easier. The ablest instructor is inevitably an individualist. He is never content to design his course to fit the idiosyncrasies of the other able man who wrote his text book. A single text, moreover, seldom contains enough material to constitute all the reading a student needs. The instructor will wish to supplement his text and lectures and to have freedom in choosing what he shall add. The availability of many small books packed with solid reading enables the instructor to choose what he wants and makes their purchase by the student practicable.

The other use of these books is to satisfy the intellectual curiosity of intelligent laymen. They are not so technical that professional men and thinking women who are keeping an eye on the advance of civilization cannot use them to understand what the psychologists think and know. The philosopher, the historian, the lawyer, the physician, and the modern mother of grown children can surely employ these books in keeping up with the scientific times.

Since World War II, psychology has been expanding in many directions, forming connections with social science, on the one side, and with biological and physical science, on the other. It has thus been said to be both "sociotropic" and "biotropic" as it turns now toward social science, now toward biological science. Scientific biology is older than scientific sociology, and thus biotropic psychology is older than sociotropic. As a consequence of its youth, scientific social psychology is at present less sure of itself than is physiological psychology or psychophysics, and for that reason Basic Topics in Social Psychology tend to stress the way in which facts are a function of method, to discuss how the facts were obtained, and sometimes to present contradictory findings. Such contradictions are no fault of the author, but rather that of the youthfulness of this science. With social psychology still waiting on maturity, these books give their readers an insight into a science that is still growing up.

Edwin G. Boring

PREFACE

THEORY IS THE NET man weaves to catch the world of observation —to explain, predict, and influence it. This is a book of theories in social psychology. The theorists represented have woven nets of different sorts. Some are all-purpose nets meant to catch many species of behavior, others are clearly limited to a few species; some have been constructed for use near the surface, others work best in the depths. All of the theorists, however, are deeply committed to the view that ideas are important and that data from the world of observation must be enmeshed in a web of ideas if there is to be a significant scientific yield.

Our aim has been to present the major ideas of social psychology in the context of the theoretical orientations from which they have emerged. We have been motivated by the belief that the theories of social psychology are both interesting and valuable. They stimulate inquiry and throw light on many different, and often puzzling, aspects of social behavior. Yet there has been a neglect of theories in social psychology; few books deal with this subject matter. The present work is an attempt to remedy this neglect.

Our coverage of social psychological theorists is representative rather than exhaustive. We have tried to get at the root ideas of social psychology, and, in so doing, we have neglected some of the branches and some of the more colorful foliage on this tree of knowledge.

Our presentation of the various theoretical orientations and theories is both expository and critical. We have attempted to present the different viewpoints on their own terms and in their own terminology, but we have not hesitated to express sharp criticisms, even as we have attempted to avoid carping and nit-picking. Although we expect that some of the theorists cited will disagree with our comments, we hope that they will take their inclusion in this volume as a mark of our esteem.

We have written this book with the student and the educated lay reader in mind. Yet we hope that what we have to say will also be of interest to our professional colleagues and will give them some new insights into familiar ideas. In writing we have striven for clarity, but we have not hesitated to ask the reader to stop and think as he reads, nor have we omitted complex or subtle material because effort is required to grasp it.

We gratefully acknowledge the help of "Garry" Boring; every page has been improved by his deft editorial touch. Mrs. George Ferguson and Mrs. John Shewmon have deciphered our handwritten scribblings and turned them into a typewritten manuscript; to them we are much indebted. Also, we are grateful to the many colleagues and students who have read, commented on, and otherwise helped us with this book.

New York City   Morton Deutsch
July 1965   Robert M. Krauss

CONTENTS

THEORIES
IN
SOCIAL
PSYCHOLOGY

I

THE ROLE OF
THEORY IN
SOCIAL PSYCHOLOGY

WHEN WE ASK ourselves "What is social psychology?" various images arise—a mother tenderly nursing an infant, an angry white man throwing a rock at a Negro student, two friends conversing, a candidate making a political speech at a street corner, a football game, a man writing at his desk, a teacher instructing students, a patient and his therapist. What is the common thread linking these diverse situations to social psychology? It is the social psychologist's interest in understanding *how people affect one another*.

The Subject Matter of Social Psychology

This very broad definition of the subject matter of social psychology is not quite satisfying, for it allows the effect of one person on another to be remote and accidental. In no way does it indicate how the relations of people differ from the relations of molecules; nor does it distinguish the relations of a person to a person from those of a person to his physical environment.

What then is distinctive about the relations of person to person? With people, as opposed to things, psychological events can take

place on *both* sides of a relationship. Each person in a relationship can perceive, think, feel, desire, and act. Each person can,
moreover, perceive that the others can perceive and act and that
their perceptions and actions can refer to him. The capacity of people to be aware of one another and to be affected by one another
as psychological beings means that in a social–psychological relationship the psychological events that occur are influenced by the
perceived or anticipated psychological activities of others (Asch,
1952).

If you push a stone, it cannot react to *you*. It cannot pursue you,
following your varying path as you try to elude it. If you push a
man, he may get angry and chase you, and, if he is fleet enough, he
will catch you no matter how you twist and turn. The outcome of a
nonpurposive system's behavior is blindly dependent upon the
presence or absence of innumerable specific conditions; in contrast, a purposive system adjusts and redirects its behavior in response to information about the discrepancy between its present
position and its desired outcome. The inanimate world—apart
from servomechanisms, cybernetic devices, and the like—is largely
made up of nonpurposive systems. Unlike a rolling stone that is
readily deflected from its course, a person with sufficient "power"
often overcomes quite varied distracting or interfering conditions
to achieve his object by one means or another. Physical objects do
not "wish" to create events that are aimed at producing a given
change in a particular person, nor can they. Only people have the
desire and power to determine the contents of another's psychological activities and experiences. Since the human being is from birth
the terminal focus of actions of others, it is evident that the understanding of human behavior requires that he be understood in his
relations with others. (This point is discussed more fully in Heider,
1958, Ch. 4.)

Person-to-person relationships are distinguished, not only by the
fact that psychological events can take place on both sides of a relationship, but also by their *social* character, that is to say, human
relationships always occur in an organized social environment—in
a family, in a group, in a community, in a nation—that has developed techniques, categories, rules, and values that are relevant to
human interactions. Hence the understanding of the psychological
events that occur in human interactions requires comprehension of
the interplay of these events with the social context in which they

occur. Just as the animal psychologist who is studying the behavior of a rat in learning a maze must know the relevant physical properties of the maze to understand or predict the behavior of the rat in it, so too the social psychologist must be able to characterize the relevant features of the social environment in order to understand or predict human interaction.

Social psychology, then, is concerned with the study of actual, imagined, or anticipated person-to-person relationships in a social context as they affect the individuals involved (Allport, 1954). This broad definition spreads into many detailed concerns when the answers are sought for such general questions as these: What are the effects whose determining conditions we wish to understand? What are the conditions whose consequences we wish to understand? What are the mediating processes that link determinants and their effects? Thus social psychologists are interested in studying the *conditions* that lead a person to conform to another's judgment, the *conditions* that determine a person's attitudes, the *conditions* that lead to cooperative or competitive interrelations. Also, the social psychologist is interested in studying the *effects* of an individual's attitudes on his relations with others, the *consequences* of competitive or cooperative interactions, and similar relationships.

Theoretical Approaches to Social Psychology

There are a number of distinctive theoretical positions that have left their mark on the literature of social psychology and that continue to influence research in this field. The social and historical backgrounds of the differing theoretical approaches are discussed by Allport (1954), Martindale (1960), and Karpf (1932). In part, these special orientations reflect differing conceptions of the nature of man, and, in part, they direct attention to different aspects of the varied subject matter of social psychology. The diverse conceptions of man, in turn, arise out of political and religious doctrines of one sort or another and buttress them. Because of their intimate link to ideological doctrines, conceptions of man are rarely free from political controversy. While there is not space here to describe the connection between political doctrines and conceptions of the nature of man, the reader will note that conceptions of man influence the choice between such political alternatives as the following: racial segregation as compared with racial integration, feudalism versus democracy, military deterrence versus fostering international cooperation as a means of preventing war.

What are some of the major issues or questions about the nature of man that are reflected in the prominent theoretical orientations in social psychology? Some of the recurring issues are listed below:

1. Is man simply a more intelligent animal than other animals, with no unique psychological processes, or do social interaction, language, and man's prolonged dependence on cooperative activities create in him unique psychological characteristics?

2. Is the behavior of man determined by egocentric motives, or may the interests of others be as basic and genuine as "self-interest"?

3. Is human behavior largely irrational and fixed by arbitrary experiences of reward and punishment, or does man comprehend and organize his behavior in the light of his experiences?

4. Is human behavior rooted in a man's biological predispositions, or do social conditions largely determine the form and content of human action?

5. Is adult behavior primarily a reflection of experiences in childhood, or does man develop and remain responsive to his current surroundings throughout his years?

Today, most social psychologists would reject the "either-or" nature of the foregoing questions. They would assert that man is *both* social and biological in nature; that he has the capacity to act in egocentric, animalistic ways without rational regard for future consequences *and* the capacity to act in ways that are distinctively human, unselfish, and rationally concerned with the consequences for himself and for others. How he will act will be determined jointly by the various physical, biological, psychological, and social influences that have confronted him in the past and that he is confronting in his present situation.

Although the current view in social psychology is to stress the conditions that lead man to be "egocentric" or "sociocentric," "rational" or "irrational," rather than to consider him as being inherently one or the other, the major theoretical orientations do indeed partly reflect differing views of man's essence. Thus, the

"Gestalt" orientations assume that man is so constructed that he is principally concerned with developing an organized and meaningful view of his world. The "reinforcement" theorists, on the other hand, posit that behavior is primarily determined by its immediate consequences for pleasure or pain. For them, man's attempt to understand his situation is a derivative of his experiences in the pursuit of pleasure. The "role" theorists start from the assumption that man is, uniquely, socially determined; in their view, the values and criteria that influence what a man will consider as pleasurable and what he will accept as meaningful are determined by his experiences in his role in a given society. The "psychoanalytic" theorists view man as a battleground between man's animal nature and society as represented by his family. According to this view, man's rational powers and adaptive capacities mediate between the conflicting forces and are, in part, molded and developed during the mediating process; experiences in his family during his childhood are regarded as crucial in determining his patterns in the resolution of conflicts and the strength of his adaptive capacities.

We shall consider the four major theoretical perspectives mentioned above in greater detail in the subsequent chapters of this book. But it should be made clear at the outset that none of them are "theories" in any strict sense. Rather they represent general orientations toward the phenomena of social psychology. They suggest types of variable that should be taken into account, but are not deductive systems from which clear, testable hypotheses can be derived. The major theoretical approaches in social psychology are the products of its infancy. It is characteristic of a science in its early stages to develop theories that are ambitiously inclusive and vague in respect of their details. There is, however, growing evidence that social-psychological theorizing is moving in the direction of developing "theories of the middle range," a phrase coined by Merton (1957) to refer to "theories intermediate to the minor working hypotheses, evolved in abundance during the day-by-day routines of research, and the all-inclusive speculations, comprising a master conceptual scheme."

Thus the theories discussed in this volume affect the working psychologist in a subtle but rather pervasive way. They guide his choice of the phenomena that he will study and his selection of the concepts that he will employ in analyzing them. To some extent they influence the choice of the techniques he uses in his research, for each theoretical pattern has its own methodological tradition.

The current trend toward "theories of the middle-range" has a tendency to blur somewhat the lines dividing the different theoretical classes. Often it is not possible to categorize a given piece of research as being in the tradition, say, of Gestalt theory or reinforcement theory. It is, however, difficult to understand fully and appreciate much of the current work in social psychology without a knowledge of its historical and theoretical antecedents.

The Nature of Theory

In discussions of the nature of scientific theory, it is common to state some ideal criteria that have to be met before a theory can be properly considered "scientific." It is well to realize that in science, as in everyday life, ideals are rarely realized. In practice, science is an untidy affair in which ideals define the objectives to strive for rather than the procedures for attaining them. Theories are intellectual tools for organizing data in such a way that one can make inferences or logical transitions from one set of data to another; they serve as guides to the investigation, explanation, organization, and discovery of matters of observable fact. (For lucid discussions of the nature of theory construction see Braithwaite, 1953; Campbell, 1920; Kaplan, 1964; Margenau, 1950; and Nagel, 1961.)

Theories in the physical sciences commonly have three distinguishable components: (1) an abstract calculus that is the logical skeleton of the theoretical system and that implicitly defines the basic notions of the system; (2) theoretical constructs that supply some flesh for the skeletal structure of the abstract calculus in terms of more or less familiar conceptual or visualizable materials; and (3) rules of correspondence that link some of the theoretical constructs to the concrete data of observation and experiment.

A "calculus" is a deductive system that is represented symbolically in such a way that for each logical principle of deduction there is a corresponding rule of symbolic manipulation. (This matter is discussed more fully in Braithwaite, 1953.) A calculus has the scientific virtue of being a deductive system in which the deductions are made according to explicit and well-defined rules; being explicit, the deductions are open to public verification and even mechanization. Moreover, the deductive process can take place without reference to any specific empirical content and is thus relatively invulnerable to the biases and preconceptions that often exist with regard to scientific subject matters. In addition, the variety of existing abstract calculi together with the possibility of creating new ones allow the scientist to search for a calculus that will be particularly fruitful in organizing the particular subject matter with which he is concerned.

The theoretical orientations and theories in social psychology do not, however, typically employ abstract calculi. Rather, almost invariably, they use the rules for deduction that are implicit in the syntax of everyday language. Thus the "derivations" from most of the theories in social psychology are usually not unequivocal, or strictly logical, for they skip steps, they depend on unexpressed assumptions, and they rest on the criterion of intuitive reasonableness or plausibility rather than on formal logical criteria of consistency. The disadvantages of everyday language in formulating a scientific theory have been noted and widely commented on by many philosophers of science.

Yet everyday language is an indispensable tool for a young science. A scientific theory, unlike a mathematical or logical system, is not purely a deductive system; it has relevance to observable events in the real world. For it to be fruitful, the "grammar," or logical structure of a theory, and its "vocabulary," or set of theoretical constructs, must somehow fit with each other in such a way that empirically meaningful predictions can be made. Since the grammar of everyday language is not illogical and since its vocabulary has relevance to significant events in the real world, the vernacular is, after all, a useful tool with which to work during the process of acquiring the insights and knowledge necessary for the formulation of a theory that is unambiguous *and* significant in its empirical implications. The usefulness of everyday language lies in its plasticity; it can be molded into more or less precise forms to fit different circumstances. It permits one, as knowledge grows, to move gradually from implicit to explicit reasoning, from vague to well-defined concepts, while maintaining contact with a constantly enlarging intuitive understanding, which is the soil from which every science grows.

Theoretical constructs or concepts form the vocabulary of a theory. A concept may be regarded as an idea that links together observations or other ideas in terms of some common property. Indeed, the development of new concepts is one of the most productive aspects of scientific theorizing. Newton's observation that the fall of an apple from a tree and the maintenance of the moon in its orbit could both be understood in terms of the concept of gravity paved the way for revolutionary changes in physical theory. The *theoretical* meaning of a construct is fixed by its interrelations with the other constructs in the theoretical system of which it is a part; its *empirical* meaning is fixed by the rules of correspondence or by such operational definitions as link the construct to observable events. An operational definition defines a concept in terms of the procedures for making the specific observations that constitute the empirical evidence for the use of the concept; for instance, there are two kinds of length, tape-measured length and triangulated length, and these lengths are not interchangeable (unless there is a further operation for identifying them). Not all theoretical constructs have direct empirical meaning; some constructs may serve only as connecting links among other concepts that do have direct empirical reference. Defining a concept is no easy matter, since a full definition requires a statement of its interrelations in the system of concepts of which it is a part (to define such a concept as "goal," one would have to define other such concepts as "motive," "intention," "success," "failure," "expectation," "attraction") as well as a statement of the procedures involved in the observation of the phenomena that refer to the concept. Thus, there is no simple way to answer such questions as "What is an electron?" or "What is an attitude?" except as one presupposes an implicit understanding of related concepts and a knowledge of the rules of correspondence linking the specified concept to observables.

Although no rules for inventing constructs can be specified, it is evident that a theory will be fruitful to the extent that it contains constructs that meet the requirements of (1) logical fertility (such constructs enable logical inferences to be made), (2) multiple connections (the constructs are not isolated from one another but, rather, are so richly interconnected that it is possible to go from one to another by various routes), and (3) empirical extensibility (some of the constructs can be related to observables in such a way that a variety of equivalent empirical definitions can be given to any specific construct). Figure 1–1 illustrates a multiply-connected, empirically extensible set of constructs. Such concepts as c′ and c″, which are not multiply-connected, have no value in a theoretical system; the set of concepts that are not connected directly or indirectly with observables (those encircled by a dotted line) form a logical, but not a scientific, system.

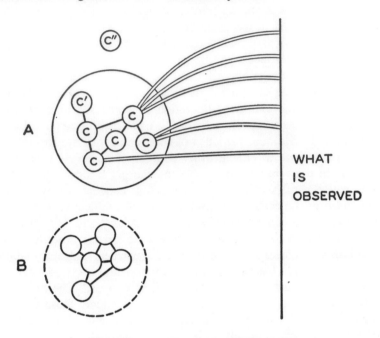

FIGURE I–I. Concepts and Systems

The double lines represent empirical connections between a concept and what is observed; empirical connections are established by rules of correspondence or operational definitions. The single lines represent logical connections between concepts; the logical connections reflect the abstract calculus or logical skeleton of the theoretical system. The set of concepts that are empirically linked to observables (system A) forms a scientific system; the set of concepts that have no linkages to observables (system B) forms a logical, but not a scientific, system. Such concepts as c′ and c″, which are not multiply-connected, are of no value. (Suggested by Margenau, 1950.)

Without rules of correspondence to link some of the constructs in a theory to observables, there is no way of ascertaining or testing its empirical consequences. Even when observables can be coordinated to constructs, however, it is rarely the case that any given observation or experiment, by itself, will be crucial in determining whether a particular hypothesis that is deduced from a theory will be rejected or accepted. If the results of an experiment are negative for a given hypothesis, one may "save" the hypothesis by rejecting as inappropriate the particular operational definition of the construct involved in the hypothesis. Whether one rejects the hypothesis or the operational definition will be determined by one's comparative investments in the operational definition and in the theory from which the hypothesis was derived and the ease or difficulty of modifying the one or the other. Thus, there is a certain arbitrariness in the empirical definition of concepts; in part, they are defined so as to enable a theory to have fruitful empirical consequences. In addition, the rules of correspondence are formulated in such a way as to enable other competent observers or experimenters to perform similar operations and get similar results; that is to say, the rules of correspondence link concepts to operations that have an objective, repeatable, and intersubjective character. Apart from the general criteria of "fruitfulness" and "objectivity," it is not possible to formalize with any precision the procedures for establishing a correspondence between constructs and observables. As Nagel (1961) has pointed out, "experimental ideas do not have the sharp contours that theoretical notions possess." The processes involved in scientific inquiry are not only or mainly those that are involved in logic; the establishment of fruitful and objective rules of correspondence is mainly an intuitive, creative affair.

Let us illustrate our discussion of the nature of theory by reference to a well-known "middle-range" theory in social psychology, the "frustration-aggression" theory (Dollard, Miller, Doob, Mowrer, & Sears, 1939). This theory employs four major concepts: "frustration," which is defined as "that condition which exists when a goal-response suffers interference"; "aggression," which refers to a class of acts that are designed to injure someone or something; "inhibition," which refers to the tendency to restrain acts because of the negative consequences one anticipates from engaging in them; and "displacement," which refers to the tendency to engage in acts of aggression that are directed, not against the source of frustration, but against another target. These concepts are interrelated by the following system of interlocking hypotheses:

1. The amount of frustration is a function of three factors: the

strength of instigation to the frustrated goal response; the degree of interference with the frustrated goal response; and the number of goal-response sequences frustrated.

2. The strength of instigation to aggression varies directly with the amount of frustration.

3. The strongest instigation aroused by a frustration is to acts of aggression directed against the agent perceived to be the source of the frustration; progressively weaker instigations are aroused to progressively less direct acts of aggression.

4. The inhibition of any act of aggression varies directly with the strength of the punishment anticipated for its expression. Punishment includes injury to loved objects and being prevented from carrying out a desired act, as well as the usual situations that cause pain.

5. The inhibition of direct acts of aggression is an additional frustration that instigates aggression against the agent perceived to be responsible for this inhibition and increases the instigation to other forms of aggression. There is, consequently, a strong tendency for inhibited aggression to be displaced to different objects and expressed in modified forms.

6. The expression of any act of aggression is a catharsis that reduces the instigation to all other acts of aggression.

From these basic hypotheses of the theory, one can "derive" a large number of subsidiary hypotheses. The derivations are plausible inferences rather than logical deductions, because they involve unexpressed assumptions and rely on the implicit meanings of everyday terms. Thus, it is plausible to infer from the above hypotheses that a man whose boss has turned down a request for a salary increase is more likely to hit his son who disturbs him while he is reading the newspaper than is a man who has not been rebuffed by his boss. There is, however, an unexpressed assumption that the salary request was made recently. Suppose, though, it had been made five years before his son had been born? Certain unstated assumptions about the effects of time are important to the theory. Also, such key terms as "interference," "goal response," and "direct" have no precise theoretical meaning, but, rather, are defined implicitly in terms of everyday usage. Nevertheless, despite these limitations, the frustration-aggression theory permits one to make plausible inferences, and it gives coherence to a variety of phenomena.

For the theory to have predictive value, it is not necessary for all of its constructs to be operationally defined. Thus, "frustration" is theoretically defined by its linking of the constructs "interfered goal response" and "aggression," each of which can be empirically defined. Of course, the theory would be empirically richer if "frustration" were also directly coordinated with observables, but even without this coordination the theory obviously has empirical consequences.

What rules of correspondence are to be used to give an empirical definition, for example, to the construct "aggression"? This is, as we have seen earlier, a matter of arbitrary choice. On the one hand, one does not want to affront common sense unnecessarily; yet, on the other hand, neither does one want to discard hastily a theory that is useful in some respects. Consider the proposition that frustration leads to aggression unless the aggressive response is inhibited. There is, of course, a good deal of evidence that the interference with a goal response often produces problem-solving behavior and constructive activity rather than activity that is commonly thought of as "aggressive." One can either broaden the empirical definition of aggression to include such activity (problem-solving behavior is designed to "destroy" the problem) or one can revise the theory. One might, for example, revise the theory by distinguishing between types of frustration (as between "threat" and "deprivation") and postulate that "threat," but not "deprivation," is linked to aggression (see Maslow, 1954, for a discussion of "threat" and "deprivation"). The revised theory might postulate that interference with certain types of goal response lead to "threat," but not "deprivation," unless the strength of deprivation exceeds a certain threshold or that specific types of interference have this result. Recent contributions to the frustration-aggression theory are contained in Berkowitz (1962) and Buss (1961).

Concluding Comment

Social psychology is in its infancy. It has only begun to identify a distinctive subject matter relating to human interaction. Being in its infancy, it is still largely dominated by theoretical approaches that are based on implicit conceptions of the nature of man. None of these approaches is sufficiently explicit in its psychological assumptions, in its mode of logical inference, nor in its empirical referents to permit unambiguous testing of its implications. In short, none of these orientations is a "theory" in the sense of theories in the physical sciences. Nevertheless, a theoretical point of view does indeed stimulate and guide research, a testimony to the human capacity to extrapolate "beyond the information given." In subsequent chapters, we shall examine the basic ideas underlying the various approaches to social psychology and explore briefly the research that they have stimulated.

2

THE APPROACH OF GESTALT PSYCHOLOGY

THE MOST PERVASIVE influence in social psychology during the past twenty years has been and continues to be the theoretical writings and research of the psychologists who have been identified with the point of view of Gestalt psychology. The reason for this extraordinary influence is probably due to the happy but fortuitous conjunction of two attributes of the Gestaltists that are only peripherally related to their theoretical orientation. Unlike both the role theorists and the psychoanalysts, the Gestalt psychologists, having always been experimentally oriented, have developed in the process of experimenting on social psychological phenomena a varied assortment of experimental techniques that make possible a laboratory investigation of problems that hitherto had not been thought of as amenable to experimental study. Studies of "democratic" and "authoritarian" group leadership, of group structure, of intragroup communication, of interpersonal trust and suspicion, of social conformity, of attitudinal change, of affiliation have now become feasible because of this Gestaltist experimental orientation.

Nevertheless, the experimental approach of the Gestaltists would not have had so great an impact on social psychology had it not been accompanied by a willingness to take naïve experience as a fruitful starting point for investigation. The reinforcement theorists, who also have an experimental approach, have been unwilling to start with naïve experience; for this reason, their work in social psychology has been remote from the significant phenomena of everyday life.

Gestalt psychology initially emerged as a rebellion against the methodological bias of the older structuralism and associationism of orthodox German psychology which assumed that psychological events have to be explained in terms of the combination of elementary local sensations and associations. The Gestaltists protested that direct experience is organized and that the experience of local events (for example, the stimulation of a sensory receptor at a given instant of time) is determined by the organized whole of which it is a component. In their rejection of elementistic doctrines, they affirmed the need to observe and understand psychological events as they occur in direct experience as a necessary first step in the development of a systematic psychology.

In effect, the Gestaltists asserted that it is scientifically legitimate to be interested in naïve experience and that a "respectable" psychologist can study the phenomena of everyday experience—hope, power, influence, leadership, cooperation, attitudinal change. This faith encouraged those who were attracted to social psychology because of their concern with existing social life to feel that a scientific attack on significant social phenomena is feasible.

Theoretical Orientation of Gestalt Psychologists

Although the theoretical orientation of the Gestalt psychologists does not explain their impact on social psychology, it is nevertheless true that Gestalt theory has affected the work of such influential social psychologists as Lewin, Heider, Asch, Festinger, Krech and Crutchfield, Newcomb, and the various investigators who have been affiliated with the Research Center for Group Dynamics, initially at the Massachusetts Institute of Technology or, later, at the University of Michigan.

The classical statements of Gestalt theory are given by Köhler (1929) and Koffka (1935). Essentially, there are two key notions. One is that psychological phenomena should be conceived as occurring in a "field"—as part of a system of coexisting and mutually interdependent factors having certain properties as a system that are not deducible from knowledge of the isolated elements of the system. The second basic notion is that certain states of the psychological field are simpler and more orderly than other states and that psychological processes act to make the state of the field as "good" as prevailing conditions allow. In other words, the conceptual model underlying the Gestalt orientation envisages a complex process with many part events that interact until a certain best end-state is reached. The means by which the best end-state is reached may vary according to the prevailing circumstances; means can be substituted, one for another, since the same end-state can be reached by different routes (there may be variability of the specific means, but invariance of their *direction* in relation to the preferred end-state).

This Gestalt view was developed from the study of perceptual processes. Its two key notions are that perception is organized and that the organization tends to be as good as the stimulus conditions permit. Let us consider some of the implications of the first notion in perceptual psychology and look for analogous implications in social psychology.

1. *If perceptions are organized, then some aspects of perception will remain constant despite a change in all of the elements in the situation being perceived, so long as the interrelations among the elements remain the same.* Thus, if all the notes in a song are raised half an octave, the melody (the organized unit) will not be changed. A square will be identified as a square if the lines composing it are colored or replaced by dots. Analogously, in social psychology, one would expect that in organized social interactions, some of the patterns of interaction will remain invariant despite replacement of the individuals participating in the interaction. Thus, a football game will still be identifiable as such even though substitutes replace the original players. A bureaucracy will retain many recognizable features despite a complete turnover in its personnel.

2. *If perceptions are organized, then the perception of any element will be influenced by the total field of which it is a part.* Thus, even though the retinal images of two objects are identical in size, the object that is perceived to be farther away will be perceived as being larger. The word "drive" will be perceived as referring to motivation or to golf depending on the organization or context in which it is perceived. Similarly, in social psychology the meaning of the behavior of an individual will be very much influ-

enced by his perceived social role and by the perceived social context or frame of reference in which it occurs. Thus, the same words will be interpreted differently if they are used by a private reprimanding a captain rather than by a captain reprimanding a private (Deutsch, 1961). A man disrobing in the locker room of a gym will be reacted to rather differently from someone doing the same thing in Times Square. The appalling poverty in Hong Kong will seem much worse if one has just come from the United States than if one has just come from India.

3. *If perception is organized, then some of its characteristics of organization will emerge; these will be the interrelations of the entities being perceived rather than the entities themselves.* Thus, a melody is the perceived interrelation among notes. Similarly, the perception of movement is a relational perception. In social relations, the role of husband cannot exist except in relation to the role of wife. Also, such social psychological phenomena as immorality, cooperation, loyalty, and leadership cannot occur in the completely isolated individual (one can only behave immorally or cooperatively in relation to one or more other persons). Social relations involve the relations of at least two people and, as such, are not completely predictable from knowledge of the isolated individuals.

Characteristics of Good Perceptual Organization

Now that we have seen some of the implications and social psychological analogies of the idea that perception is organized, let us consider the Gestalt view that the organization tends to be as "good" as the stimulus conditions permit, or, in other words, that perceptual organization is neither arbitrary nor haphazard but is directed toward achieving a certain ideal state of order and simplicity. The properties of this ideal state have never been specified with precision. Underlying the earlier Gestalt view, however, was the notion that the organization of physical events (as in a soap bubble, a raindrop, an electric field) reflects certain dynamic processes and that there is a similarity in form, an isomorphism, between these dynamic physical processes and psychological processes. Social psychologists in the Gestalt tradition are less likely to stress the isomorphism of the physical and psychological processes of organization and more likely to attribute many of the features of the perceptual organization of complex events to learning in a socially organized environment; still, like the earlier Gestaltists, most social psychologists place emphasis on the role of such central processes as perception and cognition in the understanding of behavior. Thus they are likely to use the term "perceptual field" rather than "stimulus" and "goal-directed behavior" rather than "response."

Although the properties of good perceptual organization have never been clearly specified, the Gestaltists have stated some principles of perceptual organization that have implications for social psychology. These principles are described in relation to some common phenomena to which they are applied.

   1. *Assimilation and contrast.* The "maximum-minimum" principle, the most general and most vague of the Gestalt notions, posits two basic kinds of simplicity: a minimum simplicity of uniformity and a maximum simplicity of perfect articulation. Thus, perceptual organization is, in a sense, bipolar—it will either be directed toward minimizing stimulus differences so that the perceptual field becomes homogeneous or toward accentuating them if the stimulus differences exceed a certain level or if there is an abrupt discontinuity between parts of the visual field. In Koffka's words (1935, p. 109), "either as little or as much as possible will happen." The specific form that such perceptual differentiation takes tends to maximize some stimulus differences so that parts of the perceptual field *contrast* with one another and to minimize stimulus differences within the contrasting parts (see Figure 2–1). (The tendency toward minimizing stimulus differences is referred to as the process of assimilation.) Thus, a dark gray figure on a black background may be assimilated to the background so that the entire field is perceived as black; on the other hand, if the difference between the gray and black is sufficiently great, the gray figure may be contrasted with the black background and seen as whiter than it would otherwise be seen. Similarly, in social psychology, there is considerable evidence that we tend to perceive a person in a way that assimilates him to his group (to many Americans one Chinese waiter looks very much like another Chinese waiter) or which contrasts him with his group (a red-haired Negro), depending on the extent of the differences between the person

FIGURE 2–1. Assimilation and Contrast

The ring is seen as a uniform gray in spite of the fact that contrast should be operating. That is because the ring is seen as a whole and each half is assimilated to the other half. Divide the ring by placing a pencil along the boundary between the black and the white fields. Assimilation then breaks down, since the ring no longer appears continuous and contrast is free to operate. Thus, the left half of the ring on the black ground appears brighter than the right half on the white ground. (Adapted from Krech & Crutchfield, 1958.)

and his group. Also, we tend to assimilate our perception of a person's action to our perception of the actor (the meaning and evaluation of a statement will usually be such as to be consistent with our view and evaluation of the source of a statement). Thus, the meaning of the statement, "I hold it that a little rebellion, now and then, is a good thing, and as necessary in the political world as storms are in the physical," is interpreted rather differently if it is attributed to Thomas Jefferson (its actual author) or to Lenin. When Jefferson is perceived as its source, American students usually interpret the word "rebellion" to mean "peaceful agitation and change"; with Lenin, "rebellion" is usually equated with "revolution."

2. *Perceptual grouping.* Max Wertheimer (1923), one of the founders of the Gestalt school, was the first to state a number of "principles" for determining what will be perceived as being grouped together or unified in the visual field. Others have elaborated his views so that, currently, homogeneity is thought to be

based on: (1) the *common fate* of the elements perceived (for example, they move together); (2) their *similarity* (for example, they have the same color or same luminosity); (3) their *proximity* (for example, they occur in close spatial or temporal proximity); (4) a *common boundary* (for example, the perceived elements are separated from the remainder of the field by an abrupt discontinuity); (5) the tendency to group elements that together make a *good form* (that is to say, one that is symmetrical or balanced, complete or closed, continuous or smooth, orderly or predictable rather than random, simple rather than complex); (6) the tendency to group elements functionally in terms of a *cause-and-effect relationship* (for example, to see a billiard ball that strikes another ball and imparts motion to it as being part of the same perceptual organization); (7) *past experience* or custom that has led to similar responses to the various elements; and (8) *set* or *expectation* that the elements are to be grouped together.

Some of the foregoing principles of perceptual grouping are illustrated in Figure 2–2.

It is evident that the principles for grouping may be in conflict with one another in some particular situation—for example, grouping by proximity may conflict with grouping by good form. In general, the Gestaltists consider such factors as proximity and similarity less critical than good form in determining perceptual organization. They have not, however, developed their views in sufficient detail to be able to specify with any assurance what will happen when different principles of perceptual grouping conflict with one another.

In social psychology, there has been a wide application of notions analogous to those involved in the principles of perceptual grouping. Thus, in discussions of whether a collection of individuals will form a group and of how cohesive a group they will become, emphasis is placed on such determinants as social proximity, the similarity of peoples' attitudes and backgrounds, their common experiences of success or failure, the distinctiveness of a group or person from the other people nearby, the consonance of personalities with one another, expectations about interrelationships, and other parallels of this sort. In effect, the factors determining whether an individual will perceive himself as belonging to a given group are similar to the factors that determine the grouping of elements in the visual field.

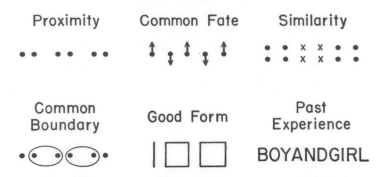

FIGURE 2–2. Examples of Perceptual Grouping

"Proximity" leads to the perception of three pairs of dots. Grouping is by "common fate," when some dots move in one way and others in another, or by "similarity," when dots that look alike are grouped together. Perceptible "boundaries" may decide which dots are grouped together. In the fifth figure, the five vertical lines are separated into groups by the fact that two pairs of them contribute to "good forms," i.e., to squares. In the last example, the ten letters divide at once into three words if the "past experience" of the perceiver has been with the English language.

The Gestalt "grouping principles" are also relevant to the study of social perception. Thus, Zillig (1928) demonstrated experimentally that poor performance is attributed to unpopular children by their classmates: *similarity* in evaluation of the act and the actor groups them together. The well-known phenomenon of "guilt by association" (the notion that a person takes on the characteristics of the people with whom he is seen) may be a kind of grouping by *proximity*. Grouping by *common fate* appears in the tendency to see the underprivileged as forming a cohesive social group. The tendency to think of Frenchmen as being alike may reflect grouping by *common boundary*.

The Gestalt view that perceptual organization tends to be as "good" as possible, that certain configurations are preferred because of their simplicity and coherence, has been the starting place for a number of influential theories in social psychology, such as Heider's theory of cognitive balance (1946; 1958), Newcomb's theory of communicative acts (1953), and Festinger's theory of cognitive dissonance (1957). These theories are all based on the central idea that an organization or structure of beliefs and attitudes or of interpersonal relations can be imbalanced, disharmonious, dissonant, or incongruous, and that when imbalance exists a tendency will arise to change one's beliefs and attitudes until they are balanced. The change may occur by alteration of the reality to which the beliefs and attitudes refer or by direct modification of the beliefs.

Like the earlier approach of Gestalt psychology to perception, these newer theories of social psychology emphasize that the *motivation* for directed action can arise from *structural* considerations. Thus, they express implicitly the belief that an important determinant of man's behavior is his requirement for an orderly and coherent view of his relations to his world. The imbalances considered in the social psychological theories are not, however, simply the dissonances in the impersonally perceived external world discussed by the earlier Gestaltists, for self-attitudes and attitudes toward others become components of the configuration that seeks consistency. In striving for a view of his world that is consistent with his view of himself, an individual may grossly distort the objective reality.

Later, in this and the next chapter, we consider the balance and dissonance theories in greater detail. Here, let us indicate the scope of these theories by citing some illustrations of their applications. Configurations that are balanced are, for instance, those that imply (assuming that we like ourselves) that we like the persons and things that "belong" to us; that our friends are also friendly to each other; that we like what our friends like. On the other hand, if we dislike ourselves, we will not like things that belong to us or like people who are friendly to us. Imbalance would be created, for example, if one learned that a good friend has stolen money from a blind beggar; that a deeply rooted habit is injurious to one's health; that one has made the wrong decision in going to one college rather than another. One exposes oneself to imbalance by belonging to a group that contains members whose opinion is markedly different from one's own, by listening to a political candidate of an opposing party, by doing something one dislikes. Imbalance can be prevented or removed by avoiding, denying, distorting, negating, isolating, or reinterpreting the dissonant information or by buttressing the challenged beliefs with social support or modifying the challenged beliefs so that they are not inconsistent with the new information. It is, unfortunately, the case that none of the balance or dissonance theories are formulated in sufficient detail to enable one to make specific predictions about how balance will be achieved when imbalance occurs. Nevertheless, some steps have been made in this direction by Rosenberg and Abelson (1960).

Among the theorists in social psychology whose work has been deeply colored by the Gestalt orientation, the names of Kurt Lewin, Solomon Asch, Fritz Heider, and Leon Festinger stand out. Lewin's work, which undoubtedly has had more impact on social psychology than that of any other theorist, will be discussed in the next chapter, as will Festinger's. Here we may briefly characterize the approaches of Asch and of Heider.

The Orientation of Solomon Asch

Much of Asch's theoretical writing, which is most fully expressed in his *Social Psychology* (1952), is a protest against those psychological formulations about human behavior and experience that derive mainly from the study of nonsocial, indeed nonhuman, behavior. He asserts that the study of man as a social being requires its own perspective, which must start from some conception, however tentative, of what it is to be human. An adequate view of man would include as a minimum that he possess unusual intellectual powers, that he can act with reference to the ideas and ideals of right and wrong, even when he violates them. He assumes that people enter into the world with a structure that can respond to social conditions and with capacities for entering into social relations.

Asch's basic contention (1952, p. 127) is:

[The] decisive psychological fact about society is the capacity of individuals to comprehend and respond to each other's experiences and actions. This fact, which permits individuals to become mutually related, becomes the basis of every social process and of the most crucial changes occurring in persons. It brings within the sphere of the individual the thoughts, emotions, and purposes of others extending his world vastly beyond what his unaided efforts could achieve. It brings him in a far-flung relation of mutual dependence, which is the condition of his development into a person. . . . It alters the psychological scene for each, since to live in society is to bring into a sensible relation private and public experience. It is also an irreversible step; once in society we enter into a circle of mutuality that cannot be undone.

Asch's view is that man's psychological processes become transformed in society. He becomes self-conscious; he becomes oriented to the future and to the past, as well as to the present; motives and goals arise out of his ability to perceive and compare himself in relation to others. Asch rejects the view of man as egocentrically oriented. He writes (p. 320): "The ego is not dedicated solely to its own enhancement. It needs to be concerned with its surroundings, to bind itself to others, and to work with them. . . . [A]ccentuation of the self is often a response, not to powerful ego-centered tendencies, but to the thwarting of the need to be a part of one's group, to know that one is respected and liked, to feel that one is playing a part in the lives of others. . . ." He rejects the thesis that a society can be based on egocentric individuals, each concerned with getting as much as possible for as little as possible.

Asch asserts further that man's enlarged sense of alternatives and possibilities introduces at the center of human life a permanent tension between what is and what might be. The ends of life are no longer merely to live, but to live a significant and meaningful life. His views, in this respect, are somewhat similar to the views of such religious philosophers as Kierkegaard, Buber, and Tillich, who stress that man is both a part of nature and apart from nature, that man is the only animal aware of his own separateness and identity, that he is the only animal aware of his mortality, and that he is the only animal aware of his imperfection and of his culpability. Out of these awarenesses, new perspectives and problems arise. Asch is one of the few experimental social psychologists who has had the boldness and imagination to recognize that an adequate social psychology must not lose sight of what is distinctly human.

Although Asch's formulation of his central thesis (the transformation of man in society) suggests a program of developmental research to study how children in different social environments acquire their particular concepts and methods of relating themselves to their social world, his research in social psychology has taken a different tack. Much of his research has consisted of demonstrating the Gestalt tenet that social experience is not arbitrary, that it is organized so as to be coherent and meaningful. Descriptions of three of Asch's important experiments follow.

The Formation of Impressions

While Asch (1946) has done a number of interrelated experiments on the formation of impressions, we shall consider only one. In this experiment, a list of personal characteristics was read to each of two groups, "A" and "B." Except for one term, the list was identical for both groups:

A. intelligent – skillful – industrious – warm – determined – practical – cautious.
B. intelligent – skillful – industrious – cold – determined – practical – cautious.

After hearing one or the other list, the subjects had to write a brief impression of the person to whom the characteristics applied. They also were instructed to select from a checklist of pairs of traits (such as "generous-ungenerous," "shrewd-wise") the item for each pair that best fitted the impression that they had formed. Rather striking differences in impression of the person resulted from the two lists. Impressions based on list "A" were generally far more positive. The subjects consider the "warm" person to be more generous, happier, better-natured, more humorous, more sociable, more popular, more humane, more altruistic, and more imaginative. Little difference is seen with regard to reliability, importance, physical attractiveness, persistence, seriousness, restraint, strength, and honesty. When "polite" is substituted for "warm" and "blunt" for "cold," the differences in impressions resulting from the two lists are relatively minor. The attribute relating to "warm-cold" is seen to be much more central to our conception of a person than that of "polite-blunt." Other experiments demonstrate how the centrality or peripherality of the "warm-cold" dimension can be influenced by the context of other terms with which it appears, and how the first terms in a series may establish a context in which successive terms are perceived.

Asch concludes from these experiments (1) that one strives to form a complete impression of a person even when the evidence is meager; (2) that the characteristics of a person are seen in inter-relation—the intelligence of a "warm" person is viewed differ-

ently than the intelligence of a "cold" person; (3) that impressions
have structure—some traits are perceived as central and determining, others as peripheral or dependent; (4) that each trait possesses
the property of a part in a whole, influencing and being influenced
by the organization of which it is a part—two people, who are
charming but otherwise dissimilar, do not appear to have the same
charm; (5) that existing impressions set the context within which
other impressions are formed; and (6) that apparent inconsisten-
cies prompt a search for a deeper view that will resolve the con-
tradiction.

The Understanding of Assertions

Asch (1948) has sharply criticized the doctrines of suggestion,
prestige, and imitation in social psychology. He has indicated
that these doctrines rest on the assumption that the association of
a statement with a person of prestige results in a "blind" change of
its evaluation; although the object of judgment itself remains un-
changed, a new evaluation arbitrarily becomes associated with it.
Asch's critique asserts that the change of evaluation of a statement
due to the influence of prestige on it results from an alteration in
the meaning of the statement. The same statement attributed to
Jefferson means something else when it is attributed to Lenin. To
demonstrate that suggestion by prestige is not a blind process resulting from the arbitrary transfer of the valuation of the statement's author to the statement itself, Asch conducted a series of
experiments. His basic method was to expose subjects to a statement (for example, "Those who hold and those who are without
property have ever formed distinct interests in society") in such
a way that some of the subjects thought Karl Marx was its author
whereas others attributed it to John Adams (the rightful author).
As a statement by Adams, subjects tended to think it descriptive of
a permanent condition of society, whereas, attributed to Karl Marx,
they thought it was a call for social change.

Asch (1952, p. 440) concludes:

> One factor seems to be fundamental in comprehending assertions:
> there are operations of fitting an assertion to its setting that establish
> its appropriate, relevant meaning. Operations of grouping and segre-
> gating, of grasping directions, of convergence and conflict occur.
> These articulate the given datum by establishing what it means in a
> given place and time. The conclusion follows that an identical datum

is not the same in different contexts. Operations also occur that work against the arbitrary joining of part to context. This became evident from the tendency to segregate parts from a context when their directions diverge or to reject their kinship altogether.

Asch indicates (p. 442) that

the conclusions reached . . . summarize a fundamental requirement for understanding social events. Whether we consider historical movements or economic and political ideas, it remains a fact that an act gains its meaning and significance from its relation to the particular conditions of time, place, and circumstance. . . . Freedom of contract meant one thing when directed against the feudal order. It meant something entirely different when used to declare unconstitutional statutes that required employers to introduce hygienic safeguards for the protection of workers—on the ground that they violated the right of the individual to work under any conditions he wished.

The Modification of Judgments by Groups

A remarkable series of experiments by Asch (1956) has stimulated a large number of experiments by other social psychologists. Asch's experimental paradigm is ingeniously simple: a single naïve subject is asked to announce his judgment of an obvious matter of fact after hearing a unanimous majority (who are accomplices of the experimenter) make a false judgment. The naïve subjects experience a profound conflict and many become emotionally upset. Although (over a series of trials) the preponderance of their judgments is correct, more than half of the naïve subjects are influenced to make errors that conform to the incorrect judgment of the unanimous majority. When an additional subject is introduced into the experiment, as an accomplice of the experimenter, and is instructed to report correct judgments, the naïve subject experiences much less conflict and is much less likely to conform to the false judgments of the majority. When the majority of the subjects are naïve and they are confronted by a single person who is instructed to make incorrect judgments, the naïve subjects react with complacency, amusement, or disdain.

Asch's explanation of his results is, in essence, that the naïve subjects are placed in conflict between two normally trustworthy sources of information—their own senses and the judgments of the others. The conflict is a profound one because, in general, individual action is based on some minimal confidence in one's own perception and judgment and social action is based on some minimal confidence in the perception and judgment of others. The experimental situation is one in which it is reasonable to have confidence in both sources; yet they disagree. Asch emphasizes the point that the tendency to reach agreement with the group is not due to blind imitative tendencies, but is rather the product of objective requirements. The group is part of the given conditions. Not to take it into account would be to disregard wilfully a reasonable view of the social situation: that each sees what the others see. There is, however, considerable evidence (Deutsch & Gerard, 1955) to suggest that conformity to the majority opinion may be based on such emotional factors as fear of disapproval rather than on the view that the judgments of the others are valid sources of information.

Asch concludes that "social life makes a double demand upon us: to rely upon others with trust and to become individuals who can assert our own reality." The achievement of agreement in social life marks the fact that a productive process which has started in one person is being carried forward in other persons. However, the meaning of agreement collapses when individuals act as mirrors to buttress one another. The social function of agreement requires that individuals should be able to refuse agreement when they see no way of reaching it.

Concluding Comment

Asch's point of view in social psychology is a generalization of the Gestalt notion that perceptual organization tends to be as good as the prevailing conditions allow. In a sense, his thesis is that man tends to be as good (as coherent, as understanding, as responsive to his social environment) as circumstances permit. His orientation is a constructive counterweight to those points of view in psychology that see man in his worst light—as being an irrational, arbitrary, egocentric animal. At the same time, Asch neglects the fact that sometimes man's behavior can be dominated by momentary considerations, can be controlled by compulsions and phobias, can be an escape from freedom and reason. Moreover, his work has not focused on certain central issues that relate to his orientation: how does man become *human?* and under what conditions will he behave *inhumanly?* Asch has not considered how man's potential for speech, friendship, and cooperative work are transformed into actualizations, nor has he indicated how these potentials can be distorted by social experience.

The Orientation of Fritz Heider

Among those acquainted with his small body of work, Heider has the reputation of being one of the most original and profound thinkers of the Gestalt school. Although his writings in the field of perception are not well known, they have had a significant influence on such important theorists as Kurt Koffka, Kurt Lewin, James Gibson, and Egon Brunswik. (For a selection of his papers on perception, see Heider, 1959.) His theoretical work in social psychology, most fully expressed in his book *The Psychology of Interpersonal Relations* (1958), is guided by the central thought-model underlying the Gestalt approach to perception. His work is primarily, but not exclusively, concerned with understanding how people perceive interpersonal events.

Heider's major thesis is that people seek to develop an orderly and coherent view of their environment, and, in the process, they build up a "naïve psychology" that resembles a science in an important respect. A science may be viewed as our attempt to represent the invariant properties of the environment lying behind the changing surface events, which give rise to the diverse events we observe. Similarly, in our naïve perception of our social environment, we look behind the surface behavior (somebody steps on one's toe) at the person who produced it, at his motives and attitudes, and at the social context in which the event occurred. In other words, we seek out these invariant relationships that can help us to understand the myriad of specific, changing events which lie within our field of observation.

Heider's work is an attempt to explicate the psychological concepts and their interrelations that are embodied in naïve psychology. In part, he is motivated by the view that to understand a person's social behavior one must understand the common-sense psychology that guides it and, in part, by the view that scientific psychology has much to learn from the treasure of insight that is embodied in common sense. His work has not, however, involved the study of the naïve psychology of specific individuals, but rather the investigation of the naïve psychology implicit in everyday language or expressed in literary, philosophical, and common-sense propositions concerning interpersonal relations. His method is to analyze the underlying psychological concepts that are used in language, and to study the interrelations of these concepts as they are employed in fables, novels, and other literary forms. Naïve psychology, he says, includes the following basic concepts (Heider, 1958, p. 17): "People have an awareness of their surroundings and the events in it (the *life space*), they attain this awareness through *perception* and other processes, they are *affected* by their personal and impersonal environment, they *cause* changes in the environment, they are able to (*can*) and *try* to cause these changes, they have wishes (*wants*) and *sentiments,* they stand in unit relations to other entities (*belonging*) and they are accountable according to certain standards (*ought*)." The italicized terms are the basic concepts whose interrelationships Heider examines at length in the successive chapters of his book.

Two major, interrelated, dynamic themes run through Heider's analysis of naïve psychology: "attribution" and "balance." In his early paper (1927), "Thing and Medium," Heider developed the theme that people tend to *attribute* happenings in their environment to central unitary "cores," which are internally conditioned and in some way centers of the causal texture of the world. They do not attribute such happenings to the mediating processes which are molded by these cores. We see a stone, not the light rays which intervene between the stone and the eyes. The mediating processes which meet our sense organs are spurious units, for they are built up of many parts that are independent of one another (the light rays reflected from one edge of the stone are independent of the light rays reflected from another edge). Without attribution to their unitary cause, the order that is imposed on the mediating processes remains unintelligible. Thus, in our perception of the physical world, perception focuses on the distal object (for example, the stone) that makes intelligible the order in the mediating processes as they impinge on our organs of sense.

Similarly, in perceiving the happenings in our social environment, we try to make sense out of the manifold proximal stimuli by focusing on the central unitary causal cores to which the surface events can be attributed. Such concepts of naïve psychology as intention ("want") and ability ("can") are at the causal cores of our social perceptions. In social perception, as compared with physical perception, there is more likely to be distortion of the underlying causal core, for two reasons. First, the relevant social context (the surrounding field) of a given event is less likely to be represented in the proximal stimuli which reflect a social event; and, secondly, the social mediating processes through which social events are often perceived are more likely to have idiosyncratic, distorting properties.

Heider points out that it is particularly important in the interpretation of social events whether we attribute an event to causal factors located in the person or to causal factors in his environment. For example, a person's enjoyment of a play may be attributed either to the play itself or to his own personal idiosyncrasies; a person's success or failure on a task may be attributed to the ease or difficulty of the task or to his ability (or lack of it); a teacher's reprimand to a student may be attributed to the personal intentions of the teacher toward the particular student or to the objective requirements of the teacher's role.

Heider (1958, p. 62) suggests that a naïve version of J. S. Mill's method of difference (more appropriately labeled as the "joint method of agreement and difference") provides the common-sense model for such causal attribution: the effect is attributed to that condition which is present when the effect is present and which is absent when the effect is absent. Thus, failure on a task is attributed to the difficulty of the task rather than to the incompetence of the person, if other people who are considered to be able also fail on it, and if the person who fails it is able to perform other tasks that are thought to require some ability.

It is evident that attribution of behavior to one or another causal source (one's self or the environment, personal idiosyncrasies or the objective requirements of the situation, and the like) will often require social comparisons. To be able to tell whether one's judgments, beliefs, or opinions are objectively right or are merely personal idiosyncrasies, it may be necessary to compare one's beliefs with the beliefs of others. To decide whether the difficulty experienced in a task lies in oneself or in the task, one will need information about how well others do. To judge whether one's emotional response to a situation is appropriate or not, social comparisons may be useful. Festinger's theory of social comparison (Chapter 3) is a more precise and more experimentally oriented formulation of the process of social comparison. Heider, in effect, indicates how these specific processes are outcomes of the more general human attempt to find an underlying causal network that will make sense of the multiplicity of surface events impinging on us.

Heider points out in his important discussion of "the naïve analysis of action" that the attribution of personal responsibility involves a decision as to which of the several conditions of action— the intentions of the person, personal power, or environmental factors—is to be given primary weight for the actual outcome. In general, the more the environmental factors are thought to influence the action, the less the person is held responsible for an action with which he is connected.

Heider also suggests that the connection between a person and an action may take a number of forms, each of which represents a different stage of conceptual development. At the most primitive level, the connection is a global one; the person is held responsible for each effect connected with him in any way; for example, a person may be accused of the wrongdoings of his ancestors. At the next level, an event is connected with the person only if he were a necessary condition for its occurrence, independently of his intentions or his ability to foresee or to alter the event's outcome; a person is judged in terms of the results of what he does; for example, a man who makes money on the stock market is enhanced in his valuation as a person. Piaget (1948) refers to this level as that of "objective responsibility." In the next stage, a person is considered responsible for an aftereffect he might have foreseen or prevented even though it was not his intention to produce it—a person's car runs out of gas because he forgot to check his meter. Next, only what the person intended is perceived as being caused by him; in Piaget's terms, this is "subjective responsibility." Finally, even actions that are intended and produced by a person are not entirely ascribed to him if his intentions are seen as having been produced by the environment, i.e., if his intention is regarded as having been provoked, coerced, or seductively induced by the environment.

The nature of attribution that occurs in any particular instance is determined not only by the stage of cognitive development, by the naïve application of the joint method of agreement and difference, by one's expectations, by personal style, but also by the need to prevent cognitive imbalance. The striving for cognitive balance is the second major theme in Heider's analysis of naïve psychology.

He points out that cognitive stability requires a congruence among causal expectations with respect to related objects. For a state of complete cognitive harmony to exist, the various implications of a person's expectations or judgments of any one aspect of the cognized environment may not contradict the implications of his expectations or judgments in respect of any other aspect of the cognized environment. Thus, if a person judges X to be of potential benefit to his welfare, he cannot at the same time judge that Y (which is judged to be of benefit to his welfare) and X are antagonistic and still maintain a stable or balanced cognitive structure. (X and Y may be things, people, the products of people, or the characteristics of people.) When the cognitive structure is in a state of imbalance or is threatened by imbalance, forces will arise to produce a tendency toward locomotion so as to change the psychological environment or to produce a tendency toward change in the cognition of the environment. Under conditions that do not permit locomotion, the tendency for cognitive change is enhanced.

In the preceding example of X and Y, cognitive change could occur by changing one's judgement of X or of Y, or of the relationship between X and Y, or by differentiating X or Y into independent or segregated subparts. Thus, instead of continuing to like both X and Y, who hate each other, one may come to dislike either X or Y, or to feel that they do not hate each other, or to feel that he likes X because she is beautiful and that Y hates X because she is wealthy and that there is no interaction directly or indirectly between these two characteristics of X—beauty and wealth. In general, the nature of the cognitive changes resulting from an imbalance will tend to produce the most congruence and least changes in the perceptual-cognitive field.

From assumptions that are similar to those just outlined, and with three hypotheses about the conditions of cognitive imbalance, Heider has been able to develop a keen insight into some of the conditions that determine perceptions in interpersonal situations. Here are three: (1) In respect of attitudes directed toward the same entity, a balanced state exists if positive (or negative) attitudes go together; a tendency exists to see a person as being positive or negative in all respects. (2) In respect of attitudes toward an entity combined with belongingness, a balanced state exists if a person is united with the entities he likes and if he likes the entities he is united with; and the converse is true for negative attitudes. (3) If two entities are seen as parts of a unit, a balanced state will exist if the parts are seen to have the same dynamic character (positive or negative); but if the two entities have different dynamic characters, then a balanced state can exist only if they are seen to be segregated (by breaking up the unit).

One may consider these hypotheses as true for various types of positive attitude (to like, to love, to esteem, to value) and also for various types of negative attitude. Similarly, the statements about belonging or being part of a unit refer to diverse types of unit (membership, belonging, causality, possession, similarity, or proximity). We must, however, not forget that the unbalanced cognitive situation produces only a *tendency* to change; whether or not locomotion or cognitive change will actually occur depends on the strength of the other forces operative in the situation.

The reader may demonstrate for himself some of the implications of Heider's hypotheses by considering three interrelated entities—his own self (P), another person (O), and a third object (X). Specify the perceived attitude (positive or negative) between any two of the entities and you can determine what the perceived relationship is likely to be between the other two. Thus, if P likes X, and P dislikes O, then one could predict a tendency to perceive O as disliking X; if P likes X and also likes O, one can predict a tendency to perceive O as liking X. The reader may introduce some additional factors by considering the relation of belongingness. For example, given that P likes O, and that O caused X, one could predict a tendency for P to like X, and so forth. The reader might find it of particular interest to consider X as an aspect of the self and to see some of the predictions one would make, from Heider's hypotheses, about attitudes toward aspects of the self under varying conditions.

Newcomb's Theory of Communicative Acts

Theodore M. Newcomb (1953) has extrapolated Heider's theory of balance to formulate a set of propositions concerning interpersonal communication. He concludes that the tendency for balance is characteristic of interpersonal as well as intrapersonal systems. In effect, he states that, when two people perceive themselves as (positively) interdependent and each is oriented toward some third entity, they will tend to develop similar orientations toward this entity. Interpersonal communication thus increases the likelihood that similar orientations will develop. On the other hand, dissimilar orientations in an interdependent pair or group tends to increase the frequency of communicative acts so as to reduce the dissimilarity of the orientations. The strength of these "strains toward symmetry of orientation" are partly determined by the strength of the bond between the two people and the strengths of their attitudes toward the third entity.

Newcomb elaborates his basic propositions to explain how the "pressure for uniformity" and the "tendency to direct communications toward deviant members" arise within cohesive groups. In a more recent work (Newcomb, 1961), he has demonstrated the great importance of perceived similarity of attitudes in determining both friendships and the structure of informal groups.

Formalizations of Heider's Theory

Cartwright and Harary (1956) have formalized and generalized Heider's theory of cognitive balance by using concepts from the mathematical theory of linear graphs. They point out that Heider's formulation has certain ambiguities and limitations. For example, Heider does not distinguish between the *complement* and the *opposite* of the "belonging" relation: the complement of "belonging" is "not belonging"; its opposite is unspecified, but probably is equivalent to "disunity" or to being "competitively linked." Also, Heider's formulation is limited to the perceived interrelations among three units (for example, three people, or two people and an object) and distinguishes only between "balanced" and "unbalanced" states, but does not make possible the identification of different degrees of imbalance. The mathematical formulation of Cartwright and Harary overcomes some ambiguities and limitations of Heider's formulation. Abelson and Rosenberg (1958) have also revised Heider's theory so as to make some of its implications more precise. Their formulation uses the formalisms of matrix algebra, which is logically similar to the linear graph formulation of Cartwright and Harary, and they have attempted to specify principles for identifying which of the various methods of reducing cognitive imbalance will be utilized in any particular instance.

Concluding Comment

Heider's theoretical work constitutes a bold and original application to social psychology of the Gestalt view that there is a tendency for orderliness and simplicity in mental organization. His ideas have a wide sweep, with implications for many aspects of social psychology. Not having formulated them in such a way as to make their implications for practice and research self-evident, the impact of his writings is largely to be found in the work of others.

3

FIELD THEORY IN
SOCIAL PSYCHOLOGY

Kurt Lewin

THE PHRASE "field theory in social psychology" is associated with Kurt Lewin and his students. Although Lewin was a member of the Berlin Gestalt group, he quickly began to break new ground by focusing his attention on motivation instead of the classical Gestalt problems of perception. The range and impact of the work of Lewin and his associates is indicated by a listing of some of the areas in psychology that they opened up for experimental investigation: dynamic studies of memory, resumption of interrupted activities, substitute activity, satiation, level of aspiration, group leadership, and group decision. Many of the terms associated with Lewin are now part of the common vocabulary of psychologists: "life space," "valence," "locomotion," "overlapping situation," "cognitive structure," "action research." Here we may briefly sketch some of Lewin's central theoretical notions as they relate to social psychology.

These terms, which have the scent of the physical sciences, do not represent an attempt to derive psychological processes from physical ones. Lewin's attack is consistently psychological. His motivational concepts are concerned with the purposes that underlie behavior and the goals toward or away from which behavior is directed. His terminology, to which we shall adhere, reflects Lewin's view that what he termed "the logic of dynamics" may be similar in the various sciences. Some of Lewin's early interests and writings (and these were much influenced by the German philosopher, Ernst Cassirer) were concerned with the nature of theory in science. He was imbued with the ambition to understand the various sciences in terms of a similar logical approach, an ambition that was fashionable in German intellectual circles after the advent of Einstein's theory of relativity. Contrary to the views held by many of his colleagues in Germany, Lewin's conception of what he termed "the comparative science of sciences" rejected the philosophical Utopia of a single universal science in which psychological explanations must rest on physics. His attempt was directed at characterizing the common modes of explanation that could be applied fruitfully in the various sciences, while he nevertheless maintained that psychological and physical phenomena must be explained within their own frameworks. Of course, he did not succeed, but his terminology is the mark of his large aim.

Dynamic Concepts

The concepts "tension," "valence," "force," and "locomotion" play a key role in Lewin's theorizing about motivation. Lewin states that a system in a state of tension exists within a person whenever a psychological need or an intention (sometimes referred to as a quasi need) exists. Tension is released when the need or intention is fulfilled. Tension has certain conceptual properties: (1) it is the state of a region that tries to change itself in such a way that it becomes equal to the state of its surrounding regions, and (2) it involves forces at the boundary of the region in tension. A "positive valence" is conceived as a field in which the forces are all pointing toward a given region of the field (the valent region that is the center of the force field), whereas all the forces point away from a region of "negative valence." The construct "force" characterizes the direction and strength of the tendency to change at a given point of the life space. Change may occur either by a locomotion (a change in position) of the person in his psychological environment, or by a change in the structure of his perceived environment.

There exists a definite relation between tension systems of the person and certain properties of the psychological environment.

In particular, a tension may be related to a positive valence for activity regions in the psychological environment that are perceived as tension-reducing and a negative valence for the region in which the behaving self is at the moment. The existence of a region of positive valence (a goal region), however, depends, not only on the existence of tension, but also on whether or not there are perceived possibilities for reducing the tension. The person who has no conception of how to reduce a tension, and who therefore perceives no goal region, will have his behavior determined by his desire to leave his present negative region for another, and to leave that for another, and so on. His behavior will be characterized by locomotion in the direction away from his present region or, in observable terms, by restless movement. Search behavior, occurring in a situation where the individual knows a goal region exists but does not know its location, has many similarities to restless activity but is distinguished from it by the fact that the direction toward the goal is dominant and the leaving of the present region is only a means to that end (Lewin, 1938, pp. 62 f.).

When a goal region that is relevant to a system in tension exists in the psychological environment, one can assert that there is a force acting on the behaving self to move toward the goal. A tension for which there is a cognized goal leads, not only to a tendency to actual locomotion toward the region of the goal, but also to thinking about this type of activity. This notion may be expressed by saying that the force on the person toward the goal exists not only on the level of doing (reality) but also on the level of thinking ("irreality").

From the foregoing assumptions about systems in tension it is possible to arrive at a number of derivations. Thus it follows that the tendency to recall interrupted activities should be greater than the tendency to recall finished ones. Zeigarnik (1927) and many others have conducted experiments in which subjects are given a series of tasks to perform and are then prevented from completing half of them. The other half are completed. Later, the subjects are asked to recall the tasks they performed. The results are presented in the form of a quotient, commonly called the Zeigarnik quotient (ZQ):

$$\frac{\text{unfinished tasks recalled (RU)}}{\text{completed tasks recalled (RC)}}$$

Zeigarnik predicted a quotient of greater than 1. The quotient obtained was approximately 1.9, clearly supporting Lewin's assumptions. Since many completed tasks were also recalled, however, it was obvious that additional factors were involved. Analyzing the situation of the subject at the moment of recall, the investigator concluded that, in addition to the force operating on the subject to think about the uncompleted tasks and hence to recall them, there was also present a force toward recall of both uncompleted and completed tasks, induced by the experimenter's instructions to "try to recall the tasks you worked on earlier." The Zeigarnik quotient can be viewed as an indicator of the relative strengths of the induced force to recall all tasks and the force to recall the uncompleted tasks. As the strength of the induced force increases in relation to the force toward the task goals, the quotient should approach one; as it decreases in relative strength, the quotient should increase beyond one. These additional predictions, which follow from an analysis of the situation at recall, were borne out in further experiments by Zeigarnik and others. Thus, when the strength of motivation associated with the interrupted task is relatively high, or when the strength of the experimenter's pressure to recall is low, or when the task is interrupted near its end, the Zeigarnik quotient will be high.

A number of more recent experiments have indicated that the situation of recall is frequently even more complex. When not finishing a task can be interpreted as a personal failure (as in an experiment where the tasks are presented as measures of a socially esteemed ability), and when recall of failure threatens one's self-esteem, or when the recall of success raises a lowered self-esteem, the Zeigarnik ratio tends to be less than one.

From the general assumption that when a need is present for a certain goal there is a corresponding force causing a tendency to move toward the goal, it follows that, as long as the tasks are psychologically incomplete, the subject will continue to try to perform the task (providing there are no sufficiently strong counterforces). Ovsiankina (1928) created conditions such that the subject thought he was interrupted by chance and at a later time was left free to do as he wished in an experimental room. There was 100 per-cent resumption of the interrupted task. When the interruption appeared to be intentional, there was still 82 per-cent resumption.

Lewin postulated that the change of the difference in tension between any two systems would depend on the time interval and the degree of interdependence of the systems. With increased time, one would expect differences in tension between interdependent systems to decrease. Thus Zeigarnik in her experiments on the recall of interrupted activities and Ovsiankina in her experiments on the resumption of interrupted activities both found that, as time elapses, there is a decreasing tendency to recall or resume the interrupted activities.

The degree of interdependence of two tension systems is conceived to be a function of the degree of fluidity or rigidity of the person and of the structural relations or connections between the systems. The fluidity of the person is affected by general states of the person. For example, a person is considered to be more fluid when tired, when he is undergoing a wave of emotional tension, when he is young, when he is in a "make-believe" or "irreal" situation, when he is more intelligent. Experiments by Zeigarnik have indicated that in the more fluid states the differences in tension between systems tend to dissipate relatively rapidly.

The structural relations between tension systems refer to such questions as whether two systems are subparts of a larger system, whether the two have a relationship of simple dependence, interdependence, or organizational dependence, and also the proximity of the regions. While the problem of characterizing structural arrangements mathematically has received only scant attention, a number of interesting experiments have been conducted that deal with structural relations. Experimental studies of substitution are relevant in this connection.

By a technique of resumption, Lissner (1933) studied the value of one activity in reducing a tension originally connected with another activity. Other experimenters have employed the technique of recall. The substitute value is measured by the amount of decrease in resumption or recall of the interrupted original activity after a substitute activity has been completed. The results of the experiments on substitute value can be summarized briefly as follows. (1) The substitute value increases with the perceived degree of similarity between the original and the substitute activity and with the degree of difficulty of the substitute activity (Lissner, 1933). (2) The substitute value increases with increasing temporal contiguity between the original and the substitute activity and with the attractiveness of the substitute activity (Henle, 1942)

(3) The substitute value of an activity (thinking, talking, or doing) depends on the nature of the goal of the original task. Tasks
that are connected with the goal of demonstrating something to
another person (the experimenter for example) require an observable substitute activity (not merely "thinking" without social
communication); "realization tasks," in which the building of a
material object is the goal, require "doing" and not only telling
how it can be done; for intellectual problems, talking (or telling
how it can be done) can have a very high substitute value
(Mahler, 1933). (4) "Magic solutions," "make-believe solutions,"
or solutions that observably violate the requirements of the task
have little substitute value for tasks at the reality level. However,
if the situation is a make-believe or play situation, make-believe
substitutions will have substitute value (Dembo, 1931; Sliosberg,
1934). (5) A substitute activity that is identical with the original
activity will have little substitute value if it does not serve the same
goal. Thus, building a clay house for John will have little substitute
value for building a clay house for Mary. If the emphasis is on building a clay house and not on the "for somebody," then, of course,
substitution will occur (Adler & Kounin, 1939). (6) Having someone complete the subject's interrupted task tends to have little
substitute value, especially when completion of the task is related
to self-esteem. When pairs of individuals work cooperatively on a
task, however, the completion of the task by one's partner has
considerable substitute value (Lewis, 1944; Lewis & Franklin,
1944).

The research findings with respect to substitute value have implications for a wide range of problems in psychology—from the
relative gratification value of individual versus socially shared projective or fantasy systems to the development of specialized roles
within a group. This point can be illustrated by the important finding that the actions of another person can be a substitute for one's
own actions if there is a cooperative relationship. The fact of such
possible substitution enables persons who are working cooperatively on a common task to subdivide the task and to perform
specialized activities, since no one of the individuals in a cooperative situation has the need to perform all the activities himself. On the other hand, the individual in a competitive situation is
less likely to view the actions of others as possible substitutes for

similarly intended actions of his own. Thus, when a competitive situation exists in a group, specialization of activities is less likely to develop (Deutsch, 1949a; Deutsch, 1949b).

The concept of tension systems has also been fruitfully employed in experimental studies of satiation. With regard to most needs, one can distinguish a state of deprivation, of satiation, and of oversatiation. These states correspond to a positive, a neutral, and a negative valence of the activity regions which are related to a particular need or tension system. Karsten (1928) has studied the effect of repeating over and over again such activities as reading a poem, writing letters, drawing, and turning a wheel. The main symptoms of oversatiation appear to be (1) the appearance of subunits in the activity leading to the disintegration of the total activity and a loss of the meaning of the activity; (2) an increasingly poorer quality and greater frequency of errors in performing the task; (3) an increasing tendency to vary the nature of the task, accompanied by a tendency for each variation to become quickly satiated; (4) a tendency to make the satiated activity a peripheral activity with an attempt to concentrate on something else while doing the task—an attempt which is usually not completely successful, for the mind wanders; (5) an increasing dislike of the activity and of similar activities with an increased valence for different tasks; (6) emotional outbursts; (7) the development of "fatigue" and similar bodily symptoms which are quickly overcome when the individual is shifted to another activity.

Satiation occurs only if the activity has, psychologically, the character of marking time or of getting nowhere. If the activity can be viewed as making progress toward a goal, the usual symptoms of satiation will not appear. Embedding an activity in a different psychological whole so that its meaning is changed has practically the same effect on satiation as shifting to a different activity. The rapidity with which satiation occurs depends on (1) the nature of the activity (with increasing size of its units of action and with increasing complexity satiation occurs more slowly); (2) the degree of centrality of the activity (other things being equal, activities which are of more significance to the person are more quickly satiated than peripheral activities); (3) the state of the person (the more fluid the state of the person, the more quickly is he satiated). The rate of satiation and cosatiation of similar activities (the spread of the effects of satiation from one activity to similar activities) decreases with a person's age and also with his lack of intelligence (Kounin, 1941a; Kounin, 1941b).

Most satiation phenomena can be explained by assuming that continued performance of a task leads to a lowering of the level of tension in the system corresponding to the task; with increasing repetition the system corresponding to the task may be represented as reaching a lower level of tension than the surrounding systems. This reduction should result in the person's turning away from the repeated task to other activities. With time, he will also turn away from such activities as are related to tension systems interdependent with the satiated system and will turn toward activities that are not thus related to the satiated activity. The general tendency is to turn away from similar activities and to turn toward dissimilar activities. This breakdown of the satiated activity into disorganized units fits in very well with Lewin's analysis of the "differentiation and unity of a whole based on simple dependence" (Lewin, 1941; Lewin, 1951, pp. 305–335).

The concept of tension system and the various experimental studies on the recall and resumption of interrupted activities, substitution, satiation, and frustration all have direct relevance to many problems of social psychology (although, as yet, their relevance has not been fully exploited). The concept of tension system is applicable, for instance, to socially derived needs and intentions, to motives that develop from belonging to a group and from participating in group activities, to interpersonal influences. The various effects of tension on psychological processes have advanced insight into those social and group factors that produce individual motivation as well as into social and group factors that facilitate the reduction of individual tensions.

Structural Concepts

Lewin attempted to develop a geometry, which he termed "hodological space," to represent a person's conception of the means-end structure of the environment—of what leads to what. Although Lewin's "hodological space" was never developed adequately from a mathematical standpoint, it highlighted the necessity of considering a person's conception of his environment in analyzing his behavioral possibilities and in characterizing the direction of his behavior. (An individual who circumvents a fence to get to a ball behind it is, psychologically, walking toward the ball even while he is physically walking away from it.)

The view that direction in the life space is dependent on its cognitive structure has been applied to give insights into some of the psychological properties of situations that are cognitively unstructured. Most new situations are cognitively unstructured, since the individual is unlikely to know "what leads to what." Hence, it follows that in such situations the individual is unlikely to know what direction he should follow to achieve his objective. As he strikes out in any direction, he does not know whether it is leading him toward or away from his goal. His behavior will be exploratory, with trials and errors, vacillating, and contradictory, not efficient nor economical. If reaching the goal has positive significance for him and not reaching it has negative significance, then being in a region that has no clear cognitive structure results in psychological conflict, since the direction of the forces acting on him is likely to be both toward and away from any given region. There will be evidences of emotionality as well as of cautiousness in such situations. In addition, the very nature of an unstructured situation is that it is unstable; perception of the situation shifts rapidly and is readily influenced by minor cues and by suggestion from others.

This characterization of some of the psychological implications of cognitively unstructured situations is of considerable usefulness to social psychology. For example, Lewin employed this concept to provide insight into the psychological situation of the adolescent (1939; 1951), of minority group members (Lewin, 1935a; Lewin, 1948), of people suffering from physical handicaps (Barker, Wright, & Gonick, 1946), of the *nouveaux riches,* and of other persons crossing the margin of social classes. The model may be applied to any situation in which the consequences of behavior are seemingly unpredictable or uncontrollable, in which benefits and harms occur in an apparently inconsistent, fortuitous, or arbitrary manner, or in which one is uncertain about the potential reactions of others.

It has also been applied by Lewin in stressing the importance of "action research" by social agencies and civic groups that are concerned with eliminating and preventing community problems. Lacking research on the effectiveness of their actions, the investigators will "feel in a fog on three counts: (1) What is the present situation? (2) What are the dangers? (3) And most important of all, what shall we do?" (Lewin, 1946, p. 34).

Lewin has also employed his structural concepts, in conjunction with his dynamic concepts, to give insight into the nature of "conflict situations." He distinguished three fundamental types of conflict:

1. The individual stands midway between two positive valences of approximately equal strength. A classical instance is Buridan's ass starving between two stacks of hay. This type of conflict is unstable, however. As the individual, because of the play of chance factors, moves from the point of equilibrium toward one rather than the other goal region, the resultant force toward that region increases; hence, he will continue to move toward that region (and therefore away from the point of equilibrium). This conclusion follows from the assumption that the strength of force toward a goal region increases with decreasing distance from the goal.

2. The second fundamental type of conflict situation occurs when the individual finds himself between two approximately equal negative valences. Punishment is an example, a type of conflict much influenced by the structure of the situation. Here are three types of conflict between negative valences: (1) A situation in which a person finds himself between negative valences with no restraints to keep him within the situation. For instance, a girl will have to marry an unpleasant suitor or become an impoverished spinster, but there is nothing to prevent her leaving the village. (2) A situation in which a person is between two negative valences and cannot leave the field. For instance a member of a group is faced with the prospect of losing social status or performing an unpleasant task, and it is impossible for him to leave the group. (3) A situation in which a person is in a region of negative valence and can leave it only by going through another region of negative valence. For instance, a man is cited for contempt of Congress for refusing to testify whether or not some of his acquaintances were members of the Communist party, and to purge himself he must become an informer.

It is evident that the situation depicted in (1) will lead to a going "out of the field." Escape behavior will follow from the fact that the resultant of the forces away from the two regions of negative valence will tend to push the person in a direction that is perpendicular to the path connecting the two negative regions. Only if restraints prevent the individual from leaving the field will such a situation result in more than momentary conflict. Restraints as in (2) introduce a conflict between the driving forces related to the negative valence and the restraining forces related to the restraining barrier. There is a tendency for a barrier to acquire a negative valence that increases with the number of unsuccessful attempts to cross it and that, finally, is sufficiently strong to prevent the individual from approaching it (Fajans, 1933a; Fajans, 1933b). Thus, the conflict between driving and restraining forces is replaced by a conflict between driving forces, as in (3). This fact is especially important for social psychology since, in many situations of life, the barriers are social. When a person turns against the barrier, he is in effect directing himself against the will and power of the person or persons, or of the social group, to whom the erection of the barrier is due. That is, when there is no way to escape the conflict between negative valences except by overcoming social barriers, both the barriers and the people with whom one perceives the barriers originate will take on negative valence as the individual is unable to escape. One of the effects of the threat of punishment is to create a situation in which the individual and the creator of the barrier stand against each other as enemies.

3. The third fundamental type of conflict occurs when the individual is exposed to opposing forces derived from a positive and a negative valence. One can distinguish at least three different forms of this conflict. (1) The situation in which a region has both positive and negative valence (a person wishes to join a social group but fears that being a member will be too expensive). The Freudian concept of ambivalence is subsumable under this variety of conflict. (2) The situation in which a person is encircled by (but is not actually in) a negative or a barrier region and is attracted to a goal that is outside the negative or barrier region (a person has to go through the unpleasant ordeal of leaving his home or his group in order to pursue some desired activity). The nature of this situation is such that the region of the person's present activity tends to acquire negative valence as long as the region that encircles him hinders locomotion toward desired outer goals. Thus, being a member of a minority group or being in a ghetto or in a prison often takes on negative valence, apart from the inherent characteristics of the region, because one can get to desired goals

from the region only by passing through an encircling region of negative valence. (3) The situation in which a region of positive valence is encircled by or is accessible only through a region of negative valence. This type of situation differs from (2) in that the region of positive valence rather than the region in which the person is to be found is encircled by the negative valence. The "reward situation," in which the individual is granted a reward only if he performs an unpleasant task, is an example of this type of conflict. Similarly, the initiation rites in many social groups —the hazing procedures of college fraternities, for example—may be viewed as exemplifying this kind of conflict.

Lewin (1946, 1951, p. 259), as well as Miller (1944), has pointed out that the forces corresponding to a negative valence tend to decrease more rapidly as a function of psychological distance than do the forces corresponding to a positive valence. The amount of decrease depends also on the nature of the region which has a positive or negative valence. It is different, for example, in the case of a dangerous animal which can move about than in the case of an immovable unpleasant object. The difference in the gradients of decrease for forces deriving from positive and negative valences accounts for the fact that a strong fear or a strong tendency to withdraw may be taken as evidence of a strong desire for the goal despite the apparent paradox. Only with a very attractive goal will the point of equilibrium between the tendencies for approach and avoidance be close enough to the negatively valent region to produce a strong force away from the goal. On the other hand, strengthening the negative valence of a region may very well have the effect of weakening the forces in conflict, since the point of equilibrium (where the force away from the negative valence and the force toward the positive valence are of equal strength and opposite direction) may be pushed a considerable distance from the valent regions.

Socially Induced Change

Lewin's concepts do not presuppose that motivation is primarily induced by physiological deficits; he leaves open the possibility that tension and valences may be aroused socially (for example, by an experimenter's instructions to perform a task). He also indictates that the forces acting on a person may be "imposed" or may directly reflect that person's own needs.

In this connection, it is relevant to introduce the concept of "power field," which, although not well defined, has been employed in many social psychological investigations (Arsenian, 1943; Cartwright, 1950; Frank, 1944; Lippitt, 1940; Wiehe, cited in Lewin, 1935b). A power field is an inducing field, which can induce changes in the life space within its area of influence.

The source of a power field is usually but not necessarily a person. It is possible to speak of a person's area of direct social influence as his power field and to speak of the changes that can be or are induced in the life spaces of other people by this person's power field. For example, where workers have no intrinsic interest in their work, not viewing it as a means to some important goal, they would be inclined to loaf were it not for the presence of a supervisor who can induce forces in the direction of performing work. When the supervisor is not psychologically present, and, when his power field is therefore absent, the workers resume their loafing.

The distinction between "own" and "induced" forces has been useful in explaining some of the difference in behavior under autocratic and democratic leadership (Lippitt and White, 1943), a difference that was a focus both for Lewin's scientific interests in the study of leadership and group processes and also for his concern about the effects of autocratic governments. This focus was extraordinarily productive. Scientifically, it helped to stimulate the development of group dynamics. The Lewin, Lippitt, and White (1939) study of various styles of leadership showed that it was possible to experiment with important properties of groups and, in so doing, revealed exciting new prospects for psychological experimentation. Socially, Lewin's interest in style of leadership and his demonstration that democratic leadership is more likely to produce groups whose members contribute to group objectives willingly and on their own initiative helped to provide a psychological rationale for democracy when it was under attack from dictatorial governments. Further, it has helped to stimulate changes in style of leadership in industrial, educational, and military groups, and it has given rise to programs of training in human relations which are widely employed in aiding people to acquire skills in group leadership.

The findings of the study of different types of leadership indicate that children in a club led by authoritarian leaders (who determined policy, dictated activities, and were arbitrary and personal in evaluation of activities) tended to develop little of their own motivation with respect to club activities. Although the children worked productively when the leader was present (when his power field was psychologically effective), the lack of personal motivation toward group goals clearly evidenced itself in (1) their change of behavior when the leader left the club, (2) their absence of motivation when the leader arrived late, (3) their lack of carefulness in the work, (4) their want of initiative in offering spontaneous suggestions in regard to the club's projects, and (5) their lack of pride in the products of the club's effort. In contrast, the children in clubs led by democratic leaders showed strong personal motivation toward group goals.

The distinction between "own" and "induced" forces has also been used to explain why workers are usually happier and more productive when they can participate in the decisions which affect their work. Apart from other considerations, participation in setting a goal is more likely to create "own" forces toward it, such that there will be no necessity to exert continuous social influence to induce forces toward the work goal or restraining forces to prevent the individual from leaving the work region (Coch & French, 1948; McGregor, 1944).

A power field may be characterized, not only in terms of its perceived source (a given person, a group, a personal value, a law), but also in terms of the regions that the power field can affect in the individual's life space (a mathematician may influence your views about the soundness of a mathematical proof, but not about the soundness of a political point of view); the strength or power of the field as indicated in the magnitude of the changes that it can induce; the conditions under which it is effective (a child is unlikely to obey his father if his mother is telling him to do the opposite); the nature of the changes induced by the field (whether barriers or valences are affected, whether the induced forces act on the behaving self or regions of the psychological environment); whether or not being in the power field of another person is positively or negatively valent (does an individual like to have decisions made for him or does he like to make them himself?); the perceived qualities of the source of the power field (friendly or hostile, personal or impersonal); the degree of correspondence or conflict between "induced" and "own" forces; and those attributes of the source of the power field that give rise to its power (physical strength, social role, personal attractiveness).

Social influence and socially induced change have been the foci of a series of investigations conducted under the direction of Ronald Lippitt and Fritz Redl (Grosser, Polansky, & Lippitt, 1951: Lippitt, Polansky & Rosen, 1952; Polansky, Freeman, Horwitz, Irwin, Papania, Rapaport, & Whaley 1949; Polansky, Lippitt, & Redl, 1950a; Polansky, Lippitt, & Redl, 1950b).

Cartwright, French, and others at the University of Michigan's Research Center for Group Dynamics (Cartwright, 1959) have systematically studied some of the phenomena related to social power and have elaborated a conception of power congruent with field theory. These studies and conceptualizations highlight the significance of social influence in eliciting and directing motivated behavior.

Level of Aspiration

Perhaps no other area of research that Lewin and his students have opened to experimental investigation has been the subject of so many studies as that of the level of aspiration, which may be defined as the degree of difficulty of the goal toward which a person is striving. The concept is relevant only when there is a perceived range of difficulty in the attainment of possible goals and there is variation in valence among the goals along the range of difficulty.

In discussing the level of aspiration, it may be helpful to consider a sequence of events that is typical for many of the experimental studies in this area. (1) A subject plays a game or performs a task in which he can obtain a score (for example, throwing darts at a target); (2) after playing the game and obtaining a given score, he is asked to tell what score he will undertake to make the next time he plays; (3) he then plays the game again and achieves another score; (4) he reacts to his second performance with feelings of success or failure, with a continuing or a new level of aspiration. In this sequence, point (4), reaction to achievement, is especially significant for the dynamics of the level of aspiration.

In outline form, the theory of level of aspiration is rather simple (Lewin, Dembo, Festinger, & Sears, 1944). It states that the valence of any level of difficulty (V) is equal to the product of the valence of achieving success (V_{su}) by the subjective probability of success (SP_{su}) minus the product of the valence of ending in failure (V_f) by the subjective probability of failure (SP_f). Algebraically, the preceding sentence may be expressed:

$$V = (V_{su} \times SP_{su}) - (V_f \times SP_f).$$

It is usually assumed that the subjective probability of success and of failure sum to one. The level of aspiration (the goal an individual will undertake to achieve) will be the level of difficulty that has the highest positive valence. The subjective experience of success or failure is determined by the relation of the individual's performance to his level of aspiration, when the performance is seen to be self-accomplished, and not simply by his absolute accomplishments.

Experimental work on level of aspiration has brought out the variety of influences that affect the positive and negative valence of different levels of difficulty. It has indicated that cultural and group factors establish scales of reference that help to determine the relative attractiveness of different points along the continuum of difficulty. Some of these influences are fairly stable and permanent in their effects. It has been found, for example, that most people of Western culture, under the pervasive cultural pressures toward "self-improvement," when first asked to consider their level of aspiration, initially indicate a level that is above the previous performance score, and, under most conditions they tend to keep their aspirations higher than their previous performances. In addition to broad cultural factors, the individual's level of aspiration in a task is likely to be very much influenced by the standards of the groups to which he belongs (Anderson & Brandt, 1939; Hilgard, Sait, & Margaret, 1940). The nature of the scales of reference fixed by the standards of different groups may vary. Reference scales do not derive solely from membership in a definitely structured social group, but may also reflect the influence of one's self-image, of other persons, or of groups that either establish certain standards for performance or that serve as models for evaluating self-performance. Thus, the level of aspiration of a college student with respect to an intellectual task will vary depending on whether he is told that a given score was obtained by the average high school student, the average college student, or the average graduate student (Festinger, 1942a; Festinger, 1942b).

Research has given some insight into the factors placing the values on the scale of subjective probability. A main factor which determines the subjective probability of future success and failure is the past experience of the individual in regard to his ability to reach certain objectives (Jucknat, 1937). If he has had considerable experience with a given activity, he will know pretty well what level he can expect to reach and the gradient of his values on the scale of subjective probability will be steep. It is, however, not only the average of past performances which determines an individual's scale of subjective probability, but also the trend—whether he is improving, getting worse, or remaining the same. Furthermore, there is experimental evidence to indicate that the last or most recent success or failure has an especially great influence on the individual's expectation of his future level of achievement. In addition, there is evidence that the scales of subjective probability of others as well as their performances can influence a subject's own probability scale. Personality factors such as self-confidence, may also affect subjective probability.

The analysis of level of aspiration has widespread implications for many social phenomena. It gives insight into the reasons for social apathy in the face of pressing political and international problems. People are not likely to attempt to achieve even highly valued objectives when they see no way of attaining them. Similarly, it sheds some light on why social revolution tends to occur only after there has been a slight improvement in the situation of the oppressed groups—the improvement raises levels of aspiration, and goals which were once viewed as unattainable can now be perceived as real possibilities.

The study of the level of aspiration suggests itself as an instrument by which to compare different cultures and by which to characterize their systems of values. Such questions as optimism-pessimism, the need for success, the fear of failure, and the influence of specific group standards also seem open to the use of this technique.

Atkinson (1957, 1964) has developed a theory of achievement motivation that is an extension and elaboration of ideas advanced in the theory of level of aspiration. His theory attempts to account for the determinants of the direction, magnitudes, and persistence of achievement-motivated performance. Achievement motivation is conceived to be the resultant of two opposed tendencies: T_s (the tendency to achieve success)$-T_f$ (the tendency to avoid failure).

The tendency to achieve success is assumed to be a multiplicative function of the motive to achieve success (M_s) which the individual carries about with him from situation to situation, the subjective probability of success (P_s), and the incentive values of success at a particular activity (I_s): $T_s = M_s \times P_s \times I_s$. Similarly, the tendency to avoid failure is assumed to be a multiplicative function of the motive to avoid failure (M_{af}), the subjective probability of failure (P_f), and the negative incentive value of failure (I_f): $T_f = M_{af} \times P_f \times I_f$.

So far, Atkinson's analysis parallels the level of aspiration theory, if one assumes, quite properly, that the Lewinian concept of valence is equivalent to Atkinson's motive times incentive: namely, that the *valence of success* $= M_s \times I_s$ and that the *valence of failure* $= M_{af} \times I_f$. He, however, introduces the additional assumptions that $I_s = I - P_s$ and that $I_f = P_s$. In other words, his theory details more unequivocally the relationship between the perceived level of difficulty and the incentive values of success and failure. (Notice that in Atkinson's theory $P_s \times I_s$ must equal $-P_f \times I_f$ and, hence, that whatever differences there are between T_s and T_f will be due solely to the differences between M_s and M_{af}.)

Atkinson (1964) summarizes a considerable body of research which is consistent with his theory. The wide applicability of the theory is indicated by the range of content to which the theory has been applied: motivational effect of ability grouping in schools, strength of achievement motive and occupational mobility, fear of failure and unrealistic vocational aspiration, preferences for degrees of risk, the effects of success and failure.

Concepts of Group Dynamics

Apart from papers dealing with group decision and social change (Lewin 1947a; Lewin, 1947b; Lewin, 1947c; Lewin, 1948), Lewin actually wrote very little on the theory of group dynamics. From the research investigations of his colleagues and students at the Research Center for Group Dynamics, however, a formidable array of concepts has been gradually emerging.

Lewin (1948, p. 54) wrote:

> The essence of a group is not the similarity or dissimilarity of its members, but their interdependence. A group can be characterized as a "dynamical whole"; this means that a change in the state of an[v]

subpart changes the state of any other subpart. The degree of inter-dependence of the subparts of members of the group varies all the way from a "loose" mass to a compact unit.

French (1944) pointed out that in addition to interdependence, membership in a group presupposes identification with the group. Deutsch (1949a) indicated that the interdependence is that of promotive or cooperative interdependence rather than, for example, competitive interdependence. Thus, a group may be defined tenta-tively as being composed of a set of members who mutually per-ceive themselves to be cooperatively or promotively interdependent in one or more respects and in some degree.

One of the key concepts, which has been the subject of much experimental investigation, is that of cohesiveness. Intuitively, co-hesiveness refers to the forces that bind the parts of a group to-gether and that, thus, resist disruptive influences. Hence, the study of conditions affecting group cohesiveness and of the effects on group functioning of variations in group cohesiveness lies at the heart of the study of group life.

Festinger, Schachter, and Back (1950) have defined cohesive-ness, in terms of the group member, as "the total field of forces which act on members to remain in the group." The nature and strength of the forces acting on a member to remain in the group may vary from member to member. These investigators make the suggestion that group cohesiveness should "be re-lated to the average magnitude of this force in all parts of the group." Deutsch (1949a), in a definition which has essentially the same implications as that of Festinger, Schachter, and Back, relates group cohesiveness to the degree of perceived cooperative interdependence among members, and to the strength of goals about which the members are cooperatively interdependent. "Mem-bership motive" in the individual is defined so as to be the counter-part of cohesiveness in the group. In the foregoing definitions, the relationship between the group attribute of cohesiveness and the individual attribute of membership motive (or cohesiveness) is not adequately handled. It is obvious, however, that the average of the various individuals' membership motives is an inadequate measure of group cohesiveness. Intuitively, group cohesiveness will be af-fected by the distribution of membership motives in a group—that is to say, whether there is much variation or little variation in membership motive among the members and whether "important" members or "unimportant" members have high or low membership motives. Parenthetically, it should be noted that in the definitions of cohesiveness the forces for remaining in the group are the resultant of the forces for both remaining in and for leaving the group. For simplicity of presentation, the discussion of cohesiveness neglects the forces to leave the group.

Various measures of group "cohesiveness" have been employed in experimental investigations: desire to remain in the group, the ratio of "we" remarks to "I" remarks during group discussions, ratings of friendliness, evaluations of the group and its product, acceptance of each other's idea, in-group sociometric choice versus out-group sociometric choice. Deutsch (1949a), in a theoretical paper, provides a rationale for the use of a wide variety of measures of membership motive by developing the hypotheses that members of more cohesive (cooperative) groups as compared with members of less cohesive (competitive) groups, under conditions of successful locomotion: (1) would be more ready to accept the actions of other group members as possible substitutes for similarly intended actions of their own (and therefore would also not have to perform them); (2) would be more ready to accept inductions (be influenced) by other members; and (3) would be more likely to cathect or value positively the actions of other group members. From these core hypotheses, with the addition of more specific assumptions, it is possible to derive the influence of the amount of cohesiveness upon many aspects of group functioning. Thus, from the hypothesis of possible substitution, it is possible to predict that more specialization of function, more subdivision of activity, more diversity of membership behavior would occur in the more cohesive groups. The hypothesis of induction leads to the prediction that members of more cohesive groups would be more attentive to one another, be more understood by one another, be more influenced by one another, be more likely to change and have more internalization of group norms than members of less cohesive groups. The hypothesis of cathexis leads to predictions of greater friendliness and greater ratio of in-group sociometric choices in the more cohesive groups. Data in a variety of experiments (Back, 1951; Deutsch, 1949b; Gerard, 1954; Levy, 1953; Schachter, 1951) support the foregoing predictions.

In a well-integrated program of research, Festinger and his coworkers have developed a series of fertile hypotheses (Festinger, 1950) and have conducted some ingenious experiments on the communication process within groups. In brief, these investigators have been concerned with three sources of pressures to communicate within groups: (1) communications arising from pressures toward uniformity in a group (Back, 1951; Festinger & Thibaut, 1951; Schachter, 1951); (2) communications arising from forces toward locomotion in a social structure (Kelley, 1951; Thibaut, 1950); and (3) communications arising from the existence of emotional states (Thibaut, 1950; Thibaut & Coules, 1952).

Festinger (1950) has noted two major sources of pressures toward uniformity in a group: social reality and group locomotion. He indicates that when there is no simple, objective basis for determining the validity of one's beliefs, one is dependent on social reality (the consensus of judgment among people whose judgments one respects) to establish confidence in one's beliefs. For example, the belief that "Negroes adversely affect property values when they move into a white neighborhood" is difficult for any white property owner to test in a simple, objective way; thus, he relies on the judgment of others as a test of its validity. Lack of agreement among members of a group provides an unstable basis for beliefs that depend on social consensus for their support, and hence (in line with Heider's discussion of the tendency toward cognitive balance) forces will arise to produce uniformity. Pressures toward uniformity among members of a group may also arise because such uniformity is desirable or necessary in order for the group to move toward some goal. Greater uniformity in opinion within a group can be achieved in either of the following ways: (1) by actions (communications) that are directed at changing one's own views or (2) by actions to make others incomparable in the sense that they are no longer effective as a comparison for one's opinions (rejecting or excluding people with deviating opinions from the group).

Experiments have shown that increasing the attraction to the group, and thus increasing the importance of the group as a comparison object, increases the amount of influence that is attempted and the amount of opinion change that occurs when there is a discrepancy of opinion within a group (Back, 1951). It has also been demonstrated that there will be more pressure for uniformity in a group, the more relevant or important the opinion is for the functioning of the group (Festinger & Thibaut, 1951; Schachter, 1951). Also, as may be expected from theoretical considerations, there is evidence that when pressures toward uniformity exist, members exert influence mainly on those whose opinions are most divergent from their own (Festinger & Thibaut, 1951; Schachter, 1951). While there has, as yet, been little research to indicate the conditions that will lead the pressure toward uniformity to manifest itself in a rejection of deviates rather than in an attempt to influence them to change, experiments by Gerard (1953) and by Festinger and Thibaut (1951) suggest that, as the heterogeneity of a group increases, rejection of deviates also increases.

The experiments revealing the tendency to direct communication toward deviants in the group, and through communication to exert social pressure on them, provide support for Lewin's theory of group decision and social change. Lewin (1947c) began his analysis of change by pointing out that the *status quo* in social life is not a static affair but a dynamic process that flows on but still keeps a recognizable form. He borrowed the term "quasi-stationary equilibria" from physics to apply to such on-going processes, which are kept at their present level by fields of forces preventing a rise or fall. The field of forces in the neighborhood of the level of equilibrium presupposes that the forces against going higher than the forces against lowering increase with the lowering (a process of negative feedback). Thus, if we assume that a group standard is operating to determine the level of the workers' productivity in a factory, any attempt upon the part of a worker to deviate from the standard by higher productivity will only result in stronger forces being exerted upon him by his co-workers to push him back into line. Thus, as Festinger's experiments have demonstrated, the deviant will be exposed to stronger pressures toward conformity the more he deviates. Nevertheless, Lewin points out that the gradient of forces may change at a distance from the equilibrium level: after an individual has gone a certain distance from the equilibrium level, the forces may push him away from the group standard rather than pull him toward it.

Lewin's analysis of the *status quo* as a quasi-stationary equilibrium has two major implications. First of all, it points out that change from the *status quo* can be produced either by adding forces in the desired direction or by diminishing opposing forces. The two methods of producing change have different consequences, however: by adding forces, the process on the new level would be accompanied by a state of relatively high tension, since the strength of forces in opposition would be greater; by decreasing the opposing forces, the new level would be accompanied by lower tension. Secondly, the analysis highlights the difficulties of attempting to change individual conduct and attitudes that are rooted in groups by efforts that are directed at the individual and not at his group. If one tries to change the prejudices of an individual without changing the prejudice of his group, the individual will either be estranged from his group or will be under pressure from his group to revert to his initial attitude. Isolated persons may perhaps change their attitudes because of their individual experiences, but the person who is deeply enmeshed in the social life of his community is unlikely to be able to resist the pressures to conform on matters of community importance if he wishes to continue in good standing.

Considerations such as the foregoing have led to experiments in various settings—in the school, with neighborhood groups, in industry, in an interracial workshop—on the relative efficacy of changing behavior by efforts directed at individuals or at a group (Lewin, 1948). A typical procedure has been to compare the results of a lecture or individual instruction in changing behavior with respect to the use of certain foods with the results of a group decision favoring the use. Results have clearly indicated that the method of group decision produces more change. Most of the experiments on group decision, however, were unfortunately not designed in such a way as to rule out the possibility that such factors as interest or decision, per se, were not the factors producing the greater change. A more carefully controlled experiment by Bennett (1952) suggests that the apparent advantages of group discussion result primarily from the fact that group discussion facilitates decision and perception of consensus. She concludes that, other things being equal, group discussion was not more effective than lecturing, nor did public identification of individuals' decisions contribute appreciably to obtained differences. In Bennett's experiment, the subjects were college students in introductory psychology classes and the content of their lecture or group discussion was concerned with a request to volunteer as experimental subjects for an unspecified psychological experiment. The "groups" were not very cohesive (introductory psychology sections) nor was the issue of volunteering group-rooted in the sense of being clearly relevant to group norms. The cumulative evidence as well as everyday experience supports Lewin's basic contention that to change group-rooted individual attitudes one must, in many instances, change the group to which the individual belongs.

Horwitz (1954) conducted a study that demonstrates some of the psychological consequences of group decision. In his experiment, it was possible for members to decide on goals for the group and, subsequently, to perceive where the group stood in regard to their attainment. In the course of working toward some of the group's agreed-upon goals, the effort was interrupted. In others, the group was allowed to complete the task. After working on a number of different tasks, a Zeigarnik-type test for memory of completed and of interrupted tasks was given to all the members. The experiment was conducted in such a way that each individual indicated by vote whether or not he wanted to complete each task. The results of a secret ballot for each task were also announced to the group. (The experimenter actually announced a falsified group vote in order to be able to study its effects under equated conditions.) The results clearly indicated the motivational effect of the groups agreed-upon goals: in general, more interrupted than completed tasks were recalled. In addition, there was clear evidence that the announced group vote (group decision) whether to complete or not to complete the task affected recall: when the announced group vote was to abandon the task, recall was less than when the announced group vote favored completion.

Much of our discussion of group dynamics, so far, has considered the group as made up of homogeneous parts. In reality, of course, groups are differentiated structures, and the behavior of any group member will be largely determined by his position in the group structure. Although the concepts of group structure and of position within the group have not been well defined in the writings of group dynamicists, a good deal of research related to these concepts has taken place. Thus Lewin, Lippitt, and White's (1939) pioneering study on the effects of different types of leadership behavior has demonstrated how crucial the position of leadership is in determining the atmosphere of the group. Bavelas

(1951) and Leavitt (1951) have demonstrated the significance of position in a communication network in determining the members' behavior and have indicated how the structure of a communication network may affect group productivity and individual satisfactions. Kelley (1951) has shown experimentally the significance of position in a status hierarchy in determining the nature and direction of communication. Polanksy, Lippitt, and Redl (1950a; 1950b), in a study of behavioral contagion in groups, have explored the relationship between status (as defined by various criteria in sociometric choice) and the ability to influence others in the group. Such studies as these provide the rationale for use of the communication process (who communicates with whom, about what, with what frequency, in what manner, in what circumstances, and with what effects) as a key instrument for characterizing group structure and for locating the occupants of various positions within this structure.

Concluding Comment

The large sweep of Lewin's work, his brilliant innovations in many areas of psychology, his experimental ingenuity, cannot but be impressive. His impact on social psychology continues to be felt in the work of his students and colleagues, including Back, Barker, Bavelas, Cartwright, Deutsch, Festinger, French, Heider, Horwitz, Kelley, Lippitt, Pepitone, Redl, Schachter, Thibaut, White, Willerman, Wright, Zander. Yet it cannot be said that Lewin's specific theoretical constructs—his structural and dynamic concepts—are central to research currently being carried on in social psychology. His impact is reflected instead in his general orientation to psychology, which has left its impress on his colleagues and students: that psychological events have to be explained in psychological terms; that central processes in the life space (distal perception, cognition, motivation, goal-directed behavior) rather than the peripheral processes of sensory input and muscular action are the proper focus of investigation; psychological events have to be studied in their interrelations with one another; the individual has to be studied in his interrelations with the groups to which he belongs; the attempt to bring about change in a process is the most fruitful way to investigate it; important social psychological phenomena can be studied experimentally; the scientist should have a social conscience and should be active

in making the world a better place in which to live; a good theory
is valuable for social action as well as for science.

Leon Festinger

Unlike Lewin and the psychological theorists of his generation,
Lewin's students have not been theorists in the grand manner.
They have not produced theoretical approaches to the general
subject matter of psychology. Rather, they have tended to develop
more limited, specific theories, theories that are oriented to
and shaped by laboratory experiments. Festinger's theory of social
communication, Deutsch's theory of cooperation and competition,
Cartwright and French's theory of social power bear these characteristics.

Of Lewin's students, Festinger is the one whose work has had
the broadest impact on social psychology. Here, we may turn our
attention to some of Festinger's more recent theoretical work,
notably his theory of the process of social comparison and his
theory of cognitive dissonance.

Social Comparison

The theory of social comparison (Festinger, 1954) is an elaboration and further development of Festinger's theory of social communication. Underlying that theory is the assumption that people
are driven to find out whether their *opinions* are correct. The theory
of social comparison assumes that this same drive also produces
behavior in people directed toward obtaining an accurate appraisal
of their own *abilities*. It also assumes that when "objective, nonsocial" means are not available people evaluate their opinions
and abilities by comparisons with the opinions and abilities of
others. (Festinger assumes that "objective, nonsocial" means are
preferred to social comparison presumably because they are
more accurate and less easily influenced.) Further, the theory
postulates that, since people want an accurate evaluation of their
opinions or abilities, they will be more likely to compare themselves with people whose opinions or abilities are similar to their
own, rather than widely discrepant: the assumption is that
greater accuracy of evaluation is possible when differences are

small, rather than gross. For example, a person who is just beginning to learn the game of chess will compare himself to other novices rather than to recognized masters of the game.

Next, Festinger draws the interesting conclusion that the drive to evaluate accurately one's own opinions or abilities may, paradoxically, lead one to change them so as to make them closer to the opinions or abilities of others who are available for comparison. He assumes here—without making his assumption explicit—that one way of reducing dissimilarity is to change and become more similar to the others. Another way is to take action to reduce the dissimilarity by changing the others. Still another way is to be attracted less to situations in which the others are dissimilar. In the case of extreme discrepancy, one would reject the situation and cease comparing oneself with others who are markedly dissimilar. One's tendency to change or to attempt to change others will be determined largely by how similar one's position is to the modal position within a group; the more at variance one's own position is, the more likely that he will change it. To illustrate, let us consider a youth who scores in the 80's for eighteen holes of golf. According to Festinger, such a youth would prefer to play with others who "shoot" in the 80's than with golfers who are considerably better or considerably worse than he. If, however, he must play in a group whose scores are discrepant from his own, he will tend to change his own performance or theirs so as to make the scores more comparable. Thus, his game may deteriorate in order to decrease the difference between his and the others' scores. Or, he may change the evaluation of his own game so as to bring it in line with the performance of the others. (Festinger, of course, recognizes that opinions, including opinions about one's abilities, are easier to change than performances or abilities. Nevertheless, his theory gives rise to the prediction, which confounds common sense, that a person will do worse than he can, not just to be "one of the group" but, rather, so as to compare himself with the group.)

Any factors which increase the strength of the drive to evaluate some particular ability or opinion (for example, by increasing the "importance" of the opinion or ability) will presumably increase the negative evaluation of dissimilarity between oneself and the others who are used for comparison purposes and, thus, increase the "pressure for uniformity." Similarly, increasing the importance of the comparison group by increasing their attractiveness or by increasing the relevance of the opinion or ability to the group will increase the pressure toward uniformity. If others are considered to be dissimilar from oneself in certain respects, however, there will be less pressure toward uniformity in other related characteristics.

Festinger points out that although the same basic processes of comparison are involved for opinions and abilities, there are critical differences. In the case of abilities, there is a value set on doing better and better ("a unidirectional drive upward") which is absent in opinions; also, there are nonsocial restraints that make it difficult to change one's ability. The drive to do better and better presumably conflicts with the need for precise evaluation of one's abilities (by comparison with the performance of others who are similar in ability). Consequently, one is led to do only slightly better than the others. It is obvious, however, that not everyone in a group can be slightly better than everyone else. Thus, with respect to the evaluation of abilities, a state of social equilibrium is never reached; competitive behavior is a manifestation of this lack of equilibrium.

Festinger points out that the theory of social comparison has clear implications for group formation and group structure. In effect, the drive for self-evaluation can lead people to associate with one another and to join groups; it is one of the factors that make persons "gregarious." The theory suggests, however, that the selective tendencies to associate with others of similar opinion and ability, together with the influence which is evoked by dissimilarity, will guarantee relative homogeneity of opinions and abilities within groups.

The theory of social comparison has been extended by Schachter (1959) to apply to the evaluation of emotions as well as to the evaluation of opinions and abilities. In a series of experiments, he demonstrated that the tendency to affiliate with others undergoing a similar experience increased when subjects were made anxious. His explanation for this finding is that the subjects were unclear about the appropriateness of their anxiety to the situation; hence, they desired to be with others undergoing a similar experience in order to compare their reactions. Schachter proposes that the emotions experienced by an individual are often very much influenced by the process of social comparison. He theorized that a state of physiological arousal (such as that induced by an injection of adrenalin) may be experienced as either euphoria or anger, depending on how it is interpreted; and, how it is interpreted may in turn depend on social cues derived from the behavior of others. This notion led Schachter to a series of experiments that indicate that subjects may, in fact, interpret a given physiological arousal so as to make it compatible with the emotions being expressed by others in the same situation (Schachter & Singer, 1962).

The theory of social comparison has stimulated a good deal of research. Much of it has focused on the effects of discrepancies of opinion within a group. (For a summary of some of this research, see the earlier discussion of the work by Festinger and his associates on the processes of social communication.) Apart from a study by Hoffman, Festinger, and Lawrence (1954), little of significance has been done with the interesting implications of Festinger's notions about the social comparison of ability. In this latter investigation, the coalition-forming behavior of subjects in a three-person competitive bargaining situation was studied. On any trial during the course of the experiment, a subject could attempt to construct a small square with his own pieces of equipment or could join with another player to attempt to construct a larger square. The rules specified that if more than one square were constructed on a trial, the larger square would "win"; if the squares that were constructed were of equal size, no points were awarded. The winning square was awarded eight points, whether constructed individually or jointly. If it were constructed jointly, the two players had to agree on the division of the points for either of them to get any. The effects of two experimentally introduced variables were studied: the importance of the task (half the subjects were led to believe that the task was a valid measure of intelligence, half that it was an invalid measure) and the "comparability" of another player (half the subjects were led to believe that one of the other two players was distinctly superior in intelligence, half were led to believe that all three players were at the same level of intelligence).

One of the subjects (*sub rosa* an accomplice of the experimenter) appeared to earn a strong initial advantage in points; on the basis of the theory, it was predicted that the other two subjects would try to make his score comparable to theirs and, thus, would be less likely to form a two-person coalition with him than with one another. It was further predicted that this pressure for uniformity would decrease if the subject who was given the initial advantage were viewed as "noncomparable" (because of his clearly superior ability) by the other two subjects or if the subjects were led to view the task as an invalid rather than a valid measure of intelligence.

The results of the experiment were in substantial accord with the theoretical predictions. As with many of the experiments performed to test the theory, however, the results are easily explained in other terms. For example, the results of the study by Hoffman et al. may be explained by assuming that the subjects have a competitive motivation to make more points than any other player and that this motivation is reduced somewhat when legitimate distinctions of status are introduced. Thus their behavior may be seen as a rational strategy in a competitive bargaining situation. A more critical test of the theory of social comparison in relation to ability would place the subject in a competitive situation that is structured so that he had to choose between harming another subject who was far ahead of him in points and helping another subject who was not far behind him in points. Comparison theory should, here, make the nonobvious prediction that the subject would prefer to help a competitor catch up with him rather than to interfere with the competitor who was further ahead of him than the other competitor was behind him.

Despite the ambiguity of many of the experimental results— often consistent with the theory but also readily explained otherwise—the central notions of the theory seem intuitively plausible. It is reasonable to suppose that people want to have an accurate appraisal of their opinions, abilities, and emotional reactions. Also, it is reasonable to expect that to appraise these attributes, they will have to compare themselves with others and, moreover, that the desire to compare themselves with others will lead to social contact.

The nonobvious aspects of the theory reside in three implicit notions. First is the idea that the accuracy of appraisal requires that comparison be confined to people with rather similar attributes. Second is the view that the necessity for comparison with similar others, presumably in order to be more precisely correct, becomes a need or motive in its own right. As such, it can motivate the individual to change his opinion away from being correct, or lead him to influence the others to change, or determine his selection of associates. Clearly, the need for similarity is being given strong motivational properties. Thirdly, the theory assumes that processes of social comparison derive from the individual's need to evaluate his opinions and abilities in order to have correct appraisals of them rather than vice versa.

Each of these three notions has its questionable aspects. Thus, there is no reason to believe that appraisal of one's opinions, abilities, or emotions is likely to be more accurate if one's knowledge is confined to comparison with others who are similar. Self-location on a scale of ability may be aided by knowing something about the extreme positions on the scale as well as knowing where one stands relative to others who are similar. For example, while it is useful for a psychologist to know how his competence as a statistician compares with the competence of other psychologists, it is also useful for him to know that mathematical statisticians are much superior to him and that the nonscientist is often vastly inferior.

Secondly, the implicit assumption of some sort of derived need for social uniformity or homogeneity runs counter to a good deal of evidence that suggests that people frequently seek out variety, novelty, and difference in their social encounters. Moreover, behavior that seeks variety, exploratory behavior, and the like, are just as much part of the process of getting to know oneself and one's environment as is social comparison with others who are similar. Furthermore, many central social processes are based on differences rather than similarities, on complementarities rather than identities. Such a relation holds in most social groups where there is role differentiation—"husband" and "wife" in the family, "teacher" and "student" in the school. That complementarity of roles does not lead to lack of interaction. Neither does it mean that the reactions of the other in the complementary role does not help to provide information for appraising one's own role behavior.

Thirdly, it is by no means self-evident that processes of social comparison derive from the need to have an objective picture of one's abilities or opinions. The causal arrow may point equally well in the opposite direction. Thus, it may be because opinions and abilities are compared socially within a group (because it is functionally useful for the group to assign group tasks in terms of the comparative abilities of its members) that a person needs to evaluate his opinions or abilities. A man who has an idiosyncratic but passionate fondness for the paintings of Hieronymous

Bosch may not and need not compare his opinions with those of others unless his views affect others or affect the way others react to him. Where the opinion or ability has little social relevance, even though it may be personally important, social comparison may not occur.

The Theory of Cognitive Dissonance

The theory of cognitive dissonance (Festinger, 1957) is, in some respects, an amplification of the theory of social comparison. It will be recalled that this latter theory assumed that the processes of social comparison develop out of the "need to know"; dissonance theory goes on to indicate that the need is to have seemingly *consistent* knowledge—cognitions that are not dissonant with one another. In its emphasis on the need for cognitive consistency, Festinger's theory of dissonance is similar to such other theories as Heider's (1946; 1958) theory of balance, Newcomb's (1953) theory of communicative acts, Kelly's (1955) theory of personal constructs, Lecky's (1945) theory of self-consistency, Osgood's and Tannenbaum's (1955) theory of attitudinal congruity, and the Gestalt emphasis of such theorists as Krech and Crutchfield (1948) and Asch (1952). All of these theories assert that a person attempts to perceive, cognize, or evaluate the various aspects of his environment and of himself in such a way that the behavioral implications of his perceptions shall not be contradictory. Festinger's theory differs from these other theories in two respects: it places unique emphasis on the consequences of decisions and it has stimulated abundant research.

Festinger (1957, p. 31) summarizes the core of the theory:

1. There may exist dissonant or "nonfitting relations" among cognitive elements.

2. The existence of dissonance gives rise to pressures to reduce the dissonance and to avoid increases in dissonance.

3. Manifestations of the operation of these pressures include behavior changes, changes of cognition, and circumspect exposure to new information and new opinions.

"Dissonance" between two cognitive elements (x and y) is said to exist if not-x follows from y. If x follows from y, the relation is defined as "consonant." If x and y are unrelated, they are "irrelevant" to one another. The magnitude of dissonance, and also the magnitude of the pressure to reduce the dissonance between two cognitive elements, is assumed to increase as the importance or value of the elements increases. The total amount of dissonance between two clusters of cognitive elements is a function of the weighted proportion of all relevant relations between the two clusters that are dissonant. The weighting is in terms of the importance of the elements involved in the relation.

In describing the reduction of dissonance, Festinger introduces a distinction between cognitive elements that refer to behavior or feelings (for example, the belief "I am going on a picnic today") and cognitive elements which refer to the environment (for example, the belief "It is raining"). He indicates that environmental cognitions are usually more resistant to change than beliefs about behavior—it is easier to change one's beliefs about what one is going to do than one's beliefs about a palpable reality. This is so because, presumably, one can more often change one's behavior than the environment. Festinger suggests that "resistance to change" of a cognitive element is determined not only by the individual's inability to influence the events to which the belief refers, but also by how much new dissonance the change will introduce into the relations with other cognitive elements. He asserts (1957, p. 28):

> The maximum dissonance that can possibly exist between any two elements is equal to the total resistance to change of the less resistant element. The magnitude of dissonance cannot exceed this amount because, at this point of maximum possible dissonance, the less resistant element would change, thus eliminating the dissonance.

Up to this point, the implications of dissonance theory are basically similar to the other theories which posit some need for cognitive consistency. These theories—including dissonance theory —provide many useful insights into processes of attitude formation and change, the pressure for uniformity within groups, the formation of personality impressions, the development of interpersonal relations. Dissonance theory also shares many of the defects of other consistency theories: a rather vague definition of the meaning of psychological inconsistency or dissonance which does not consider the "degree of inconsistency," an inadequate specification of the conditions that will lead to one or another form of reduction of dissonance, an unsatisfactory conceptualization of the type of motivation that is involved in the pressure for the reduction of dissonance. For example, although dissonance is conceived to be a motivating state, there is no attempt to characterize it as an innate or an acquired motivation, nor any inquiry into the conditions that sensitize or desensitize individuals to dissonance. Like most tension-reduction theories, moreover, the "paradise" of dissonance theory is a state of lack of tension. As Festinger's personal style clearly indicates, however, the production of dissonance can stimulate interest and arouse curiosity. People seek out dissonance as well as avoid it.

Dissonance theory differs from other consistency theories in its distinction between predecision and postdecision processes. Earlier, Lewin (1951, p. 176) had suggested in his discussion of the behavior of a housewife who buys food, that predecision differs from postdecision:

> For example, if food is expensive, two forces of opposite direction act on the housewife. She is in a conflict. The force away from spending too much money keeps the food from going into that channel. A second force, corresponding to the attractiveness of the food, tends to bring it into the channel. Let us assume that the housewife decides to buy an expensive piece of meat: the food passes the gate. Now the housewife will be very eager not to waste it. The forces formerly opposing one another will now both point in the same direction: the high price that tended to keep the expensive food out is now the reason why the housewife makes sure that through all the difficulties the meat gets safely to the table and it is eaten.

Festinger's theory generalizes the idea that the situation after decision may differ from the situation before decision. He makes the unique and original assumption that making a decision per se arouses dissonance and pressures to reduce the dissonance.

Dissonance after decision results, according to Festinger, from the fact that the decision in favor of the chosen alternative is counter to the beliefs that favor the unchosen alternative(s). To stabilize or freeze the decision after it has been made, a person will attempt to reduce dissonance by changing his cognitions so that the relative attractiveness of the chosen as compared to the unchosen alternative is increased, or by developing cognitions that permit the alternatives to be possible substitutes for one another, or by revoking the decision psychologically. In Festinger's (1964) view, the crucial difference between the states before and after decision is that the conflict before decision is more "impartial" and "objective," since it does not lead to any spreading apart of the attractiveness in favor of the alternative presently to be chosen. Festinger writes (1964, pp. 8–9): "Once the decision is made, however, and dissonance-reduction processes begin, one should be able to observe that the differences in attractiveness between the alternatives change, increasing in favor of the chosen alternative." According to this view, after a student has decided to go to one college rather than another, the college he has chosen will seem to him to have increased in attraction compared to the college that he did not choose.

A variety of interesting and ingenious experiments have been stimulated by Festinger's view of the postdecision process. These experiments have often involved "nonobvious" predictions that appear to defy common sense. Many of these derive from the notion that if a decision produces insufficient rewards, the person will change his beliefs so as to make the decision seem more rewarding. Festinger (1961) writes: "Rats and people come to love the things for which they have suffered." Presumably they do so in order to reduce the dissonance induced by the suffering and their method of dissonance-reduction is to enhance the attractiveness of the choice which led to their suffering.

In a widely quoted experiment by Festinger and Carlsmith (1959) the prediction was made that the *smaller* the reward that was used to get a subject to do something that he would ordinarily be opposed to doing, the greater would be his change of opinion. Subjects were given an extremely boring task to do and then asked by the experimenter, as a favor, to tell other subjects how enjoyable and interesting the experiment had been. One group of subjects was hired to tell the deception at a rate of $1.00; a second group of subjects was hired at a rate of $20.00; a third, control group were not asked to engage in the deception. Subsequently, measurements were made of the subjects' attitudes toward the monotonous task. Those who deceived others for only $1.00 rated the task as being somewhat enjoyable, the group who received $20.00 for the deception and the control group rated the task "neutrally," that is to say, less favorably. In other words, the results of the experiment seem to support a rather surprising prediction: a small reward may be more effective in producing attitudinal change than a larger one. Chapanis and Chapanis (1964), however, point out that the results are explicable by

assuming that many of the subjects (college students) had suspicions about a $20.00 payment for a few minutes' work, and these
suspicions could have lowered their ratings of the task. Their critique does not seem applicable, however, to other experiments
which have used smaller rewards varying from $.50 to $5.00 and
found essentially the same results as were obtained by Festinger and
Carlsmith. (See Silverman, 1964, for a summary of several of these
experiments.)

Brehm and Cohen (1962, pp. 308–309), in a book summariz-
ing the research stimulated by the dissonance formulation, indicate that many of the major derivations of the theory have been
tested and confirmed. Some of the supported derivations concerning the arousal of dissonance in a "free choice" situation are: (1)
a choice between attractive alternatives creates dissonance; (2)
dissonance arising from a choice is proportional to the attractiveness of the rejected alternative; (3) dissonance arising from a
choice is proportional to the qualitative dissimilarity of the alternatives of choice; and (4) dissonance arising from a choice is proportional to the importance of the choice.

Supported derivations concerning the arousal of dissonance in
a situation of "forced compliance" include: (1) dissonance from
commitment to comply decreases as rewards, incentives, or justifi-
cations for compliance increase; (2) dissonance from commitment
to comply decreases as coercive forces to produce compliance increase.

With regard to studies of "exposure" to dissonant information,
the following additional derivations—among others—have been
confirmed: (1) the amount of dissonance consequent to exposure
to discrepant information is a direct function of the importance of
the issue; (2) dissonance in the communicatee is a direct function of the difficulty or effort involved in exposure to the discrepant information. Evidence has also supported the contention
that dissonance is a direct function of choice in situations of both
"free choice" and "forced compliance."

Chapanis and Chapanis (1964), in reviewing some of the same
experimental literature described in Brehm and Cohen (1962),
come to a rather different conclusion, asserting that "as a body of
literature, it is downright disappointing. Too many studies have
failed to stand up to close scrutiny." Their criticisms of many experiments on dissonance are trenchant. They point out inadequa-

cies in the research designs, in the statistical treatment of the data, and in the interpretation of the results of many of the widely cited experiments. Nevertheless, it is only fair to note that their criticism ignores studies of dissonance which are less vulnerable to methodological criticisms. (See Silverman, 1964, for a rebuttal of the Chapanis and Chapanis criticism.) These less vulnerable studies suggest that dissonance after decision and reduction of dissonance *can* occur. They do not indicate, however, that dissonance *must* occur as a result of decision-making.

Festinger, in a recent statement, revised his earlier view (1957, p. 35) that "dissonance then will be a result of the simple act of having made a decision." He wrote (1964, p. 156): "On the whole, the evidence is clear that simply making a decision does not guarantee the onset of dissonance-reduction processes." He goes on to suggest, in agreement with some ideas proposed by Brehm and Cohen (1962, p. 300), that "commitment" is necessary for the occurrence of dissonance. He indicates that a decision carries commitment if it "unequivocally affects subsequent behavior. This is not intended to mean that the decision is irrevocable, but rather that the decision has clear implication for the subsequent unrolling of events as long as the person stays with that decision." Unfortunately, Festinger has not yet gone beyond this vague and rather unsatisfactory definition of "commitment."

It is especially unfortunate because the uniqueness of Festinger's theory of consistency—the emphasis on postdecisional dissonance—necessarily is linked to the meaning of the phrase "decision with commitment" once one has abandoned the notion that all decisions produce dissonance. Nor is the discussion of commitment by Brehm and Cohen of much help; they use the term more or less as a synonym for "decision." Thus, they write (1962, p. 7): "A person is committed when he has decided to do or not do a certain thing, when he has chosen one (or more) alternatives and thereby rejected one (or more) alternatives, when he actively engages in a given behavior or has engaged in a given behavior."

Festinger concludes his latest work on dissonance with the following sad comment (1964, p. 158): "There is an old joke, which is not very funny, about the monograph that concludes by saying that it has created more problems than it has solved." Dissonance theory has indeed solved no problems, but it has pointed to some very interesting questions about postdecisional processes. It has stimulated research which suggests that there may be less objectivity and more partiality and bias in the way the person views and evaluates the alternatives *after* he makes his decision than *before* he makes it. So far, however, the theory has not been specific enough to state the conditions under which the "rationalization" of decision will occur nor detailed enough to state what kind of rationalizing process will occur.

The psychoanalytic term "rationalization," used to refer to the processes involved in the reduction of postdecisional dissonance, clarifies the discussion because it is useful to think of postdecisional dissonance as a form of "defensiveness" and to think of "dissonance reduction" as a "mechanism of defense." According to this view, which has been presented more fully elsewhere (Deutsch, Krauss, & Rosenau, 1962), when a person experiences dissonance after making a choice, he is attempting to defend himself against a perceived implication of his choice which is contrary to his self-conception. It is the inconsistency between the cognitions of self and of the choice, rather than the inconsistency in selecting one alternative rather than another that is critical to the occurrence of postdecisional dissonance.

More generally, one may state the proposition, adapted from Heider (1958), that any event (X) which is conceived to be a function of the characteristics of a person (P) and of his environment (E) will tend to be perceived in such a way that the perception of the $P, E, X,$ and their interrelationships are not inconsistent with one another. The more general formulation implies that an individual may experience dissonance in relation to his conception of another, that is to say, when P is another person. Thus, it is dissonant with one's conception of a friend to see him cheat or to see him make a choice in poor taste. It further implies that an individual may experience self-dissonance (the need to defend his self-conception) even when X is produced by another person, as long as he attributes X to some characteristics of himself. Thus, it is dissonant with one's conception of himself as a father to learn that his son has stolen some money. It is dissonant with one's conception of himself if someone he respects (a teacher, an experimenter, an expert) thinks that one may have shown poor judgment in making a choice.

The general proposition implies that the arousal of dissonance or defensiveness can occur with or without there having been a decision made. Dissonance is, thus, not unique to the postdecisional process nor is it inevitable as a consequence of decisions. This conclusion should not suggest, however, that decision and the actions which follow from it have no consequences. The frequent necessity to justify one's actions to oneself as well as to others may produce the subtle, nonobvious changes which have been the focus of the experiments on dissonance. In addition, the actions which follow from decisions may change the reality confronting the individual and may, as a consequence, make it difficult for him to alter or reconsider his decision. Thus, if a person decides to accept a dinner invitation rather than go to a concert, his decision becomes stabilized as a result of such activities as telling his host that he will come to dinner (going to the concert will now have the new, additional negative consequences of breaking a promise) or as a result of not having gotten tickets for the concert (which may make it unlikely that he will be able to get in). The changes in reality resulting from decisions may generally be expected to increase the relative psychological potency of the chosen alternative, which enters more into the focus of attention and activity.

In a well-constructed world, increased attention would lead to increased interest and attraction. Thus, if a student chooses psychology rather than physiology as his major, he will take more courses in psychology as a consequence. In this way, his attention and activity become more focused on psychology. Presumably, his activity and focused attention will lead him to discover unexpected pleasures and interests in his study, whereas the unexpected pleasures and interests inherent in physiology remain undiscovered simply because of his lack of exploration. Of course, the world is not perfectly constructed: increased attention does not always lead to the discovery of new pleasures. Indeed, it may lead to the negation of fantasied expectations, to regret, and eventually to an attempt to undo what was decided.

Concluding Comment

Festinger's theories have been stimulating to experimental investigation even though the theories, as such, are often vague, overgeneralized and, in some respects, obviously incorrect. Why, then, have they been so productive of further research? The answer lies in Festinger's unusual ability to go beyond the obvious and to make challenging predictions, combined with his talent for

creating striking experimental formats that readily suggest interesting experimental variations.

Undoubtedly Festinger would rather be stimulating than right.
This attitude is entirely sensible. In the present stage of development of social psychology, no one is ever "right" for very long.
The life span of any theory is short. By its very provocativeness
and bold generalization, Festinger's work stimulates the research
which will create new ideas, some of which constitute a more systematic development of ideas that he first brought to life.

4

THE
REINFORCEMENT
THEORISTS

ONE OF THE MOST productive focuses of research in modern American psychology has been the study of phenomena associated with the acquisition of responses—or learning. The importance of such phenomena is clear. In the human being, at any rate, little behavior seems to be strictly determined by the organism's genetic background, least of all its social behavior. Such socially important characteristics as a person's language, values, or attitudes have all been acquired through his experience with a particular set of social environments. Thus, a knowledge of how people acquire behavioral predispositions is of great relevance for understanding the social nature of man.

Until recently, rather little of the learning psychologists' efforts have been concerned with learning which is specifically social. Instead, they have sought to develop a set of basic principles which explain learning in every situation. To a great extent, the subjects of such investigations have been lower organisms, such as the pigeon and albino rat, although human investigations have by no means been neglected.

Underlying Orientations of the Reinforcement Theorists

The study of learning has been set by three major orientations: the methodological point of view of *behaviorism;* the elementistic structural principles of *associationism;* and the motivational principle of *hedonism.*

Methodologically, behaviorism arose as a revolt against the subjective procedures of introspectionism and the mentalistic concepts of "sensation, perception, attention, image, will, and the like" (Watson, 1919, p. xii). In place of subjective procedures, behaviorism stressed the point that psychology should deal only with observables that everyone can see—with the stimuli that impinge on an organism's sense organs and the observable responses or behavior elicited as responses to stimuli. The wholesome emphasis of behaviorism on objective methods of observation that could be reliably repeated by different observers has had a salutary effect on the rigor of research in psychology. Even now in social psychology, research conducted by those in the behaviorist tradition tends to be noted for its tough-minded focus on observations which do not require complex judgments by the observer.

Early behaviorism, by its emphasis on external observables, tended indirectly to minimize the significance of the organism's inherent internal structure and to neglect the central processes that give coherence and versatility to the "input" from the environment and the "output" to the environment. The term "stimulus-response" or "S-R," which is often used to characterize the orientation of some learning theorists, itself connotes a relative lack of interest in the characteristics of the organism which enable it to organize incoming stimuli so as to refer them to stable, distal objects and to coordinate and direct responses toward goal objects. This lack of interest in what the organism contributes to the integration of sensory input and behavioral output reflects, in turn, the elementistic structural doctrine of associationism. The essence of associationism, which is one of the oldest doctrines in psychology, is that the elementary units of mind, like sensations or ideas, are linked or associated by their contiguity in space and time: internal structure is developed by the experience of elementary units having been associated. The behaviorists, while rejecting these mentalistic units of classical associationism, nevertheless accepted the principle of association, substituting for it the "conditioned response" as the basic unit of analysis.

The third orientation underlying the approach of several, but not all, of the well-known learning theorists is a utilitarian emphasis on the role of "reward," "drive-reduction," "pleasure," "reinforcers," or "satisfiers" in establishing and strengthening stimulus-response connections. The doctrine of psychological hedonism, which maintains that pain and pleasure are our "sovereign masters" (Bentham, 1789, p. 1), has a long history and has taken many forms. In psychology, as early as 1898, Thorndike proposed his famous dictum, "Pleasure stamps in; pain stamps out," which subsequently became one of Thorndike's basic laws of learning, the "law of effect"; similar notions today are usually referred to as "reinforcement theory." In social psychology, the point of view of hedonism has commonly been expressed in terms of the doctrine of "economic man." This doctrine, as Homans has stated so succinctly (1961, p. 13), envisages "human behavior as a function of its payoff; in amount and kind [human behavior] depends on the amount and kind of reward and punishment it fetches." The doctrine of economic man underlies the work of such social psychological theorists as Homans (1961) and Thibaut and Kelley (1959). As a consequence, their writings in social psychology share a common underpinning with the work of the social psychologists who employ the more traditional "reinforcement theory."

Two Basic Procedures for Learning Experiments

The experimental study of learning has been dominated by the use of two paradigms, known as classical conditioning and instrumental conditioning. The first of these procedures stems from the work of the Russian physiologist, Pavlov; the latter derives largely from the work of E. L. Thorndike of Columbia University's Teachers College.

Classical Conditioning

The paradigm for classical conditioning is well known: meat powder, an "unconditioned stimulus" (UCS), is placed in a dog's mouth and automatically elicits a flow of saliva, an "unconditioned reflex" or "unconditioned response" (UCR); a neutral stimulus, such as the sound of a bell, which does not ordinarily elicit the flow of saliva, is presented just before each presentation of food and comes presently to elicit the saliva without the UCS. The new response to the bell is called a "conditioned reflex" or "conditioned response" (CR) and the sound of the bell is called a "conditioned stimulus" (CS). The neutral stimulus (CS), by being associated with the unconditioned stimulus (UCS), elicits a response (CR) resembling the one originally made to the unconditioned stimulus (UCR).

Operant or Instrumental Conditioning

In instrumental or operant conditioning, the procedure entails the presentation or omission of reward or punishment after the animal, has made some specific response. The response to be conditioned must occur before it can be rewarded or punished. Hence, it must have been in the animal's behavioral repertory before the experiment and must be "emitted" by the animal during the course of an experiment. In a typical experiment, a hungry rat is placed into a specially constructed box. Whenever it presses a bar in the box some food pellets are delivered into a tray for the rat to consume. The bar-pressing response, which first occurs accidentally during the rat's exploration of the box, soon becomes the dominant instrumental response: the rat presses the bar, goes to the tray and consumes the food pellets; when the food tray is withdrawn it goes back to pressing the bar. In avoidance training (as contrasted with reward training), the animal might be exposed to a noxious stimulus—for example, an electric shock—which it can prevent or terminate by pressing a bar. In instrumental conditioning, the animal's behavior is instrumental to the procurement of reward or the avoidance of punishment. It should be noted that instrumental responses are usually specified in terms of their consequences (for example, all behaviors which depress the bar in such a way as to elicit a reward, no matter how much they differ otherwise, are called bar-press responses) rather than in terms of the specific movements involved in the response.

Basic Concepts of Learning

Although there are differences between the two kinds of conditioning, there are also many similarities between them. These similarities are apparent in the technical vocabulary which is used to describe phenomena found in both types of conditioning. Such terms as the following are part of the basic vocabulary applied to learning phenomena in diverse contexts.

1. *Response strength.* As a result of learning, the strength of the tendency to make a specified response (in a given situation, given certain motivation) tends to increase. The strength of a response tendency is measured in terms of (1) the *probability of its occurrence* (for example, in what percentage of trials it occurs), (2) the *rate of responding* (for example, the number of responses made in a given period of time), (3) its *latency* (how long it takes for the response to occur), (4) its *magnitude,* or the intensity of the response, and (5) its *resistance to extinction.* In experimental work, the various measures of response strength often show little intercorrelation (see Kimble, 1961) and are themselves conditionable (the subject can learn to respond with a given latency, or with a given intensity, or at a given rate). These facts make it difficult to state unequivocal, general rules for coordinating the empirical measurements of a response with the concept of "response strength" (or "reaction potential").

"Response strength" is usually linked to such other concepts as "habit strength," "drive," "incentive motivation," or "stimulus intensity," all of which are considered to be determinants of "response strength." These concepts are, in turn, linked to "observables": "habit strength" may be taken as the number of times a given response has been reinforced (Hull) or the number of times a given response has occurred in conjunction with a given stimulus (Spence); "drive" may mean "hours of food deprivation," "percentage of normal body weight," "blood sugar level," or "intensity of stomach contractions." The various learning theorists differ among themselves as to how "response strength" is related to such other concepts as "habit strength" and "drive" and as to how these other concepts relate to one another and to observables. Few of them would disagree, however, that performance of a given response in a given situation can be influenced by such factors as the amount, kind, immediacy, and distribution of reward associated with prior performances; the kind and intensity of the subject's motivation; the amount of work connected with making the response; the distinctiveness of the stimulus situation from other situations to which competing or interfering responses have been learned, and the similarity of the stimulus situation to other situations in which similar or facilitating responses have been learned. The term "performance" indicates that what a subject does in a situation is partly determined by prior learning, but also partly by current motivations, current incentives, and the current situation.

2. *Extinction* refers to the decrease of response strength with nonreinforcement. Since conditioned responses show little tendency to be forgotten, it is evident that extinction must be the result of some active process. Various opinions exist as to the nature of this process. Some attribute extinction to the development of a "conditioned inhibition" for avoiding the work involved in making the unreinforced response; others urge that the absence of reward is frustrating and that frustration acts as a drive and produces responses that interfere with the conditioned response; still others suggest that extinction occurs as the subject learns to *expect* that reinforcement will no longer follow the conditioned response. Despite these theoretical differences, most learning theorists agree that the factors influencing the extinction of a response are similar to those influencing its acquisition.

3. A *discriminative stimulus* is one which defines the occasion on which a response will be reinforced—it helps the subject to distinguish between those situations in which a given response will be reinforced and those in which it will not. Learning theorists have done very little research on the properties of stimuli which relate to their ease of identification or to their discriminability, apart from study of the effects of quantitative variations in the psychophysical properties of stimuli (intensity, wave length). This kind of perceptual research has been of more interest to the Gestalt psychologists (see Ch. 2).

4. *Reinforcement.* Any event which follows a response and makes it more likely that the response will be repeated is called a reinforcer. In practice, reinforcement is usually achieved by arranging circumstances so that after making a given response the subject gets something he wants (food after food deprivation, approval from the experimenter) or avoids something he dislikes (a noxious stimulus, an electric shock, disapproval). A "secondary reinforcer" is any stimulus which derives its reinforcing properties from association with a primary reward. The concept of secondary reinforcement is of especial importance in the application of reinforcement theory to social behavior, since it is quite clear that the sorts of reinforcers which operate in social situations (praise, disapproval) are qualitatively quite different from such primary reinforcers as food or electric shock. Reinforcement theorists usually assume that such "social" reinforcers as praise and disapproval derive their power from association with primary reinforcers.

The main charatceristics of reinforcement which have been singled out for investigation are (1) the amount and quality of the reinforcement, (2) the extent of the delay of reinforcement, and (3) the way reinforcement is scheduled or programmed. There are various types of reinforcement schedule: "continuous reinforcement" involves administering a reinforcement on every trial or after every correct response; "partial" (or "intermittent") reinforcement is the administering of reinforcement according to some particular schedule. The reinforcements may be scheduled to occur only after a specified period of time has elapsed ("interval schedules") or only after a given number of responses have been made ("ratio schedules"); the time interval or ratio may be *fixed* so that it does not vary from reinforcement to reinforcement, or it may be *varied* randomly in such a way that only the average of the time intervals or response ratios between reinforcements is a specified interval or ratio.

A vast amount of research has been done on reinforcement. This research has not produced any consensus as to whether *rewards* are necessary for learning. There is, however, agreement that the availability of rewards for a given response will affect the subject's readiness to perform it. The evidence in respect of *punishment* suggests that it acts only to inhibit performance; it does not (unlike nonreinforcement) permanently weaken habit strength. *Immediate* reward or punishment is more effective than *delayed*

Research on lower animals suggests that delays in reinforcement of more than a few seconds make primary learning unlikely. Instances of learning with protracted delays of reward are assumed to be cases where immediate *secondary reinforcement* occurs. *Intermittent,* compared with *continuous,* reward of a response leads to a slower rate of extinction after nonreinforcement has begun; *intermittent* punishment leads to a more prolonged inhibition of the response after the punishment has been discontinued than does *continuous* punishment.

The mechanisms of reinforcement have been studied extensively. The research has not revealed, as yet, any single mechanism. Rather, the evidence is that a great variety of physiological processes, of internal and external stimuli, of responses, can serve as reinforcers. Thus, for a hungry animal, the smell of food, its taste, introduction of food directly into the stomach, change of its blood sugar level can each independently serve as a reinforcer. So can electrical stimulation of certain parts of the brain; so, too, the opportunity to explore a maze or the opportunity to see new stimuli. The point to be made is that the diversity of reinforcers indicates that no single explanatory notion like "tension reduction" or "need reduction" is adequate.

5. *Drive* is used variously to refer to (1) the underlying physiological conditions that activate and energize behavior (for example, the physiological conditions which accompany food deprivation), (2) the stimuli (for example, stomach contractions) which, if sufficiently intense, activate behavior, and (3) the tendency of behavior to have a goal-directed character (to persist until a given end-state is attained). Many reinforcement theorists—a notable exception is Skinner—consider that the mechanism of reinforcement somehow entails drive reduction.

The search for the relationship between drive and learning is usually expressed in two questions: How do drives affect learning? How are drives acquired or learned? Unfortunately, the answers to these questions are not univocal. Ambiguity results partly from the lack of clarity of the concept itself and of the conditions which affect a given drive and partly from the fact that different measures of the intensity of a given drive often show little correlation with one another ("hours of food deprivation" as against "amount of food eaten"; "activity level" as against "maze performance"). The evidence concerning the effect of the drive level on response acquisition is inconclusive: many experiments show no effect, other experiments suggest that intense motivation may unduly restrict attention and interfere with learning, whereas still other experiments indicate that learning improves as the strength of drive increases up to a moderate intensity. There is more clear-cut evidence demonstrating that different drives (like "hunger" and "thirst") can provide distinctive stimuli to which the subject can learn to respond and that such learnings can occur quickly.

Common sense supports the view that drives can be acquired or learned. Much of the research on acquired drives has been concerned with the acquisition of fear. This research indicates that a conditioned fear can be evoked by stimuli associated with painful events, that conditioned fear will serve as a motive for learning and that fear reduction is a reinforcer. Other unconfirmed research has suggested that such social drives as "aggression" and "affiliation" possess the normal properties of other drives, that is to say, they can be satiated by "consummatory behavior." For example, the need for aggression or for affiliation can be satiated by aggressing or affiliating and when satiated the need will not instigate aggressive or affiliative responses. There has been, however, little research that demonstrates the processes by which social motives are acquired.

6. *Generalization.* "Stimulus generalization" refers to the fact that a response which is conditioned to a certain stimulus tends also to occur with similar stimuli; the more similar are the two stimuli, the more likely is the response. "Response generalization" means that a given stimulus may not only elicit the response directly associated with it but may also increase the likelihood that similar responses will be elicited. Generalization occurs in the extinction process as well as in the acquisition or eliciting process.

In the preceding paragraph, we have seen that a response is often generalized to *similar* stimuli, but it is also evident that responses are often generalized to stimuli which have no physical similarity to the original stimuli—responses acquired in relation to an intense light may be generalized to intense auditory or tactile stimuli, responses acquired for the word "barn" may be generalized to other rural words. To explain the occurrence of generalization to physically different stimuli, the S-R theorists have developed the view that such generalization is "mediated"—that, intervening between the observable stimulus input and the observable response output, there is some mediating process, such as the stimulus eliciting an internal response that produces internal stimulation, which then elicits the observable response. Generalization would occur because the internal response and the internal stimuli elicited by the different observable stimuli are similar.

7. *Discrimination.* If a subject is reinforced for responding to one stimulus and not to another, or for making one response rather than another to a given stimulus, a discrimination gradually develops. The end result is that he learns to discriminate between the occasions for making a given response ("stimulus discrimination") or between the responses appropriate for a given occasion ("response discrimination"). Paralleling the development of discrimination is the gradual extinction of the response to the inappropriate stimulus or the gradual extinction of the inappropriate response.

Few of the learning theorists have contributed greatly to social psychology. Much of their writing in this area consists of attempts to translate psychoanalytic concepts into the concepts of learning theory. This approach has been especially characteristic of such learning theorists as Tolman (1951), Mowrer (1960a; 1960b), Sears (1943; 1951), and, to some extent, Miller and Dollard (1941; Dollard & Miller, 1950). More relevant here, however, are the work of Miller and Dollard and of Bandura and Walters on social learning and imitation, the writings of Hovland and his associates on communication and persuasion and the work of Skinner and his associates on verbal behavior, and the contribution of Homans, a sociolgist who has been strongly influenced by Skinner's point of view. Finally, we turn to the work of Thibaut and Kelley, who analyze social interaction in terms of its rewards and costs.

Neal E. Miller and John Dollard

Miller and Dollard (1941; Dollard & Miller, 1950) point out that four factors are exceedingly important in learning: drive, cue, response, and reward or reinforcement. They define drive as a strong stimulus which impels a response; the stronger the stimulus, the more drive function it possesses. Cues are distinctive stimuli which determine which response will be made, and when it will be made.

The most likely initial response in a given stimulus situation is the dominant response in the initial hierarchy of responses. If the initial response is not rewarded, the connection between the stimulus and response is weakened. If a response is followed by a reward, the connection is strengthened so that the next time the same drive is present with other cues this response is more likely to occur: with the rewarding or nonrewarding of responses the hierarchy of responses to a given situation may be altered. The effects of rewards taper off in a gradient so that the connections of the cue response immediately associated with a reward are strengthened more than remoter connections.

Miller and Dollard explain the acquisition of social drives and social rewards essentially in terms of the notion that a neutral cue can acquire the property of a drive by being connected or associated with a drive stimulus; it acquires reward property by being associated with the reduction of a drive stimulus. Thus, a child may learn to fear dogs after having been bitten by one, and the fear of dogs can thereafter motivate him to make certain kinds of response (such as running to his mother) that may reduce his fear. In effect, "dogs," a previously neutral cue, elicits internal responses (similar to those elicited by pain) which produce strong stimuli which function as a drive; the drive in turn evokes responses which are more likely to be repeated in similar situations if they are rewarded by reduction of the drive stimuli. Cues associated with the drive reduction—like the mother—take on reward value. Thus, more generally, if the mother has been repeatedly associated with drive reduction, her presence and her approval come to have reward value. On the other hand, her absence or disapproval may elicit internal responses (such as anxiety) that produce drive stimuli.

Miller and Dollard stress the importance of language as a "cue-producing response" in mediating responses to remote rewards or punishments and in eliciting acquired drives, responses that are foresightful. Thus, a child who has acquired a fear of dogs may have his fear elicited by the statement "There is a dog in the next room," once he has acquired an understanding of language. The child's ability to make a foresightful response (such as locking the door to the next room) is enormously facilitated by the possibility of his making anticipatory covert verbal responses ("Dogs cannot go through locked doors"; "The door to the next room has a lock on it"; "I can lock the door"). Also, verbal statements—"The dog has a muzzle and cannot bite"—may help reduce the fear. Verbal responses can, moreover, greatly facilitate the processes of discrimination and generalization by categorizing stimuli as calling for similar or dissimilar responses. Thus, the words "friendly" and "fierce" as applied to a dog help to discriminate between the occasions for approach and avoidance responses. Labeling a dog as "friendly" makes it equivalent in this regard to other dogs that have been similarly labeled and facilitates the transfer of responses previously learned in relation to dogs who were labeled "friendly." The difference in effort between making the verbal responses "friendly" and "fierce" is trivial, yet it is evident that the cues produced by one label or the other may lead to major differences in the way a person responds to the dog.

Verbal responses in language are especially useful cue-producing responses, not only because they are easy to make and can be made covertly as well as overtly, but also because they are social in character. The social character of language means that one person's verbal responses, if made overtly, can function as cues for others as well as for himself. (It should be noted that Miller and Dollard here begin to provide a rationale for learning theory that rejects the methodological bias of early behaviorism against verbal report and introspection.) The social character of language means that it is possible for one person to transmit economically to other people enormous amounts of information (and misinformation) by the use of language.

Miller and Dollard also show that social imitation plays a central role in the process of learning to talk and a considerable role in all social learning. Imitation is also important in maintaining social conformity and discipline. They say (1941, p. 10): "Individuals must be trained, in many situations, so that they will be comfortable when they are doing what others are doing and miserable when they are not."

The term "imitation" refers to two important types of action: "matched-dependent" behavior, in which the followers must depend upon the leader for the cues as to what act is to be performed and where and when; and "copying" behavior, in which the imitator attempts to produce responses which are an acceptable reproduction of the behavior of a model. Essentially the same concepts are used to explain how both forms of imitation are acquired. These authors illustrate their thesis that imitative behavior occurs

because the individual is rewarded when he imitates and not rewarded when he does not with a series of parallel experiments on
albino rats and young children. In the experiments with albino rats,
the response selected for study was that of turning in the same direction as a leader at the junction of a T-maze. It was found that,
before specific training, the rats showed no marked tendency either to imitate or not to imitate the behavior of the leader. One
group of hungry rats were then rewarded by being given food
only if they went in the same direction as a leader; another group
of hungry rats were rewarded by food only if they went in the opposite direction. Under these conditions, the first group learned to
imitate and the second not to imitate. Further tests indicated that
the learning to imitate (or not to imitate) had been generalized.
Thus, animals that had learned to imitate white rats also imitated
black rats without any additional training; animals that had
learned to imitate when motivated by hunger, imitated when motivated by thirst; animals that had learned to imitate on the T-maze
tended to imitate on another task. Parallel experiments with children indicated that they could learn to imitate or not to imitate a
leader in order to get a reward of candy. Further experiments indicated that children could learn to discriminate between leaders so
that they would copy one leader (a tall person, perhaps) and not
copy another leader who was distinctly different (a small person).
Once such learning occurs, there is some generalization, so that
children are more likely to copy leaders who are similar rather
than dissimilar in appearance to the leaders whom the children
were initially rewarded for copying. Also, a child who is rewarded
for copying a leader in one situation will show a tendency to imitate his behavior in other situations.

Miller and Dollard point out that imitation can greatly hasten
the process of independent learning (making correct responses
without the presence of a model) when the occurrence of the correct responses by trial-and-error procedures is improbable. However, if the subject is rewarded for performing an incomplete copy
of the model's responses, independent learning may be retarded.
Thus, if watching the model prevents the subject from copying the
model's response of looking at the relevant cues, imitation may
delay the learning of independent responses.

The Miller-Dollard theory of social imitation has been severely
criticized as, in effect, requiring the person to be able to make a re--

sponse before he can learn it through imitation. Thus, Bandura (1962, p. 217) asserts that the Miller-Dollard theory implies that for a child to learn to say "symposium" imitatively, he would first have to emit the word "symposium" in the course of random vocalization, match it accidentally with the model's verbal response, and secure a positive reinforcement. From his own extensive program of research on social learning through imitation, Bandura (1962, p. 260) concludes that "the process of response acquisition is based upon contiguity of sensory events, and that instrumental conditioning and reinforcement should perhaps be regarded as response-selection rather than response-acquisition or response-strengthening procedures." He also points out that models who are attractive, rewarding, prestigeful, or powerful, are likely to command more attention and therefore elicit more imitation than models who lack these qualities. Similarly, persons who are dependent, lacking in self-esteem, incompetent, and who have been frequently rewarded for imitative behavior are apt to be highly attentive to the cues produced by the behavior of others. In other words, reinforcement may function as causal agent in learning through imitation primarily by augmenting or reducing the arousal and maintenance of the observing reaction.

The Yale Communication Research Program

Carl Hovland and his colleagues at Yale University have engaged in a systematic program of research on the effects of different kinds of communication upon opinion and attitude change (Hovland, Lumsdaine, & Sheffield, 1959; Hovland, Janis, & Kelley, 1953; Hovland, 1957; Hovland & Janis, 1959; Hovland & Rosenberg, 1960). Their theoretical position is often referred to as "the instrumental learning model," because it treats attitudinal dynamics in terms similar to those employed by Hull (1943) and by Miller and Dollard. The central notion of this approach is that an opinion (an habitual judgment or prediction) or an attitude (an habitual evaluative orientation) becomes habitual because its overt expression or internal rehearsal is followed by the experience or anticipation of positive reinforcement. They use the term "incentive" rather than "reinforcement" because they are concerned with anticipated reinforcers, which are brought into play by a message from a communicator who is trying to change the opinions or attitudes of an audience.

Hovland and his associates point out that the techniques of opinion change involve obtaining the audience's attention, comprehension, and acceptance of the communication. Although they clearly state the significance of nonmotivational influences (particularly as they affect attention span, memory, and comprehension), their stress is on the determinants of the incentives to attend, comprehend, and accept a communication. They recognize that existing attitudes are supported by incentives and that, as a consequence, attempts to change attitudes will often be resisted. In studying the process of attitude change, they have investigated primarily three types of incentive: direct gains of money, health, security, or the like if the attitude is altered; social approval, prestige, and group acceptance resulting from attitudes similar to those held by respected individuals or groups; and self-approval, such as feeling right or wrong or feeling that one is being manipulated or treated with respect.

The Yale group has studied experimentally how the process of persuasion is affected by variations in the characteristics of the communicator (his credibility, the amount of change he advocates), the communication (its one-sidedness, its explicitness in drawing conclusions, the type of incentive it appeals to, its ordering of pro and con arguments), and the audience (its personality dispositions, the salience and strength of its group memberships, its role—active or passive—in developing support for the advocated position). These studies and their results have been thoroughly summarized and evaluated in Cohen's (1964) book, *Attitude Change and Social Influence,* and will not be detailed here.

However, we note some of the major findings below, with the comment that they are both consistent with common-sense observations and not surprising: attitude change is more likely when the credibility of the communicator is high rather than low; the amount of attitude change that can be induced increases with the amount advocated if the communicator's credibility is high, but not if it is low; fear appeals that are not immediately followed by reassuring methods of reducing the fear often boomerang; conclusion drawing is more appropriate when the issues are so complex that the audience is not likely to draw the desired conclusion; "inoculation" of the audience against opposing viewpoints by presenting two rather than one side of an issue is desirable when the audience is likely to know of or to be exposed to counter arguments; the strength of group-conformity motives affects the willingness to accept attitudinal positions that are concordant or discordant with group norms; people who experience success or receive approval for an attitudinal position that they are induced to take are more likely to maintain the new attitude than those who do not get rewarded; active participation in rehearsing and improvising support for the new attitudinal position produces more attitudinal change than passive listening to or reading similar material.

There has been an interesting controversy between the proponents of dissonance theory and of instrumental learning theory. The two theories lead to opposite predictions concerning the way in which incentives produce attitudinal change when used to induce behavior that is discrepant with a pre-existing attitude (for example, a prohibitionist being induced to favor lowering the age at which minors could buy liquor by the promise of a reward). Dissonance theory predicts that small rewards are more effective than large rewards in inducing such attitudinal changes. Instrumental learning leads to the opposite prediction. On pages 68–75, we describe some research that supports the theory of dissonance. Here we note that recent research by Janis and Gilmore (1965) and Rosenberg (1965) challenges it.

The study by Janis and Gilmore investigates the influence of incentive conditions on the success of role playing in modifying attitudes. They reason that, when a person accepts the task of improvising arguments in favor of a point of view at variance with his own convictions, he becomes temporarily motivated to think up arguments favoring the new position and to suppress opposing ones. This biased scanning increases the salience of favorable arguments and enhances the chance of attitude change. However, they hypothesized that, if the sponsor of the role-playing assignment were viewed negatively, the resulting negative incentives would elicit responses that would interfere with attitudinal change. Instrumental learning theory also suggests that a large positive incentive should facilitate attitudinal change more than a small one. In their experiment, they studied the effects of (1) unfavorable (blatantly commercial) versus favorable (public welfare) sponsorship of the role playing; (2) small monetary reward ($1) versus a large one ($20) for carrying out the task; and (3) overt role playing versus passive exposure to the same material. In general, the results of the experiment fail to support the predictions from dissonance theory. The unfavorable sponsor does not produce more dissonance reduction than the favorable sponsor and the $1 reward is not more effective than the $20. However, the results provide only weak support for incentive theory. Neither sponsorship nor reward in itself produces significant effects; the combination of favorable sponsorship and a large reward does, however, produce more attitudinal change than unfavorable sponsorship combined with small reward.

Rosenberg's (1965) experiment provides somewhat more clear-cut evidence about the effects of incentives than does the Janis and Gilmore study. He reasons that the promise of excessive reward in the experiments supporting dissonance theory, which show greater attitudinal change with less reward, was unwittingly creating evaluation apprehension and hostile attitudes toward the experimenter. These, in turn, would make the subjects' attitudes more resistant to change; thus, the lesser change in attitudes by subjects who were promised a larger reward would be an artifact of the coincidental evaluation apprehension and suspiciousness toward the experimenter. To eliminate these hypothesized biasing factors, Rosenberg arranged his experiment so that subjects saw no connection between the part of the experiment in which they were induced to write an essay opposing their views and were paid $.50, $1, or $5 and the part in which their attitudes were measured. A different experimenter was employed for each part, and they were also disconnected in other ways. The results show that the amount of changes in attitude is directly proportional to the amount of payment received by the subject. Moreover, they support Rosenberg's suggestion that evaluation apprehension may underlie some of the phenomena of the dissonance experiments. This suggestion is similar to our proposal that self-defensiveness may be central to the occurrence of postdecisional dissonance.

Concluding Comment

Hovland and his associates have not developed any systematic theory of the process of persuasion, but, nevertheless, they have been guided by the central notion of learning theory: that the consequences of behavior, particularly those relating to reward and punishment, affect subsequent behavior. However, they have formulated many of their propositions in terms of anticipated consequences or incentives rather than in terms of actual rewards. As a result, they have been able to readily absorb into their conceptions some of the more phenomenologically oriented notions of personality theory and group dynamics. Thus, their research has often greater immediate relevance to everyday experience than the work of the more traditional behaviorists. At the same time, their formulations have an *ad hoc* quality that, although consistent with common sense, does not go very far beyond it.

Albert Bandura and Richard H. Walters

Unlike many other learning theorists who have written about human social behavior, Bandura and Walters have done their extensive investigations primarily on persons rather than animals. Much of their research is summarized in two co-authored books, *Adolescent Aggression* and *Social Learning and Personality* (Bandura & Walters, 1959; Bandura & Walters, 1963) and in Bandura's *Behavioristic Psychotherapy* (in press). Their studies have been conducted in natural field settings, in the laboratory, and in the clinic with children and adolescents. As a consequence, among the learning theorists, their work shows most clearly the relevance of this approach to the understanding of human social behavior. Their own studies are not, however, uncritical of prior applications of learning theory. They write (Bandura & Walters, 1963, pp. 43-44):

> Previous attempts to conceptualize social phenomena, including deviant patterns of response, within the framework of modern learning theories have, generally speaking, relied on a limited range of learning-theory principles that have largely been developed and tested on the basis of studies of animal subjects and of human subjects in one-person situations. Because of their neglect of social variables, these attempts have been particularly ineffective in accounting for the acquisition of novel social responses. Moreover, the exponents of learning-theory approaches to the problems of social and antisocial behavior have, for the most part, tacitly accepted the basic tenets and concepts of psychodynamic models and have merely translated these into terms familiar and acceptable to the learning

theorist. In this book we have attempted to extend and modify existing learning-theory principles and to suggest additional principles in order to account more adequately for the development and modification of human responses.

The Role of Imitation

The approach of Bandura and Walters to the study of social behavior places a unique stress on the role of imitation in the acquisition of behavior, deviant as well as conforming. Unlike Miller and Dollard's theory of imitation (which, as we have seen, assumes that the imitated responses are already in the subject's behavioral repertory), Bandura and Walters assert that novel response patterns that are precise imitations of another's behavior can be acquired through observation. They emphasize, moreover, that usually the learner successfully imitates more or less the entire response pattern of a model, even though he performs no overt response and receives no reinforcement during the demonstration. Thus, the acquisition of novel responses through imitation is not the slow, gradual process based on differential reinforcement which has usually been postulated by other learning theorists.

In a series of experiments by Bandura and his associates (summarized in Bandura, 1962), they exposed nursery-school children to different kinds of models (human adults in person, human adults on film, cartoon figures on film), with different patterns of behavior in the model (aggressive or nonaggressive), which had different kinds of consequences for the model (rewarding or punishing). The results indicate that children who have observed aggressive models (as they punch, sit on, throw, or kick a large inflated plastic doll) respond to subsequent frustration with considerable aggression, much of which imitates the observed behavior precisely, whereas equally frustrated children who have observed models displaying inhibited behavior tend to match the nonaggressive behavior of the inhibited model. The viewing of cartoon figures and films of human adults produced as much postfrustration aggressive behavior as did the observing of similar behavior in a physically present adult. These findings suggest that children's behavior may be much influenced by what they see portrayed on television programs.

In addition to teaching children entirely novel responses, the presentation of models may have "inhibitory," "disinhibitory," or "eliciting" effects on their behavior; that is to say, observing an aggressive model may release or disinhibit some of the child's inhibitions toward aggressive behavior or may simply elicit aggression that is already in his behavior repertory. Similarly, observations of the inhibition of aggression in a model may increase the tendency to inhibit already learned responses. Although a response may be acquired by merely observing a model's behavior, the readiness to perform it is partly contingent on whether the model is seen to be rewarded or punished as a result of his behavior. Observation of rewarding consequences to the aggressive model produces substantial imitative aggression and releases previously learned aggressive behavior; the observation of punishing consequences may lead to the rejection of the model as a basis for emulation.

Rewarded models are more likely to elicit imitative behavior than unsuccessful ones; so, too, are rewarding models more likely to be emulated than nonnurturant ones. Bandura and Walters indicate, however, that a wide range of imitative responses may be elicited without the necessity of first establishing a nurturant-dependent relationship between the model and the observer.

The Role of Reinforcement

Although Bandura and Walters emphasize that reinforcement (either observed or experienced) does not play a dominant role in the acquisition of novel responses, they give a central role to patterns of reinforcement in strengthening and maintaining different behavioral tendencies. They describe research demonstrating that positive reinforcement in the form of verbal approval or material rewards will increase the frequency of children's aggressive responses; that reinforcement of one class of aggressive response may result in an increase in another class of aggressive response; and that reinforcement of aggressive behavior in one situation may lead to its increase in other situations.

These results are contrary to the frustration-aggression theory, which posits that frustration is an inevitable antecedent of aggression. Bandura and Walters (1963, p. 135) suggest that the relationship between frustration (defined by them as delay of reinforcement) and aggression should be conceptualized as follows:

> Frustration may produce a temporary increase in motivation and thus lead to more vigorous responding. The dominant response to stimuli present before frustration may be one that when mild is not

classed as aggressive, but when strong is so categorized. Frustration also changes the stimulus situation and consequently changes in the kind as well as in the intensity of responses may be expected. Interference with a response sequence may be a stimulus for eliciting response hierarchies in which, because of past learning, pain-producing responses tend to be dominant. Modification of the associative strength of responses through stimulus change can thus, independently of changes in the motivational level of the subject, lead to the occurrence of aggressive behavior. Prior experiences of frustrated subjects, and particularly their "personality characteristics" (that is, the response patterns that are dominant in many of their response hierarchies), should consequently determine to a large extent the nature of their response to frustration.

According to Bandura and Walters, one can readily produce a highly aggressive child merely by exposing him to successful aggressive models and rewarding the child intermitenly for aggressive behavior, even if frustration is kept at a very low level. The importance of the schedule of reinforcement in producing persisting aggressive behavior is demonstrated in an experiment by Walters and Brown (cited in Bandura & Walters, 1963). Seven-year-old boys who were rewarded with a marble every time they hit an automated doll (they were on a "continuous" schedule of reinforcement) were less aggressive in a subsequent play session with another child then were similar boys who were rewarded with a marble for every six times they struck the doll (they were on an "intermittent fixed-ratio" 1:6 schedule). The intermittent schedule produced more subsequent aggressive behavior, a finding that is in keeping with other research on the effects of different schedules of reinforcement. These other studies, furthermore, suggest that among intermittent schedules the "variable" schedules (in which the ratio of reinforcement to responses or the time interval between reinforcements is allowed to fluctuate around some average value) elicit more persistent response tendencies than the "fixed" schedules. Thus, one way for a mother to create persistent demanding and attention-seeking behavior in a child is for her usually to reward such behavior erratically, after the child has sought attention many times. Bandura and Walters suggest that the genesis of much "troublesome" behavior results from parents' employing, unwittingly, schedules of reinforcement that intermittently reward undesirable responses of high magnitude and frequency.

The Development of Self-Control

In a discussion of the influence of models on the acquisition and maintenance of self-controlling responses, the authors cite evidence demonstrating that children not only imitate what adults and peers do (and do not do) in relation to others, but that they also imitate the self-directed actions of others. Thus, Bandura and Kupers (cited in Bandura & Walters, 1963) showed that the higher the bowling score that a model required himself to achieve before he rewarded himself by taking a candy, the higher the score the child required of himself before he would take a candy in a subsequent game (when the model was no longer present).

They discuss different forms of disciplinary interventions in the development of self-control, distinguishing between the use of a negative reinforcer or aversive stimulus and the withdrawal or withholding of positive reinforcement. They point out that the effects of disciplinary acts will depend, not only on the type of discipline employed, but also on its timing. Punishment occurring early in a response sequence conditions anxiety to the response-generated cues and thus produces response inhibition. If punishment occurs, however, after the commission of the undesired act and is only withdrawn when the recipient makes a self-punitive, self-critical, or apologetic response, "guilt" reactions, self-criticism or "apologies" may be strongly reinforced. Of course, if punishment can be avoided by "excuses," "concealment," or avoidance of the punitive agent, these responses—if they occur—will be strengthened.

While disciplinary methods may be most effective when punishment occurs early enough to inhibit the undesired behavior or when its termination is made contingent on the child's compliance with parental demands, it is well to note that anxiety-motivated avoidance behavior is often resistant to change. Thus, a child whose fear of punishment inhibits him from exploring certain areas—intellectual, social, or biological—may refrain even when the threat of punishment is no longer existent because his anxiety has not permitted him to find out that his explorations would not be punished. Bandura and Walters suggest that the techniques of eliciting positively reinforcing, desirable responses from a child that are incompatible with his ongoing or incipient antisocial activity might be more advantageous. Unfortunately, there has been little relevant research on this latter topic.

Methods of Producing Behaviorial Change

Bandura and Walters detail five major ways of modifying behavior: (1) *extinction,* by removing the positive reinforcement or anxiety-reduction which maintains the behavior (not responding to the baby who cries when he is put to bed will often, after a week or so, extinguish the crying response in relation to going to bed); (2) *counterconditioning,* which involves eliciting in the presence of the fear-arousing stimuli responses that are incompatible with anxiety or fear reactions: through the classical conditioning of these incompatible responses to the fear-arousing cues, anxiety is eliminated or reduced (Wolpe, 1958, used relaxation to produce responses which are incompatible with mild fear-arousing situations and then gradually increased the strength of the fear-arousing situations until the most potent phobic stimulus could be presented without disrupting the relaxation state, with relaxation coming eventually to be attached to the original fear-arousing stimuli); (3) *positive reinforcement,* which entails the use of rewards to increase the strength of a response tendency (rewarding a withdrawn child whenever he participates in a social activity); (4) *social imitation* (providing disadvantaged youths with successful adult models whose behavior they can emulate); and (5) *discrimination learning,* which uses positive reinforcers to reward desired responses to given stimuli and negative reinforcers to punish undesired responses or lack of reward to extinguish them.

Concluding Comment

The work of these authors is a fine integration and summary of the application of the behavioristic orientation to socialization and personality development, as well as an original contribution to it. Their own research is stimulating and immediately relevant to important issues in childrearing and psychotherapy. A careful examination of their ideas and their research suggests, however, that their research involves less systematic theory and more common sense than meets the eye. It is, after all, a common observation that children imitate and that they often model themselves after parents, older siblings, teachers, scout leaders, fictional heroes, and so forth. (Sartre's *The Words,* 1964, gives an illuminating account of the significance of fictional heroes in shaping his aspirations.) Bandura and Walters illustrate the imitative process profusely in their experiments and in the literature which they cite, but they do not explain it.

The notion of contiguous sensory stimulation as a sufficient condition for the acquisition of imitative responses (even when attention-producing variables are also considered) is obviously not adequate. It does not explain why people do not imitate everything they attend to, nor does it throw light on the fact that imitation is often unsuccessful. (One of us has been trying unsuccessfully for years to imitate a French accent when speaking French, even though he has often heard French spoken well.) That is to say, Bandura and Walters' discussion of imitation is graced by common sense (the introduction of common sense into learning theory is, itself, no minor achievement), but it does not adequately explain common sense. It falls down in explicating the process of imitation, in clarifying the conditions which relate to the ability to imitate, and does not do as well as the more traditional social psychological approaches in handling the motivation to imitate (or to conform). It does little to explain why imitation seems more common among children than adults or why children seem so much better at it.

Bandura and Walters have ingeniously explored the implications for social learning and personality development of the recent empirical work on schedules of reinforcement. Here, their discussion of the persistence of intermittently reinforced behavior throws new light on the causes of stubbornly resistant, undesirable behavior. Their application of reinforcement theory runs, however, into the typical problems confronting such theories: (1) the lack of specifications of the conditions under which a "reinforcer" is reinforcing (does praise after admittedly poor work lead to reinforcement or to contempt for the praiser?); (2) the tendency to treat human cognitive abilities as though they were the same as those of lower animals and, thus, to assume that man reacts only to the immediate consequences of his behavior; and (3) the avoidance of the central questions concerning the processes involved in determining which particular aspects of a complex stimulus situation, of a complex response, and of a complex reinforcing event will be selected to be linked together. (If a four-year-old is praised for putting away his toys after playing with them, will the praise be connected with the activity of "submitting to an adult," "making mommy happy," "putting away the toys," "doing something my younger brother doesn't do"? And what will be rewarding about the praise—the sense of recognized personal achievement, mommy's happiness, the implicit promise that Santa Claus will bring a desired toy?)

B. F. Skinner

In his novel *Walden Two*, Skinner (1948) describes himself through one of its characters as having had only one idea in his life—a true *idée fixe*—which is expressed in the word "control": the control of behavior. There is little doubt that a central theme of Skinner's extensive and careful experimental work with animals has centered on the question: How can an animal's behavior be brought under experimental control so that it will be predictable and "shaped up" according to the experimenter's specifications? His general answer, which his research has attempted to specify in more detail, has been that it is achieved by the experimenter's manipulation of environmental conditions in such a way as to control the contingencies of reinforcement that are associated with the animal's behavior. In Skinner's words (1953, p. 64): "The barest possible statement of the process is this: we make a given consequence contingent upon certain physical properties of behavior . . . and the behavior is then observed to increase in frequency." As Skinner indicates, this is a restatement of Thorndike's law of effect: a restatement in the rhetoric of radical behaviorism.

The rhetoric and methodology of behaviorism have dominated Skinner's approach to psychology. Methodologically, his emphasis has been placed on the description of the rate and number of occurrences of a given behavior (for example, a disk-pecking response by a pigeon) as a function of variables that are readily controlled by an experimenter in the radically simplified laboratory environment in which the experimental animal is placed. His emphasis on positivistic description is also reflected in his view that psychological theories should be nothing more than statements about facts that express the experimentally observed relationship between dependent behavioral variables and independent environmental variables. He has rejected hypothetico-deductive theory, with its explicitly stated axioms and formal derivation of logical consequences, as a distraction from the scientific work of describing the lawfulness to be found in experimental observation. Description of this orderliness can be made without reference to events dealt with primarily by other sciences (physiology, physics); behavior is to be dealt with at its own level.

Similarly, description of the orderliness of behavior does not require mentalistic or psychic explanations; conscious content must be described in behavioral terms, such as the "behavior of seeing-that-we-are-seeing"; we learn to "see-that-we-are-seeing" only because a verbal community arranges for us to do so. Skinner rejects the view of the more traditional behaviorists that private events (events taking place within the skin of the organism) cannot be included in a true science of behavior. His view is, rather, that they should be approached as forms of behavior that are not essentially different from behavior that is publicly observable. He asserts (1963, p. 953): "An organism learns to react discriminatively to the world around it under certain contingencies of reinforcement. . . . So far as we know, the same process of differential reinforcement is required if a child is to distinguish among the events occurring within his own skin." Nevertheless, in attempting to establish a repertoire of verbal behavior, the "verbal community" works under a severe handicap when dealing with private events. "It cannot teach a child to call one pattern of private stimuli 'diffidence' and another 'embarrassment' as effectively as it teaches him to call one stimulus 'red' and another 'orange,' for it cannot be sure of the presence or absence of the private patterns of stimuli appropriate to reinforcement or lack of reinforcement." Thus, awareness, or, in Skinner's terminology, "self-descriptive behavior" is a social product much the same as publicly observable verbal behavior, except that the social community is less able to shape with precision the private behavior to private events.

Skinner's rigorous emphasis on the description of behavior and the contingencies which affect it, combined with his genius for technical invention, have produced important contributions to the field of psychology. Methodologically, his technique of experimenting has become one of the standard techniques for the experimental study of behavior. His technique essentially involves the use of an impoverished laboratory environment whose features can be precisely controlled, the limiting of the variety of stimulation and of behavior that are possible in this environment, the use of animals whose prior history and, particularly, whose state of deprivation can be controlled, the isolating for investigation a simple behavioral act (a rat pressing a bar, a pigeon pecking at a disk) that can be studied quantitatively in terms of its frequency and rate of response, and the introduction as experimental variables of various contingencies between the simple behavioral act and experimenter-controlled reinforcing and discriminative stimuli. His antitheoretical bias and his lack of interest in the work of other investigators have enabled him to explore and investigate such phenomena as schedules of reinforcement that had been ignored by other theorists. He was one of the first to distinguish classical or respondent conditioning from operant or instrumental conditioning, and, he emphasized this distinction clearly, with great impact on the field. Similarly, although his emphasis on the role of reinforcement was not unique in the field of learning, his detailed investigation of how behavior can be shaped by reinforcement techniques has had widespread effects: it has led to ingenious techniques for training animals; it has stimulated the rapidly growing field of "automated teaching"; and it has led to the study of how verbal behavior is influenced by reinforcement procedures.

More than most animal experimentalists, Skinner has been willing to extrapolate his concepts from the situations in which they have been developed to the more complex situations involving verbal and other forms of social behavior. His often expressed antitheoretical bias, combined with his rhetorical preference for a behavioristic, descriptive positivism, thus has put him in the awkward position of doing what his rhetoric condemns. In *Verbal Behavior,* for example, Skinner (1957) states that the book is not theoretical nor is it a presentation of obtained relationships and facts based on the actual experimental study of verbal behavior. Nevertheless, he asserts (1957, p. 3): "The basic processes and relations which give verbal behavior its special characteristics are now fairly well understood. Much of the experimental work responsible for this advance has been carried out on other species, but the results here proved to be surprisingly free of species restrictions." (This experimental work used rats and pigeons, as subjects, species neither of which exhibits verbal behavior.)

Skinner's characterization of his book as being neither empirical nor theoretical is apt. It is rather an extrapolation without any explicit rules for extrapolation—without any way of knowing whether the terms one has employed in his description of his laboratory experiments are being appropriately applied in the description of human behavior in a complex social situation. The notions of "stimulus," "response," and "reinforcement" are relatively well defined in terms of observable relationships in the controlled and impoverished environments used in Skinner's laboratory experiments, but they are not, otherwise, given an independent definition. Hence, they occur only analogically when applied to more complicated human situations. There is, of course, nothing wrong with the use of analogies; it is often a fruitful way to orient oneself to a new area of investigation. Analogical statements are not, however, statements of obtained relationships, but only speculations about what might be true if the analogies were valid.

In *Verbal Behavior,* Skinner presents a set of terms for describing verbal behavior and an orientation for identifying how the specific characteristics of verbal behavior arise. The key question with which Skinner concerns himself is: what reinforcement does the listener give the speaker for speaking and what is accorded the listener for listening and reinforcing the speaker? His central assumption is that the operant repertory for the speech of the child (the sounds it emits during its vocalizations) are the raw materials on which the contingencies of reinforcement provided by the child's verbal community (its immediate social environment) operate to mold and determine its verbal behavior. This assumption asserts that language is acquired as a result of the slow and careful shaping of verbal behavior through differential reinforcement.

Consistent with his emphasis on the role of reinforcement, Skinner defines "verbal behavior" as behavior on the part of a speaker which is reinforced through the mediation of other persons (listeners) who have been conditioned precisely in order to reinforce the behavior. He identifies a number of types of functional relations in verbal behavior: the two basic types are the "mand" and the "tact."

A mand is a verbal operant in which the response is reinforced by a characteristic consequence and is therefore under the functional control of relevant conditions of deprivation or aversive stimulation. In the grammarian's terms the mand is in the imperative mood: it includes demands, entreaties, requests, questions, commands. Mands are the first functional elements to appear in the language behavior of the child. They are the first verbal responses to be reinforced by such hearers as the mother or nurse. Presently, the mother differentially reinforces the infant by supplying it with milk when the infant says something vaguely resembling milk. In the conditioning of mands the form of the response is specific to the particular reinforcement obtained. The "meaning" of a mand is given by what consequences follow its emission in a particular verbal community. The emission of mands is controlled by the organism's needs, since these mands have a history of appropriate reinforcement under these needs.

The tact is related to *particular discriminative stimuli* (usually nonverbal in nature); it is given generalized rather than specific reinforcement. "Tacting" is a "naming function": if the speaker emits the required sound when a given discriminative stimulus is present, he is reinforced by "approval" or some other generalized conditioned reinforcer. (Any event which characteristically precedes many different reinforcers and which can be used as a reinforcer to bring behavior under control is termed a "generalized conditioned reinforcer.") The tact relation is that of the declarative sentence: it is an announcement of fact representing relatively disinterested behavior for which the speaker gets nothing in particular, but only something in general from the listener. Responses under the control of verbal stimuli are distinguished from tacts and are labeled in terms of the kind of verbal stimuli determining the response: an "echoic operant" is a response that generates a sound pattern similar to that of the stimulus; a "textual" operant is a verbal response which corresponds to a written stimulus; an "interverbal" operant is a verbal response which is under the control of both auditory and written verbal responses.

A special class of operants, called "autoclitics," are responses which are evoked by and act upon other behaviors of the speaker: they are responses to covert, incipient, or potential verbal behavior. They include negation, qualification, quantification, construction of sentences, as well as grammatical processes of ordering and arrangement. They account for the highly complex manipulations of verbal thinking.

Skinner's approach to verbal behavior is open to criticism on many fronts. One such criticism relates to the well-established process of semantic generalization. Semantic generalization is a specific sort of stimulus generalization (see above) in which generalization goes along a dimension of "closeness of meaning" rather than one of physical similarity. As Osgood (1963, p. 739) puts it:

> Having learned a novel response to the word "joy" (for example, lifting a forefinger to avoid shock), the normal adult speaker of English will promptly transfer this response to the word "glee"—but not to the physically more similar word "boy." The basis for the transfer is obviously similarity of meaning, but there is no place for such symbolic processes in Skinner's behaviorism.

Noam Chomsky, the linguist, in a sharp critique of *Verbal Behavior,* has stated (1959, p. 54):

> If we take his terms in their literal meaning, the description covers almost no aspect of verbal behavior, and if we take them metaphorically, the description offers no improvement over various traditional formulations. The terms borrowed from experimental psychology simply lose their objective meaning with this meaning, and take over the full vagueness of ordinary language.

That is to say, the rhetoric of behaviorism without the detailed observation of specific relationships among variables produces no increase in the precision and objectivity of statements.

Skinner's key assumption, that the acquisition of language is acquired through the slow and careful shaping of behavior by reinforcement, is also open to question. There is ample evidence of the ability of young children to acquire language by casual observation and imitation of adults and other children, without any precise shaping of their behavior on the part of listeners—some young children begin to speak by speaking in sentences or, in other words, without much in the way of external shaping of their speech through differential reinforcement. Skinner's emphasis on the external control of behavior through reinforcement leads him to neglect the significant contribution of internal processes and structure. As Chomsky points out (1959, p. 57):

The child who has learned a language has in some sense constructed a grammar for himself on the basis of his observations of
sentences and nonsentences. . . . [The] young child has succeeded
in carrying out what from the formal point of view, at least, seems
to be a remarkable type of theory construction. Furthermore, this
task is accomplished in an astonishing short time, to a large extent
independently of intelligence, and in a comparable way by all children. Any theory of learning must cope with these facts. . . . [A]
refusal to study the contribution of the child to language learning
permits only a superficial account of language acquisition, with a
vast and unanalyzed contribution attributed to a step called "generalization" which in fact includes just about everything of interest in
this process.

As we noticed above, Skinner's *Verbal Behavior* presents no evidence to support his theory, except for a rather gross analogy to
operant conditioning in pigeons. Nor in the years which followed the
publication of this fundamental text have Skinner or his students
made any appreciable effort to provide an empirical base for the
main body of the theory. (For sympathetic reviews of the literature on verbal conditioning see Krasner, 1958, and Salzinger, 1959;
critical comments may be found in papers by Spielberger, 1962,
and Dulany, 1962.) The one area where Skinner's ideas have had
real influence is in the study of the effects of "generalized reinforcers" on verbal conditioning. A wide variety of studies have demonstrated that the procedures of operant conditioning can be
utilized to modify subjects' verbal behavior. In a typical study of
verbal conditioning, subjects are asked to say words or numbers,
or to construct sentences employing a choice of words, or to engage in some other specified verbal activity. The subject may be
aware that an experiment is taking place or, in some cases, he is
led to believe that he is undergoing an interview or a session in
psychotherapy or is being engaged in an informal conversation.
The experimenter reinforces responses selectively from some predetermined class of verbal responses (such as plural nouns or
personal pronouns), employing a "generalized conditioned reinforcer" (a statement of "good," "mmmhmmm," or a nod of approval).

Such studies suggest striking parallels between the behavior of
subjects in an experiment on verbal reinforcement and the behavior of pigeons in operant conditioning in the laboratory. Subjects

show a grad al increase in the frequency of the reinforced response during the phase of acquisition, and a gradual diminution of the response during extinction. Such conditioning seems to affect many diverse classes of response including expression of opinion, personal pronouns, and plural nouns. A number of investigators, moreover, have reported that their subjects were neither aware that conditioning had taken place nor that they had modified their verbal behavior in any systematic manner.

Although such studies seem to provide support for Skinner's approach to verbal behavior, some psychologists have taken exception to them. Both Spielberger (1962; Spielberger, Levin, and Shepard, 1962) and Dulany (1962) have criticized the techniques employed by many investigators to detect their subjects' awareness of the contingency between the reinforcer and the class of reinforced responses. Their data suggest that when a more sophisticated technique is used almost all subjects whose behavior is modified show at least some degree of awareness of the response-reinforcer contingency. Dulany argues that, rather than an automatic and unconscious strengthening of stimulus-response connections, subjects deliberately attempt to formulate hypotheses about the "correct" response, which then serve to guide their behavior.

Bandura, a critic of these studies of verbal conditioning, has suggested that if the experimenter simply and politely asked subjects to emit personal pronouns, it is a safe prediction that the subject would respond with the requested behavior immediately, making it unnecessary to engage in the whole tedious process of verbal conditioning which makes it more difficult for the subject to discover what the experimenter wants. The implication of Bandura's comment is that reinforcement may not be necessary to lead a subject to increase the frequency of a given kind of response. Nor, of course, may the procedures of operant conditioning be particularly effective or economical in influencing human behavior.

A number of studies of a somewhat different sort create additional difficulties for the proponents of the notion of verbal conditioning. These studies indicate that whether a subject emits the desired response depends importantly on the characteristics of the person who dispenses the reinforcers. In a study by Sapolsky (1960), subjects who were told that they were "compatible" with the experimenter were "conditioned" rapidly during the acquisition phase, while subjects who were told they were "incompatible" with the experimenter did not; but, in the "extinction" phase, during which the "compatible" or "incompatible" experimenter left the room, the response curves for the two groups converged. The "compatible" subjects emitted fewer of the reinforced responses while the "incompatible" subjects emitted the reinforced response with greater frequency than they had during acquisition. Clearly, Sapolsky's subjects had learned what was the "correct" response in both conditions. The *emission* of the correct response, however, was determined not by simple conditioning, but by the nature of the subjects' relation to the experimenter. Nor is this an isolated finding. Numerous studies suggest that the subject's attitude toward the reinforcing agent determines whether or not he will show a modification of his verbal behavior.

George C. Homans

Homans, a sophisticated and urbane social psychologist, identifies himself professionally as a sociologist. Neither the subtlety of his description of human values and human sentiments nor his professional identity would suggest that he would find in Skinnerian psychology a congenial set of explanatory principles for his own views of elementary social behavior. Homans explains his attraction to the Skinnerian orientation in terms of his own felt necessity to find higher-order propositions from which the empirical findings of small-group research, social anthropology and history (the three fields in which he has undertaken research) could be derived. He uses the admittedly unattractive term "ultimate psychological reductionism" to characterize his view "that the ultimate explanatory principles in anthropology and sociology, and for that matter in history . . . [are] psychological" (Homans, 1962, p. 61). His selection of the Skinnerian system rather than some other psychological point of view is probably a result of the accidental circumstance that Homans and Skinner are well acquainted, both having been members of the Harvard Society of Fellows. In any case, before swallowing Skinner's system, Homans seems to have chewed it beyond clear recognition.

Homans' interest lies in *elementary social behavior:* the face-to-face contact between individuals in which the reward or punishment each gets from the behavior of the others is relatively direct and immediate. In his view, the most convenient locale for studying such behavior is in small groups and, thus, the data he draws on are largely from observational and experimental studies of small groups. In *The Human Group* (Homans, 1950), he examined five detailed field studies of human groups to see into what basic classes the observations can be divided and what propositions can be inferred about the relations among the classes of variables. He employed four basic categories: "activity," a kind of behavior, "sentiment," an activity that is a sign of attitudes and feelings, "interaction," which occurs when an activity of one person is rewarded or punished by an activity of another, and "norm," a statement by group members of how members ought to behave in certain circumstances. In addition, he made a distinction between "the external system" ("the behavior of a group so far as that behavior represents one possible answer to the question: How does the group survive in its particular environment?"; Homans, 1950, p. 109) and "the internal system" ("the elaboration of group behavior that simultaneously arises out of the external system and reacts upon it").

Homans employs his concepts to state a number of generalizations based upon the field studies summarized in *The Human Group*. Here are some of them.

"[The] more frequently persons interact with one another, the stronger their sentiments of friendship for one another are apt to be" (p. 133).

"[Persons] who interact with one another frequently are more like one another in their activities than they are like other persons with whom they interact less frequently" (p. 135).

"[The] higher the rank of a person within a group, the more nearly his activities conform to the norms of the group" (p. 141).

"[The] higher a person's social rank, the wider will be the range of his interactions" (p. 145).

"[A] person of higher social rank than another originates interaction for the latter more often than the latter originates interactions for him" (p. 145).

"[A] person who originates interaction for another in the external system will also tend to do so in the internal" (p. 146).

"[The] sentiments of the leaders of a group carry greater weight than those of the followers in establishing a social ranking" (p. 181).

"[The] closer an individual or a subgroup comes to realizing in all activities the norms of the group as a whole, the higher will be the social rank of the individual or subgroup" (p. 180–181).

"[The] higher a man's social rank, the larger the number of persons for whom he originates interaction, either directly or through intermediaries" (p. 182).

"[The] higher a man's social rank, the larger will be the number of persons that originate interaction for him, either directly or through intermediaries" (p. 182).

"[If] a person does originate interaction for a person of higher rank, a tendency will exist for him to do so with the member of his own group who is nearest to him in rank" (p. 184).

"[The] more frequently persons interact with one another, when no one of them originates interaction with much greater frequency than the others, the greater is their liking for one another and their feeling of ease in one another's presence" (p. 243).

Faced with these and other empirical generalizations from *The Human Group* and from experimental studies of small group behavior, Homans sought an underlying set of explanatory propositions, finding them in behavioral psychology and elementary economics. He says (1961, p. 13):

> Briefly, behavioral psychology and elementary economics envisage human behavior as a function of its payoff: in amount and kind it depends on the amount and kind of reward and punishment it fetches. . . . Thus the set of general propositions I shall use . . . envisages social behavior as an exchange of activity, tangible or intangible, and more or less rewarding or costly, between at least two persons.

Homans (1961) enumerates five basic propositions from which he believes the empirical findings of social psychological research can be explained. These five are:

1. *"If in the past the occurrence of a particular stimulus situation has been the occasion on which a man's activity has been rewarded, then the more similar the present stimulus situation is to the past one, the more likely he is to emit the activity, or some similar activity now"* (p. 53).

2. *"The more often within a given period of time a man's activity rewards the activity of another, the more often the other will emit the activity"* (p. 54).

3. *"The more valuable to a man a unit of the activity another gives him, the more often he will emit activity rewarded by the activity of the other"* (p. 55). ("Value" here refers to the degree of

reinforcement that is received from a unit of another's activity. "Cost" refers to the value obtainable through an alternate activity which is foregone in emitting the present activity. Profit equals reward minus cost.)

4. *"The more often a man has in the recent past received a rewarding activity from another, the less valuable any further unit of that activity becomes to him"* (p. 55).

5. *"The more to a man's disadvantage the rule of distributive justice fails of realization, the more likely he is to display the emotional behavior we call anger"* (p. 75). (The "rule of distributive justice" is stated thus: "A man in an exchange relation with another will expect that the rewards of each man be proportional to his costs—the greater the rewards, the greater the costs—and that the net rewards, or profits, of each man be proportional to his investments—the greater the investments, the greater the profit.")

Homans' first four propositions are attempts to restate in everyday language a Skinnerian point of view about the interrelated effects of deprivation or satiation and of frequency and quality of reinforcement on the frequency and rate of a given behavior. It is easy to criticize these propositions. Some of their key terms are neither conceptually nor operationally defined—"unit of activity," "value," "reward"; there are obvious counterexamples to his propositions—the second proposition links frequency of emitted behavior to frequency of reward. Yet one of Skinner's notable contributions in psychology has been the demonstration of the more potent effects of intermittent as compared with continuous reinforcement in delaying the extinction of a response.

Despite the criticisms that can be made of them, Homans' propositions are used to explain many aspects of social behavior. One gets the flavor of his analysis of social behavior as an exchange of valued activities by considering the reward-cost contingencies that are involved in an encounter between two people, "A" and "B." With regard to any act, it is relevant to think of its cost to the producer and its reward-value to its consumer. Thus, if "A" asks "B" for help, this act costs "A" a certain amount (by his admission of inadequacy or inferiority) and rewards "B" a certain amount (by the recognition of his superiority); if "B" supplies "A" with help, this will cost "B" something (plus his putting off some other activity while helping "A") and reward "A" (who is helped) a certain amount. From the basic propositions, one can infer plausibly that the exchange will not continue unless *both* are making profits from the interaction. (Homans does not suggest that the profits, jointly or individually, have to be maximized.) His proposition about distributive justice (or fair exchange) implies, moreover, that, if the investments or social statutes of the interactors are equal, the profits should be equal; if the investments or social statuses (age, sex, seniority, acquired skill) are different, the profits of each should be proportional to his status. Thus, presumably, a boss should profit more than his subordinate in an interaction with his subordinate. Similarly, the ability and willingness to supply services for others that are in short supply (to supply valuable activities) will lead others to return high esteem; doing so maintains a fair exchange. "For high value received, men will return high esteem."

Homans indicates (1961, p. 264) that

> As a practical matter, distributive justice is realized when each of the various features of his investments and his activities, put into rank-order in comparison with those of other men, fall in the same place in all the different rank-orders. This condition which we call status congruence, is not only the condition of distributive justice but also that of social certitude: the status of a man in this condition is secure, established, unambiguous in the eyes of his fellows. . . . Congruence facilitates social ease in the interaction among men, and . . . should encourage their joint efficiency.

Homans assumes that incongruence of status produces conflicting stimuli. For example, a father who acts as a buddy to his son presumably confuses the son and makes it likely that some of his responses to his father will be inappropriate; these inappropriate responses will, in turn, annoy or frustrate the father. Thus, status incongruence is a generator of social friction.

Homans applies his basic propositions to varied social phenomena by suggesting a wide range of activities which can be rewarding—approval, agreement, change of opinion to conform with the opinion of another, esteem, similarity, help, status congruence, cohesiveness. Thus, he interprets the research of Festinger and his coworkers on social influence as being supportive of his view of social behavior as exchange. Their finding that more cohesive groups can exert greater influence upon deviant group members to change their opinions, he renders as "the more valuable the activities that members get, the more valuable that they must give." That is to say, for the deviate to continue to receive the valuable sentiments and activities that relate to group cohesiveness, he must return the rewarding activity of agreement. On the other hand, if the deviate fails to supply this reinforcement to the others by changing his opinion so as to agree with them, then they will withhold social approval and communication from him.

From the proposition that a person will emit an activity the more he is rewarded for it, Homans develops a number of corollaries about social interaction. If one assumes that the more people like one another the surer they are to reward the acts of one another with approval, then, Homans points out, it follows that the more they like one another the more they will interact. Also, if receiving approval for an act leads one to give approval, then it also follows that the more a person interacts with another the more he likes him. Homans elaborates his hypotheses about interaction by assuming that men differ in their ability to reward others. A man who controls scarce resources (ability, experience, wealth) is able to provide more valuable rewards and will, thus, obtain high esteem. As a result, he is almost certain to receive more interactions directed to him than is a man of lower esteem. Since, by definition, rare and valuable services are controlled by few, only a few can come to be esteemed highly. Requests, esteem, obedience, and loyalty flow from the many to the few, while advice, valuable services, orders, and emotional support go from the few to the many. The costs of giving and receiving orders, advice, and so on are such that they introduce ambivalence into the relationships between leader and follower, introducing a tendency to avoid interaction in the social sphere with people who differ in status in the public sphere of life (the sphere "in which esteem is won and lost").

The preceding summary of the central ideas in Homans' work does little justice to the sophistication and insightfulness of his writing. Interlaced among his systematic generalizations are perceptive comments, subtle elaborations, and qualifications which shed much light on the intricacies of social life. Moreover, his delightful and elegant prose neatly conceals the rough and ragged edges of his theoretical formulations.

However, if we look at his theoretical statements per se, it is evident that they have a number of defects. As Homans points out, his theory has two main variables: the *value* of a unit of activity and the *number* of such units received within a period of time. His theory implies that there is a common *currency* or a single dimension to which the value of different experiences ("getting a B+ on an exam," "being kissed by one's sweetheart," "hearing a Beethoven quartet," "being served a cold beer") can be coordinated so that the value of a "unit" of one such activity received can be compared with the value of another unit. If there is such a common currency of "value," it has not yet been identified nor have methods of unitizing activity been worked out (is the kiss or the date the unit? the symphony or the movement?). Nor can Homans, without being circular, say that value is measured by the frequency of acts emitted after an act has been reinforced by rewarding a person with a given value. He cannot, because he indicates that he has not tried to answer the question of how values are acquired or, in other words, what (apart from immediate deprivation or satiation) determines the value of an act. That is to say, without some conceptual and empirical definition of reinforcement, Homans is in the position of defining a value as that which is valued, paralleling the Skinnerian circularity of a reinforcer as that which reinforces. Lacking any clear-cut definition of his basic terms, Homans employs them in their everyday meanings, stretching them to fit the particular research he cites. As a result, there is an *ad hoc* quality to the research findings that he uses as evidence to support his basic propositions and their corollaries.

The lack of specification of a common currency for the measurement of value creates serious problems for such notions as "profit" (reward minus cost), "rate of exchange," or "distributive justice." These notions imply an ability to compare, to add and subtract, and to divide value. The assumption that values are directly additive is common to many economic theories. These theories tend to ignore such psychological processes as inner conflict and ambivalence. For example, if one adds a negative value or cost (an electric shock) to a positive value or reward (obtaining food), the result is not simply the smaller positive value that is implied in the formula, Profit $=$ Reward $-$ Cost; rather, the subject experiences conflict and manifests symptoms of stress.

The defects of vagueness, lack of adequate conceptual and empirical definitions, incompleteness, and inconsistency which can be pointed out in Homans' theory are not in any way more characteristic of his theory than of most other theories in social psychology. More than most theoreticians, his theoretical net has been spread widely in an attempt to catch a great range of social psychological phenomena, and although the net is not closely woven it does touch, if not catch, the major research findings in the area. Also, unlike most of the theories, his is based on a fairly specific image: the image of a market transaction involving the exchange of commodities. Like most analogies that are not far-fetched, this one has had fruitful consequences: for instance, it gave rise to the concept of "distributive justice." Homans, in identifying this concept and in relating it to such other established phenomena as status congruence, has suggested one of the central conditions of group equilibrium. If the concept of distributive justice is to become more than a suggestive metaphor, however, the related concepts of "profit," "investment," "reward," and "cost" will have to be given more specific empirical and conceptual definitions.

The link between Homans' theory and a behavioristic psychology is a brittle one. Although Skinnerians emphasize the role of reinforcement in controlling behavior, they would blanch at the way Homans freely uses such words as "reward," "cost," "expect," and "justice." Homans not only abandons the methodology of behaviorism in his social psychological research but also abandons its rhetoric. He neglects, moreover, the central contribution of the Skinnerians, their fine-grained study of the effects of different contingencies of reinforcement—for example, of different schedules of reinforcement. The only link between Homans and behavioristic psychology is the psychological hedonism which underlies both the law of effect and the doctrine of economic man.

John W. Thibaut and Harold H. Kelley

Thibaut and Kelley, both of whom were students of Kurt Lewin, present in their book, *The Social Psychology of Groups* (1959), a modified doctrine of economic man. Like Homans, they explain social interaction in terms of its "outcomes": the rewards received and the costs incurred by each participant in an interaction. (Homans uses the terms "payoffs" or "profits" instead of "outcomes.") These authors, and Homans also, assume that social behavior is unlikely to be repeated unless its rewards exceed its costs. The value which a person places upon a given outcome, however, will not be determined, according to Thibaut and Kelley, by its absolute magnitude but rather by comparison against two standards.

One standard, called the "comparison level" (abbreviated "CL") is defined as (Thibaut & Kelley, 1959, p. 81) "some modal or average value of all the outcomes [of the given social situation] known to the person (by virtue of personal or vicarious experience), each outcome weighted by its salience (or the degree to which it is instigated at the moment)." With this concept, they are trying to define a neutral point on a scale of satisfaction: the higher an outcome is above the CL, the more satisfying it is; the lower an outcome is below the CL, the more dissatisfying it is.

The concept of the comparison level is modeled after Helson's early psychophysical concept of "adaptation level" (Helson, 1948), which has now been elaborated into a widely ramifying theory (Helson, 1964). The essential point underlying both the CL and Helson's concept is that what a person experiences when he is exposed to a given stimulus will be determined by what he has become adapted to. After driving at 60 miles an hour for several hours, 40 miles an hour seems rather slow; after creeping along in a traffic jam, it seems quite rapid. Thibaut and Kelley suggest that current experience plays an important role in determining the CL: after the immediate experience of smoking a really good cigar, a cheap cigar, even though once enjoyable, may be distasteful; similarly, after the experience of intense criticism from a teacher, faint praise, once viewed as damning, may become desirable.

The second standard against which a person appraises his outcomes is termed the "comparison level for alternatives": this standard is used in deciding whether to remain in a social relationship or to leave it. It is the lowest outcome a person will accept in the light of the best alternative opportunities available to him. With this idea, which resembles the concept of level of aspiration, Thibaut and Kelley are attempting to specify a neutral point on a scale of acceptance-rejection. Presumably, a person will not stay in a satisfactory job if he can have a more pleasing one, nor will he leave a dissatisfying position if the only available alternatives are even more unpleasant.

As a way of characterizing social interaction, Thibaut and Kelley use a matrix (see Table 4–1) that describes the outcomes of satisfaction or dissatisfaction to each participant when the actions of each are known. Table 4–1 is an example of such a ma-

trix for two persons, A and B, interacting socially. The rows specify A's possible actions, and the columns B's. The cells of the
table provide further information, giving the amount of satisfaction
or dissatisfaction that A and B would each feel if the contingent
conditions (row and column) for that cell were actually realized.
In the instance of Table 4–1, A, a seller, is envisaged as capable

TABLE 4–1. An Interaction Matrix Showing the Outcomes to a Seller
            (A) Who Can Set the Price and to a Buyer (B) Who Can
            Set the Quantity of Goods to Be Purchased

		B	
		Quantity to Be Purchased	
Selling Price	10 Yards	15 Yards	Don't Buy
A $1.00 per yard	A=+1, B=+1	A=+3, B=+4	A=−2, B=−1
$1.25 per yard	A=+2, B=0	A=+4, B=−2	A=−2, B=−1
Don't sell	A=−2, B=−1	A=−2, B=−1	A=−2, B=−1

of three possible actions, and B, a buyer, also with three possible
contingent behaviors that could be associated with each of A's
choices. The cells show the corresponding outcomes, the combined
costs and rewards, in satisfaction and dissatisfaction for every
combination of behaviors by these two people. If A decides to sell
his fabric at $1.00 per yard and if B buys 15 yards, then the ma-
trix asserts that A will evaluate the outcome as equivalent to three
units of satisfaction on his satisfaction-dissatisfaction scale,
whereas the buyer, B, will appraise his outcome as four units on his
scale.

Thibaut and Kelley indicate that the payoffs that are represented in their matrices are, in their phrase, "the objectively available outcomes" which the interactors would actually experience if
they behaved in a given way; that is to say, the outcomes listed in a
matrix do not necessarily correspond to what is expected or anticipated by the social participants before the actual interaction. A
person may have little knowledge of what to expect, or he may
have faulty anticipations of what he will get from a social encounter. Thus, the seller in Table 4–1 may not realize before he makes
his choice that choosing "not to sell" will leave him feeling dissatisfied. It is not clear from the authors' discussion of outcomes
whether they have considered the possibility that the immediate

and the delayed outcomes of a given social interaction may differ from each other and that, moreover, the appraisals of a given outcome may differ at different times. In other words, not only may the anticipation differ from the experience of a social encounter, but the experience may vary at different times after its occurrence.

Presumably, it is only by repeated experience in a given social relationship or with relationships of similar type that a person is able to predict accurately the consequences of his behavior for himself. The outcome experienced in the early stages of interaction may not, however, be a good sample of the possible outcomes which exist in a dyadic relationship; nevertheless, it may determine whether the relationship will continue or it may confine the interaction to certain activities. A man and woman, for example, who might find one another awkward and undesirable as social companions if they met as strangers at a large, impersonal gathering, might discover one another's wit and charm in a different social setting. Thibaut and Kelley consider in some detail the kinds of factor that affect the formation of first impressions (which they describe as a "process of exploring the matrix of possible outcomes"), and they discuss the course of development of relationships as a function of the outcomes which the participants actually experience.

The representation of social interaction by a matrix, which has its origins in mathematical game theory (Luce & Raiffa, 1957; Shubik, 1964), has proved to be a useful tool for describing, abstractly, different types of social interdependencies, and for stimulating research. Matrices 2a, 2b, 2c, and 2d illustrate several different types. The reader may visualize some of the experiments (Deutsch, 1958; Deutsch, 1962; Rapoport & Orwant, 1962) which have employed matrices by imagining two players ("A" and "B") in a game, each of whom has to choose between pressing either a black or a red button. The payoff to each player is determined by the choices of both players and by the matrix which says what the value-outcomes are in the game. In experiments the outcomes are specified in points or in money rather than in units on a scale of satisfaction-dissatisfaction. Usually, the players are given a complete description of the matrix before they are asked to make their choices. They are required to make their choices simultaneously and, frequently, without any opportunity to communicate with one another (although some investigators have studied the effects of communication upon the behavior of the subjects). The game is often played for many trials, and after each trial the outcomes for the two subjects are made known to each of them. Sometimes a player, instead of being just a single subject, is a team of two or more people which has first to agree among itself about what choice to make.

Thibaut and Kelley have used matrices experimentally, as well as in theoretical analysis, to give insight into different types of interdependency and especially into types of control that a person may have over another's outcomes: "fate control" and "behavior control." Person A has fate control over person B if, by varying his behavior, A does not affect his own outcomes directly but does affect B's outcome regardless of what B does. A has behavior control over B if, by varying his behavior, A can make it desirable for B to vary his behavior too. In a situation of behavior control, B's outcomes vary not solely as a function of A's choices (fate control), nor solely of his own, but rather as a function of both persons' choices.

Table 4–2a illustrates a situation in which A has fate control over B but B has no control over A; B is completely at A's mercy. B's choice of black or red will not alter his outcome. For B everything depends on whether A chooses red or black. Table 4–2b shows mutual fate control: if A chooses black, B always benefits, no matter what B does; and if B chooses black, then A always benefits, no matter what A does. Mutual behavior control is illustrated in c and d of Table 4–2. In these two matrices, which are discussed more fully later, it is evident that in order to predict what outcome B will get, it is necessary but not sufficient to know A's choice; B's choice must also be known. Similarly, to specify A's outcome, it is necessary to know the decisions of both A and B. Presumably, for example, in the Matrix c of Table 4–2, by choosing black, A can make it more desirable for B to choose black also. It is well, however, to note that if A does so, B might perceive A's action as a challenge to a contest of wills.

Thibaut and Kelley suggest that in a situation where a person has no direct control over his own outcomes, he can use his ability to control the other's outcomes so as to influence his own payoffs indirectly. For example, in the situation depicted in b of Table 4–2, A can persuade B to choose black by choosing black if B chooses black and red if B chooses red. More generally, they

TABLE 4-2. Several Different Types of Social Interdependence

(a)

FATE CONTROL

		B	
		black	red
A	black	A=+5, B=+5	A=+5, B=+5
	red	A=+5, B=+1	A=+5, B=+1

(b)

MUTUAL FATE CONTROL

		B	
		black	red
A	black	A=+5, B=+5	A=+1, B=+5
	red	A=+5, B=+1	A=+1, B=+1

(c)

BARGAINING

		B	
		black	red
A	black	A=+4, B=+2	A=−1, B=−1
	red	A=−1, B=−1	A=+2, B=+4

(d)

TRUST AND SUSPICION

		B	
		black	red
A	black	A=+1, B=+1	A=−2, B=+2
	red	A=+2, B=−2	A=−1, B=−1

suggest that even when people do not know how their behaviors affect one another, the strategy which is most likely to lead to a stable, mutually rewarding interaction for each party is one in which each person changes his behavior after receiving a punishment (an outcome that is not preferred) and maintains the same behavior after receiving the preferred reward. With this matrix, if both players used such a strategy and if A chose red and B chose black, B would be dissatisfied with his outcome and would change his next choice to red while A would continue his choice as red. This "red-red" combination would lead both participants to their least preferred outcomes, causing each to choose black on the next trial, and this latter combination would produce the outcomes preferred by each and, thus, would lead to repetition of the same rewarding choices.

Although they do not make any specific suggestions about the types of situation depicted in matrices c and d of Table 4–2, it is evident that the strategy described in the preceding paragraph would not produce stable patterns of mutually profitable interaction unless one or both players were to settle for less than his preferred outcome. Matrix c is labeled a bargaining situation because, as in most bargaining situations, the participants will be better off if they can agree (in this instance, if both agree to choose the same color), yet agreement is difficult because they have opposed preferences with regard to what kind of agreement to make: A would prefer both to choose black, B would prefer both to choose red. As an illustration of Matrix c, imagine a husband and wife who would like to spend an evening out together; the husband would prefer that they go to the movies, the wife would prefer that they attend a concert. In such a situation, the crude insistence on "doing it my way or not doing anything at all" may lead to a deadlock because such insistence may change the meaning of the alternatives: the choice becomes one of whose "will" is stronger rather than one of going to the concert or to the movies. (Kelley, 1964a; Kelley, 1964b; Kelley, Thibaut, Radloff, & Mundy, 1962; and Thibaut & Faucheux, 1965, report relevant research.)

The situation portrayed in Matrix d is especially interesting because it poses a problem for the conceptions which favor the doctrine of economic man. An examination of this matrix will reveal that, by choosing red, each player can win the most he can (+ 2 rather than + 1) or lose the least he can (− 1 rather than − 2);

yet, if each player chooses red, both players will lose. Clearly, a strategy which emphasizes mutual reward (the choice of black), if pursued mutually, may lead to greater individual reward than a strategy which stresses individual gain. Unless, however, each participant can trust and behave in a trustworthy manner toward the other (or unless virtue is taken as its own reward), it may be difficult indeed to avoid the choice of red. At least, that is what a good deal of research indicates.

The dilemma posed in Matrix d is sometimes called "the prisoner's dilemma." A. W. Tucker, the mathematical game theorist who originated this type of matrix, illustrated it in terms of two prisoners who are suspected of committing a crime. They are placed in separate cells by the district attorney who then tells both prisoners that each will be offered the choice to "confess" or "not confess." The prisoners are informed (1) that if both choose not to confess they will both be released; (2) if both choose to confess, they will each get a light sentence; and (3) if one chooses to confess but the other does not, the one who confesses will go free and be rewarded, whereas the other prisoner will be given a stiff sentence. Matrix 2d depicts the prisoner's dilemma by allowing black to represent "not confess" and red to represent "confess." It is clear that in such a situation what each person believes about the other's motivation, and also what each thinks the other believes about him, may influence whether he chooses to confess or not.

Although *The Social Psychology of Groups* contains many insightful discussions of the processes and determinants of social interaction, the theoretical position of its authors presents many of the same problems as does Homans' formulation. Thibaut and Kelley's central concept—the matrix of objectively available outcomes—is circular: they indicate no way of ascertaining "objectively available outcomes." Their suggestion that the matrix of outcomes becomes increasingly useful in predicting behavior as relationships become stable (therefore, as social behavior repeats itself) indicates, unwittingly, that behavior is predictable directly from knowledge of past behavior without reference to the matrix. Their theoretical analysis of social interaction, moreover, treats it as though it were an interaction between persons who pursue their self-interests mechanistically, without any psychological response to their awareness that they are thinking about one another and trying to anticipate one another's behavior. Their analysis often appears to assume that it makes no difference to a person whether he is interacting with another person or with a thing that has no ideas about him or about the interaction. As a consequence, their book mostly ignores the role of communication in social interaction, as if the opportunity to discuss matters of mutual relevance did not have much significance for social behavior.

The merit of the position advanced by Thibaut and Kelley lies not so much in the theoretical concepts set forth, but rather in its emphasis on how social interaction is influenced by the interdependence of the participants. Their stress upon the two comparative standards against which outcomes are evaluated highlights the fact that rewards and costs are not experienced as absolutes: the psychological significance of a reward varies with the person's past experiences and present opportunities. By broadening the concept of outcome in this way, Thibaut and Kelley have established a bridge between the views of the Gestalt theorists and the reinforcement theorists. Traditionally, the Gestaltists have emphasized that rewards are perceived relationally, but they have neglected the study of the consequences of reward on behavior, whereas the reinforcement theorists have stressed the consequences of reward, but not the conditions that determine the way it is perceived.

An Overview

Learning theories, as we noted at the outset, deal with the processes by which behavior is acquired. There is no doubt that the bulk of social behavior is indeed learned. It may seem surprising, therefore, that the impact of learning theory upon social psychology has not yet been great. Perhaps this paradox can be explained in terms of the fact that, until recently, the learning theorists undertook little research on the social behavior of human beings. The behavior of rats and pigeons seemed too remote from everyday human interaction to serve as its model. In addition, there is little doubt that the conceptions, so long dominant, of the learning process as dependent on reinforcement have been phrased in terms which treat human cognitive abilities as though they are the same as those of lower animals. This phrasing has alienated many social psychologists on humanistic as well as on scientific grounds. Furthermore, these conceptions have often, in their own circularity, ignored questions that are central to human social psychology; the questions, for instance, of what *is* rewarding or reinforcing for a given person and of what determines how a person will respond to the consequences of his own behavior.

Today learning theorists are beginning to undertake systematic research on human social behavior. Their attack has already generated new insights into significant issues relating to childrearing and to the modification of behavior, as well as into the processes of social interaction. It seems likely that learning theory and the field of social psychology will both become more sophisticated as a result of closer contact with each other.

5

PSYCHOANALYTIC THEORY

ONE NAME TOWERS above all others whenever psychologists or the general public seek to identify a major contributor to the understanding of human behavior: Sigmund Freud. Freud's acclaim did not come easily nor quickly. His most original and profound work, *The Interpretation of Dreams,* sold 600 copies in the first eight years after its publication, fewer than it now sells each month. Today, with the widespread acceptance and popularization of psychoanalytic ideas, it is difficult to appreciate the revolutionary impact of Freud's theories. This chapter will outline his major con- tributions, discuss classical psychonanalytic theory and some of its offshoots, and consider psychoanalytic contributions to social psy- chology.

Freud's Major Contributions

Many psychologists accept the following ideas which Freud em- phasized and illustrated persuasively in his voluminous writings:

1. *Psychic determinism.* Trained in the naturalistic methods of physiological science and imbued with the scientific determinism of the latter half of the nineteenth century, Freud extended de- terminism to the heart of human affairs. Dreams, the embarrass-

ing mistakes of everyday life, wit, the bizarre symptoms of mental disorder, religion, myth, art, and literature were to be viewed as determined by lawful psychological processes common to mankind. The titles of some of his writings indicate the scope of his attempt to extend systematic psychological explanation: *The Interpretation of Dreams* (1900), *Psychopathology of Everyday Life* (1901), *Wit and Its Relation to the Unconscious* (1905), *Leonardo da Vinci* (1910), *Totem and Taboo* (1913), *Group Psychology and the Analysis of the Ego* (1921), *Civilization and Its Discontents* (1930), *Moses and Monotheism* (1939).

2. *Psychodynamics*. Although the purposive, goal-directed quality of behavior was also emphasized by other early psychological theorists (notably such functionalists as James, Dewey, Angell, and Woodworth), Freud's attempt to specify the instincts, their derivatives, and their vicissitudes was unique. His use of the term "instincts" is similar to the notion of "drive." For him it did not connote a genetically-determined specific goal object or specific mode of behavior, but rather a persistent, somatically derived pressure to change an internal state by external activities. We shall not err if for Freud we use "drive" and "instinct" interchangeably.

Psychological structure as well as psychological process were, for Freud, to be explained largely in terms of the fate of the drives as they are directed toward satisfaction in the external world, and by their interplay in conflict or support of one another. Interests, defense mechanisms, character traits, and personality organization all reflect the experiences of the individual in seeking gratification of his basic drives and their derivatives. They represent an attempt to mold the reactions of the external reality and to reshape the drives so as to maximize the benefits to the psychic economy by reducing threat or danger and enhancing drive satisfaction. Later psychoanalysts (Kris, Hartmann, Rapaport, Erikson), those identified with "psychoanalytic ego psychology," have modified Freud's almost exclusive emphasis on drive by suggesting that much of the perceptual-cognitive-motoric apparatus which relates man to his external reality (the "ego") is not a mere product of the interaction of the drives with reality, but rather has autonomous origins and functions.

This psychodynamic approach has led to an appreciation of the roles of frustration and conflict in mental development, which were seen to be important determiners of both normal and pathological development. Frustration may lead to aggression, but it may also produce greater responsiveness to reality. Conflict may lead to neurosis, but it may also lead to a creative elaboration of thought. Psychoanalysis was the first psychological system to focus systematic attention on the causes and consequences of frustration and conflict.

3. *Unconscious mental activity.* Freud made man aware of how little he is conscious of the roots of his own behavior. He demonstrated that man often cannot allow himself to know what he does, nor why he does what he does. This demonstration led many to conclude that Freud was emphasizing the irrational nature of man. Of course, it is true that by showing that man's conscious thought controls his behavior only to a limited degree, Freud undermined the rationalistic conception that man is dominated by reason. Yet, paradoxically, even in his psychoanalytic work Freud was a rationalist emphasizing the role of reason. Freud's unmasking psychology was rooted in his opposition to deception. Moreover, the Freudian view of the unconscious is that "unconsciousness" is dynamically determined; that is to say, an idea or drive remains or becomes unconscious because by being unconscious it is less damaging to the individual's psychic economy. It would seem that, by being unconscious, it causes less anxiety, guilt, or pain than it would were it conscious. Repression and the other mechanisms of defense are conceived to be the barriers which keep potentially damaging ideas or drives unconscious. Unconscious mental activity is often reflected in behavior that is "defensive"—behavior that gives evidence of an active use of a defense, presumably to ward off an unconscious idea. It also may be detected when the usual defenses are relaxed—in dreams, in reveries, in slips of the tongue, under drugs or intoxication, and in nonthreatening environments. Unconscious mental activity does not follow the logical forms of conscious, communicated thought, but rather tends to the metaphorical, concretistic, and poetic, expressing ideas and feelings in figures of speech and visual images.

4. *Psychosexual development.* Psychoanalytic theory is a developmental theory which is concerned with identifying the critical stages of psychosexual (or more aptly "psychosocial") development and the conditions and experiences which lead to initial fixation at a given state, or to later regression to such a state. In plac-

ing its emphasis on the importance of the early experiences of the child, psychoanalysis has stimulated much study of the family and of the effects of different child-rearing practices. Although Freud and many of the earlier analysts were inclined to stress the influences of experiences of the first five years of life, more recently Sullivan (1953) and Erikson (1963) have emphasized that developmental problems confront the individual throughout his life.

5. *Sex and aggression.* Freud's writings unmasked the role that sexual and aggressive impulses play in the mental life of man. In so doing, he provoked a storm of protest. People were shocked to read that the thoughts of children were not so innocent, that the hysterical seizures of women were often disguised expressions of repressed sexual feelings, and that behind a façade of excessive kindness and consideration there were often murderous impulses. Now, however, it is commonplace for psychologists and nonpsychologists alike to search with a detective's zeal for the sexual or aggressive feelings behind the seemingly most innocent and mundane actions.

6. *Psychoanalytic technique.* In addition to his contributions to psychological theory, Freud made many important contributions to the technique of psychotherapy. Three of his most important are the development of the method of free association, the systematic interpretation of dreams and fantasies, and the analysis of the phenomena of transference and countertransference. All three are methods of getting at unconscious material. In free association, the patient is asked to report whatever thoughts, sensations, or feelings come to his mind, under the assumption that undirected meanderings of the mind in a relaxed atmosphere will flow naturally to the emotional tensions and problems of the person. In actual practice, few patients can associate freely, and associations are usually focused on a given topic. The difficulties and resistances encountered in the course of free association, as well as the actual associations, are part of the grist for analysis. While the specific use of dream interpretation varies considerably among different analysts and different analytic groups, all utilize the interpretation of dreams as a basic tool for uncovering attitudes and feelings that the patient may not be able to express otherwise.

Perhaps Freud's most important therapeutic contribution was his recognition that the therapeutic situation is an interpersonal situation and that a tendency exists for the patient to transfer some of the feelings and attitudes he has acquired in his childhood family situation to his relationship with the therapist. Thus, the therapist may be seen as similar to the patient's seductive mother or to his critical, rejecting father. Analogously, the therapist may respond to the patient with feelings and attitudes based upon his own personal needs and earlier experiences—a response known as "countertransference." Presumably, the therapist who has been successfully analyzed will experience little countertransference, will be aware of tendencies toward it and thus able to suppress or control it.

Classical Psychoanalytic Theory

Psychoanalytic theory has evolved and has been modified during its evolution by both Freud and his followers. The derivative variations of such theorists as Adler, Jung, Rank, Horney, Fromm, and Sullivan will be considered later in this chapter only insofar as they illustrate criticisms of classical psychoanalytic theory. It is difficult to write about psychoanalytic theory because, as Rapaport (1959b, p. 57) pointed out, "neither Freud nor other psychoanalysts' writings give a systematic statement of the psychoanalytic theory." The most systematic attempt at such a statement is found in Rapaport's own writings (1951; 1959a; 1959b; 1960) to which this summary is much indebted.

The core of psychoanalytic theory is in Freud's theory of instincts or drives. This theory has a number of interrelated facets: (1) the theory of the transformation of instinctual energy into derivative motivations and structures, (2) the theory of the structural organization of the personality, (3) the theory of the stages of psychosexual development, and (4) the theory of consciousness. In the following sections, we shall consider the first three of these theories. The theory of consciousness, having been largely ignored until recently, is only now, in the work of such psychologists as Klein (1959a; 1959b) and Holt (1963; 1964), beginning to receive the systematic attention it warrants. Yet even now the approach to it does not pay sufficient heed to the role of social factors in influencing consciousness; in short, the thinking of George

Herbert Mead (see Ch. 6) has not yet had sufficient impact on psychoanalysis.

Basic Psychoanalytic Model of Instinctual
Drives and Their Derivatives

According to this model, an instinct is "the psychical representative of the stimuli originating from within the organism and reaching the mind" (Freud, 1915, pp. 121f.). The *source* of an instinct is the somatic process which gives rise to the stimuli that are represented in the mind as an instinct. (Freud believed that the knowledge of sources was not necessary for psychological purposes and that the study of sources lies outside the scope of psychology.) An instinct exerts pressure on the psychic apparatuses of perception, memory, affect, and motility to do work to achieve the *aim* of the instinct ("satisfaction," which can only be obtained by removing the source of stimulation). The recognition that an instinctual drive can manifest itself in different types of psychological activity or work led Freud to postulate an underlying displaceable quantitative entity of instinctual energy or "drive cathexis" which can be transformed or utilized in different forms of activity. Whenever drive cathexis has risen above the constitutionally determined threshold of discharge, the drive cathexis will, by definition, initiate psychological activity. The natural flow of instinctual energy is entropic, that is to say, its *aim* is to seek discharge. The "pleasure principle" is the term used by Freud to characterize this entropic tendency of instinctual energy. While the pleasure principle describes the inherent tendency of the drive cathexis, the *object of an instinct* determines the specific direction of drive-determined activity. The object of an instinct is the thing in regard to which the instinct is able to achieve its aim. "It is what is most variable about an instinct and is not originally connected with it, but becomes assigned to it only in consequence of being peculiarly fitted to make satisfaction possible. . . . It may be changed any number of times in the course of the vicissitudes which the instinct undergoes during its existence" (Freud, 1915, pp. 122f.).

Thus, the basic psychoanalytic model is one in which drive cathexis seeks immediate discharge through attainment of a drive object. If the drive object is absent or if the discharge of cathexis must be delayed for some other reason (such as internal conflict), some of the available cathexis may be expressed in the cathexis of the memory trace of a drive object (in making conscious the image of a desired object), or in an affect discharge. That is to say, drive cathexis can be expressed in ideation and affect, as well as in overt activity, and is likely to be so expressed in the immature psyche whenever immediate gratification is not possible. Only relatively small amounts of drive cathexis, however, can be absorbed in ideation and affective discharges. Thus, when an instinctual drive reaches threshold intensity and the drive object is absent, reestablishment of equilibrium by discharge is not possible. As a consequence, a new method of establishing equilibrium develops: the threshold for discharge of cathexis is raised by means of a superimposed cathectic barrier termed "anticathexis" or "countercathexis."

The countercathexis derives its energy from the very drive cathexis whose attempt at immediate discharge it seeks to prevent. The repeated absence of immediate gratification results in "binding" the drive cathexis into countercathectic defensive and control structures which block direct attempts at immediate instinctual gratification. Defensive structures function to block immediate or delayed drive gratification so that gratification does not occur even when the drive object becomes available again. (The various kinds of defenses—repression, denial, isolation, reaction formation, rationalization, and undoing—are described in most textbooks of abnormal psychology.) Control structures, on the other hand, provide for the possibility of delayed discharge and for the development of the motives and techniques of finding in reality the object which permits discharge.

Although little is known about the circumstances which lead to the development of defensive rather than control structures, it is commonly assumed that defensive structures are more likely to develop if the intensity of the instinctual drive is so high that the drive seems "uncontrollable," or the reality is so intensely frustrating that there is little hope of drive gratification, or if the instinctual drive is in irreconcilable conflict with another important instinctual or derived motivation. Each of these three conditions is likely to evoke anxiety, which may in turn stimulate the development of a defensive structure.

Both types of derived countercathectic structure are energy structures and manifest themselves as motivations of behavior.

Just as countercathectic structures can develop in relation to the direct discharge of cathexis, so also can defensive and control structures develop in relation to more primitive defensive and control structures. Layer on layer of derivative motivational structures can emerge this way. To illustrate the layering of defenses, let us consider a hypothetical case. Suppose that as a defense against the social disapproval expressed toward any manifestation of her sexual drives, a young girl represses her sexual drive (erects a countercathexis against the manifestation of her drive in behavior, thought, or affect). Later, in college, she becomes aware of her lack of sexual interest and feeling and is disturbed by this lack; as a defense against this disturbance she erects another defense, the reaction formation of nymphomania or compulsive sexual indulgence. Then, becoming anxious about being socially respectable, she erects the defense of appearing excessively prim, proper, and sexually unappealing.

Her motivation to be prim and proper could, in psychoanalytic terms, be viewed as a remote derivative of the encounters between the external reality and her sexual drive (and the more immediate derivatives of her sexual drive). In effect, the countercathectic structures are internal representations of the perceived facts of external reality; that is to say, they modify the discharge of cathexis so as to permit discharge only in accordance with the perceived reality. With the development of these internalized representatives of reality, the pleasure principle becomes modified by the "reality principle." Once established, defense or control structures can become independent of the instinctual drives from which they are derived. If, in effect, a derived structure establishes connections with other instinctual drives and their derivatives, it can survive the loss of its original connection or function.

Freud's theory of instinctual drives is sometimes confused with his "libido" theory. "Libido" is a word used to refer to the cathexis or energy of those instincts which have to do with all that may be comprised under the words "sexual" or "love." Freud used the term "sexual libido" to refer, not only to the desire for body or organ pleasure, but also to affectionate impulses, self-love, love for parents and children, friendship, and so on. That is, the term is employed to refer to any drive energy which presumably has as its sources erotogenic stimulation arising within the body, no matter how transformed its manifestation or how remote its connection to the originating biological source. The libido theory does *not* say that the indirect aim of behavior is sexual union; rather, it posits that libido which is initally dischargeable only through sexual objects can be transformed and find gratification in nonsexual objects. Sex, so to speak, is at the root of much nonsexual behavior but is not necessarily its objective. It was boldly original and, initially, rather shocking of Freud to advocate the view that polymorphous desire for body or organ pleasure was a major concern of the "innocent" child and that the more adult forms of sexual activity and of affectionate relationships derive from these "innocent" concerns. The impact of this view has given psychoanalytic theory its sexual coloring.

Freud, however, did not assume that the sexual instincts and their derivatives were the only kind of motivation. In his early formulations, he posited ego instincts related to self-preservation which quickly were molded to conform to the requirements of reality. Later, in an unsatisfactory attempt to explain the phenomena of sadism and masochism, he introduced the concept of the "death instinct" (*Thanatos*) which he contrasted with the "life instincts" (*Eros*). *Eros* includes both the sexual and the ego instincts; they represent all the constructive, unifying forces in the organism. *Thanatos* represents the tendency of organic matter to return to a state of inorganic matter; this tendency, when diverted outward, is expressed as aggression; if it remains internalized, it leads to self-destruction. Although the notion of inborn aggressive tendencies has been accepted by many psychoanalysts, few have accepted the concept of a death instinct. Many see this concept as a reflection of Freud's pessimism after World War I and as expressing a feeling that man's nature is such as to lead him to destroy others or to destroy himself.

Any assessment of the psychoanalytic theory of instincts must acknowledge that its emphases were important and valuable, even if somewhat one-sided. The psychodynamic approach and the Freudian emphasis on sex and aggression in mental life have given psychologists and nonpsychologists insight into many puzzling aspects of pathological behavior and have provided a useful way of thinking about everyday behavior and some of its determinants.

Critics, who may or may not acknowledge that some of the emphases of the theory of instincts have been valuable, make the following kinds of criticism:

1. *The theory is too vague; the concepts are poorly defined; the theory is not predictive but only explanatory after the fact.* These criticisms are valid, but to a greater or lesser degree they are applicable to many other psychological theories. Although Freud rooted instincts in somatic processes, he provided no characterization of these processes, nor did he indicate how variations in these processes systematically affect the instinctual drives. Neither he nor his followers indicated the conditions under which instinctual energy would be displaced from one activity or object to another, nor did they specify the circumstances which would transform drive cathexis into one rather than another type of countercathexis—into a control or a defense structure, into a defense of reaction formation or a defense of rationalization. The various instincts—sexual, ego, and aggressive—are so vaguely defined that there is no way of identifying whether a given instinct is operative in a given behavior. Although the concept of cathexis is a quantitative one, it presents no method of translating the different forms in which cathexis is manifested into a common currency. Nor is there any suggestion as to how the various instinctual energies—sexual, ego, and aggressive—summate, fuse, or interact with one another in determining behavior. These and other formal defects make the theory extremely wobbly as a platform for prediction and, in fact, psychoanalytic theory is not noted for its predictive successes.

2. *The view that the aim of instincts is the decrease or abolishment of excitation or tension has been much criticized.* It is evident, as many critics (among them Harlow, 1953; Piaget, 1952; Schachtel, 1959; White, 1959; White, 1960) have pointed out, that animals and human infants show persistent tendencies toward activity, exploration, manipulation, and exposing themselves to new stimulation, even when all known primary drives have been satiated. The Freudian theory of motivation assumes, as do the various other theories of tension reduction or need reduction, that all drives result from unpleasant somatic stimulation. The implicit corollary of this assumption is that the individual relates to the world and people about him as though they were mere need objects that might relieve his organic discomfort. Critics (like Schachtel) point out that the curiosity, the delight in activity and exploration shown by infants, suggest inborn motivations that lead the infant to have a direct interest in the world about him.

Such critics contend that neither interest in the external world nor pleasure from effective activity (White, 1959; White, 1960) are secondary motivations, derived in the pursuit of instinctual gratification.

To some extent, the leading proponents (Hartmann, Rapaport, Erikson) of what is termed "ego psychology" in psychoanalytic circles have also recognized the necessity of positing autonomous energies at the disposal of the perceptual-motor apparatus to explain the obvious facts of infant behavior. It is, however, only a timid recognition—one which still clings firmly to the basic doctrine of equating pleasure with tension reduction.

3. *The theory commits the genetic fallacy of assuming that adult motives and concerns are merely derivatives of the drives and motives of early childhood.* Although Freudian theory allows experience to have a role in modifying the expression of instinctual drives and in producing derivative motivations, its point of view is that "the child is father to the man." In everyday experience, the man is father to the child, rather than vice versa. A child does not have the perspective, cognitive capacities, and social roles underlying the stable motivational orientation necessary to being an effective father. The extension of the psychological field as the child develops into an adult affects both the structure and content of human motives. For example, the enlarged capacity of the adult to see his actions in the perspective of time, to anticipate his own death, may have profound motivational consequences. This is not to say that early childhood experiences may not influence the adult's conception of the meaning of death. Nevertheless, the awareness of its possibility may alter the meaning and value of one's actions and give rise to activities and plans in which one would not have otherwise engaged.

4. *The libido theory* is rejected as being too biological, too sexual, and too substantive by many "neo-Freudians" (such as Adler, Fromm, Horney, Kardiner, Sullivan). For example, Fromm (1941, p. 9), in emphasizing the social determinants of motivation, has written: "Although there are certain needs, such as hunger, thirst, sex, which are common to men, those drives which make for the *differences* in men's characters, like love and hatred, the lust for power and the yearning for submission, the enjoyment of sensual pleasure and the fear of it, are all products of the so-

cial process. . . . Man's nature, his passions, and anxieties are a cultural product."

Psychoanalysts who reject libido theory for the most part place their emphasis on the social needs and attitudes which develop in the parent-child interaction. These are partly stimulated by the child's biological needs and partly by the parents' conception of their social roles. The biological needs structure the interaction of parent and child and, thus, lead to the development of interpersonal attitudes and self-conceptions which then become the basic motivators of behavior. Clearly the modes by which biological needs are fulfilled vary more among adults than among infants, and this fact is consistent with the neo-Freudian emphasis on the social rather than the biological determinants of motivation. The neglect of biological processes by many of the neo-Freudians results, however, in a lack of attention to the detailed processes of interaction, which in the earliest stages of development uses the medium of bodily contact and sensory stimulation rather than language for the communication of attitudes. Further, it has led to a lack of specific understanding of the processes by which the social attitudes are communicated and formed.

The libido theory is thought, by some, to be based upon an adultomorphic misinterpretation of infantile sensory pleasure. As Schachtel (1959, p. 133) writes: "There is nothing primarily sexual in the pleasure of the infant's grasping, with mouth or hands, of the mother's breast." Sensory pleasure furnishes "an important link in the infant's motivation of the continued exercise of its muscles and senses, its motor coordination, and its exploration of the environment as well as of its own body and physical capacities." Sensory pleasure is, of course, a component of sexual pleasure at a later stage of development. Nevertheless, to call infantile sensory pleasure "sexual" because it enters into sexual pleasure at a later stage makes about as much sense as calling it "athletic" since it also enters into athletic pleasure at a later stage; calling the infantile sensory pleasure "athletic pleasure" would, by analogy, lead one to think of sexual pleasure as a derivative of athletic pleasure.

A third major criticism of libido theory is that it employs a concept that is substantive and limited in quantity. If a person libidinally cathects another, he should have less cathexis available for himself or for others. On the contrary, it is fallacious, as Fromm has pointed out, to assume that love and self-love are incompatible. Love is not a substance; one does not necessarily have less of it by sharing it. In terms of a physical analogy it is more like "information" than it is like "energy"; one does not lose one's own information by communicating it to another.

Structural Organization of the Personality

Freud distinguished three major structures of the mind: the "id," the "ego," and the "superego."

The id consists of all the various drive cathexes which seek immediate discharge. It abides by the pleasure principle, is unconscious, and is dominated by "primary process" organization—the organization of memory and thought in terms of drives and the affects associated with their frustration or gratification.

The ego consists of the psychic apparatuses (perceptions, memory, motility, and so on) which enable the individual to perceive, to think, and to act upon his environment. It also includes the psychic structures of defense and control which have resulted from the id's previous encounters with reality. The ego is governed by the reality principle and has the function of serving both the id and reality and of harmonizing their potentially conflicting requirements. It acts for the id by seeking gratifications for it in reality and it acts for reality by containing and delaying inappropriate drive discharge and by transforming the drives so that they are more concordant with social reality. In addition, it has the function of harmonizing existing ego structures, including the superego, with the id and reality.

Although Freud's view was that the apparatuses of the ego emerged out of the id's contacts with reality, the widely accepted view, advanced by Hartmann (1939), is that these apparatuses have a primary autonomy. They have emerged in the course of the evolution of the human species and are "preadapted" to function appropriately under "the average expectable environmental conditions" confronting the human species. The ego apparatuses initially function independently of the id. As they become closely involved with the drives, however, the ego apparatuses may become objects of cathexis or countercathexis. Hysterical blindness is a striking illustration of how the perceptual apparatus may be influenced by motivational processes; so, of course, are the more subtle variations of what a person attends to and what he ignores.

The superego is an outgrowth and a modification of the ego. It is commonly thought of as an internalized authority which evaluates id impulses and ego activities in terms of standards and values acquired as a result of the individual's experiences in social groups, particularly in his early family. There are two aspects of the superego: the "conscience" (the internalized prohibitions) and the "ego ideal" (the internalized ideals). The ego attempts to avoid disapproval by its superego (experienced as guilt feelings) by erecting defenses against unacceptable id impulses and by transforming or sublimating unacceptable drives into socially approved derivatives. The child who says "No-no" to himself as he experiences his hand reaching for a forbidden object illustrates the functioning of the unformed superego and provides a clue to its formation. In saying "No-no," the child is acting toward his own behavior as his parents have previously acted toward similar behavior; the child has identified himself with his parents and has internalized a value which leads him to disapprove behavior which would be disapproved by them. The values internalized are, of course, not necessarily the actual values of the parents but reflect the meaning of the parental behavior to the child. In experiencing the event as an activity of his hand which is disassociated from himself, the child is erecting a defense against the superego's disapproval.

Although precursors to the superego exist in the loosely organized system of primitive morality of isolated "do's" and "don'ts," according to Freud the superego does not become an integrated system until the passing of the Oedipal stage of development, at about four to six years of age. At this stage, the child identifies itself with the organized complex of attitudes and values associated with one or another of its parents (preferably the like-sexed parent) as a means of coping with its sexual feelings toward the opposite-sexed parent. By identification with the like-sexed parent, the child obtains vicarious gratification by being like the envied parent and internalizes the obstacle to direct expression of the sexual impulses, the adult rival who would oppose and punish any attempts to replace him. In effect, Freud assumed that conscience could not be fully formed until the child had developed some con-

ception of its future adult role in the family and had internalized
the values governing this role by identification with the envied
parent.

In discussions of psychoanalytic theory it is often pointed out
that the superego is the central social institution of the personality
and that identification of one individual with another is one of the
central psychological processes by which social values and traditions are incorporated into the personality. Although this is a
valid emphasis in the theory, it should also be recognized that the
development of the ego largely reflects the vicissitudes of the instinctual drives in external reality—a reality which is largely social
in nature.

The ego, apart from its inborn apparatuses of perception, memory, motoric activity, and so on is thus largely formed by social
experience. Presumably, of the three major institutions of the personality, it is only the id which remains immutable and invulnerable to social experience. Yet, as we have seen in our discussion
of the instincts and their vicissitudes, Freudian theory posits that
instinctual energies or cathexes can be transformed and instinctual
objects can be changed in the course of experience: the only immutable aspects of the id are its aim (immediate gratification), its
mode of functioning (primary process), and the biological processes which are the sources of the instincts. As research on conditioning of visceral processes has demonstrated, however, it is
likely that even the "sources of the instincts" are influenced by
experience.

Are the concepts of id, ego, and superego necessary to psychoanalytic theory? Probably not. The foregoing discussion of the instincts and their vicissitudes suggests that the emergence of personality structures could be characterized in more useful detail as a
consequence of the interplay between specific social experience
and specific, genetically determined biological processes and structures. The global structural concepts of id, ego, and superego gloss
over the detailed processes that are involved in motivation,
adaptation, and self-evaluation. Furthermore, they suggest spurious entities instead of concepts which refer to different aspects of
a complex process.

The substantivity of these Freudian concepts does in fact,
however, capture aspects of the actual phenomenological experience of the divided self under conflicting pressures from desire.

perceived reality, and conscience. The dramatic imagery of the pleasure-seeking id, the strait-laced superego, and the adaptable, influenceable ego suggests a cast of characters (external and internal) with which most of us are familiar. With a little specification of the setting, moreover, it is not difficult to imagine a particular dramatic interplay among the characters. The rich connotations of the three concepts make them suggestive, but, unfortunately, not clear, for their meanings shift as one or another connotation becomes prominent.

Psychosexual Stages of Development

In the course of his therapeutic work with neurotics and deviates, Freud observed that his patients were not only immature in their social attitudes, but also impaired in their sexuality and given to overt or covert gratifications from other than genital body zones. Their impairment, moreover, appeared to be related systematically to their early childhood experiences, in particular to the fate of their urges for bodily pleasure under the training methods employed by their parents. He concluded that, as a result of a maturational sequence, different zones of the body become the source of sexual pleasure as they are endowed successively with libidinal energy. First, the mouth, then the anal zone, and finally the genitals become the dominant source of libidinal gratification. Constitutional predispositions or early experiences of excessive frustration or gratification may, however, distort the normal sequence of change: too much libido may become *fixated* on a given zone so that subsequent stages of development may have an insufficient supply available, or, under severe frustration, libido may be withdrawn from the painful zone and lead to a *regression* to an earlier stage of development. The symptoms of psychopathology reflect the stage of psychosexual development an individual is fixated on or regressed to. Only if he achieves the psychoanalytic utopia of full genital sexuality is he likely to be completely free of neurotic symptoms.

Concomitant with libidinal development, but not necessarily subservient to it, is a development of the ego, of social attitudes, and of social relations. The concise summary of different aspects of the theory of psychosexual development which follows seeks to incorporate the more recent extensions of the Freudian theory of development as exemplified in the works of Erikson (1950;

1959), White (1960; 1963), and Parsons and Bales (1955). It should be noted, however, that the stages overlap considerably: a sequential presentation cannot bring out the overlapping with sufficient emphasis.

Psychoanalytic theory has concentrated mainly on the three earliest stages of development—the oral, the anal, and the phallic. The later stages—latency, adolescence, young adulthood, adulthood, maturity, old age—have only recently become foci of interest. Of necessity, these later stages are characterized much less systematically. Each of the earlier stages is described in terms of the items on the list which follows; the later stages of development are characterized in less detail.

- The name of the stage.
- Its age level.
- The bodily zones involved.
- Its central core of activities.
- The general mode of approach reflected in these activities.
- The object of these activities.
- The normal frustration or threat to continuation of the given stage.
- The defense mechanisms typical of the stage.
- The social attitudes and character traits derived from the stage.
- The developmental problem posed by the stage.
- Ego development.
- The social subsystem involved.
- Psychopathology.

1. *Oral Stage.* This stage is usually subdivided into the "oral-erotic" and "oral-sadistic" periods.

(1) The oral-erotic period lasts from birth to about eight months; the mouth, lips, tongue, skin, and sense organs become the loci of libidinal energy; the *mode* of obtaining pleasure is passive incorporation (receiving) and is expressed through such activities as sucking, swallowing, bodily contact, and observing; the *object* of libidinal energy is primarily autoerotic ("autoerotism" is the utilization of local erotic excitability without any accompanying relation to the self or outer world, neither of which is as yet distinguished as such). The main *normal frustration* during this stage is the lack of continuous and exclusive availability of the

mother to satisfy the infant's needs. The *defense mechanisms* which characterize this stage are: apathy, or withdrawal of libidinal energy, denial (that the desired gratification is missing, accompanied by hallucinatory gratification), and introjection (internalization of the missing loved object as a compensation for its loss). The latter two mechanisms imply some minimal differentiation between the self and the outer world. Adult *social attitudes and character traits* which represent perpetuations, sublimations, or reaction formations (turning an impulse into its opposite) against the original impulses include passivity, dependency, receptivity, curiosity, generosity, compliance, optimism, haste, restlessness, smoking, overeating, food faddism, talkativeness.

(2) The oral-sadistic period extends from about six to eighteen months; the teeth, jaws, skin, and sense organs are the primary source of libidinal energy; the *mode* of obtaining pleasure is active incorporation (seizing) and is expressed through biting and chewing; *object cathexis* is largely autoerotic, but some of the energy branches off in the direction of the ego (ego cathexis is termed "narcissism") and some in the direction of the external object (the mother as perceived by the infant). The major *normal frustrations* are weaning and the birth of a new child. Characteristic *defense mechanisms* include withdrawal, denial, introjection, and projection (the attribution to the external environment of one's own unacceptable impulses). Adult *social attitudes and character traits* reflecting this period include demandingness, clingingness, exploitativeness, ambivalence, enviousness, jealousy, cynicism, pessimism, sarcasm.

The oral stage, taken as a whole, presents the infant with the *developmental crisis of trust versus mistrust*. During this period, the infant establishes enduring (but not necessarily unmodifiable) dispositions to be more or less trusting or mistrusting of the outside world and of his own capacity to cope with his urges and to elicit response from others. *Ego development* is reflected in the gradual emergence of the distinction between inner experience and outer reality; his recognition of external objects; his beginning awareness of an objective reality, not dependent upon his perception; the development of his capacity to signal his needs ("to ask") and not merely to utter reflex cries of distress; the development of his primitive dual conception of the mother as "good" when she gratifies and as "bad" when she frustrates; the development of his dual conception of himself as omnipotent or helpless depending upon his state of gratification or frustration.

During the oral stage, the infant and mother form a relatively isolated subsystem of the family. From the point of view of the more inclusive social systems of family and community, the mother's role is to care for the child so that he thrives and develops social needs for her presence and approval. These will later enable her to motivate the child to endure the frustrations and demands he will encounter as he moves from the isolated and protected mother–child subsystem to more inclusive subsystems containing siblings and other adults. The infant's role is to learn to expect "care," to become dependent upon, and to organize his segmental needs in terms of the socially determined rhythms of expectable maternal care. The more inclusive social systems of family and community facilitate this stage by valuing "mother love" and by reducing other responsibilities of the mother during this period.

Severe impairment of development during the oral stage is reflected in *schizophrenia* (characterized by a denial of and withdrawal from reality, hallucinatory experience, excessive ideation, inability to distinguish clearly between an inner and external reality, primary-process thinking), *the depressive states* (characterized by intense depressions, self-abuse, agitation, distorted body images), and *manic-depressive psychosis* (characterized by intense swings of mood from elation to depression, and by a markedly ambivalent view of oneself as both omnipotent and helpless and of one's environment as both beneficent and hostile). Although psychoanalysts link psychosis with impairment in the earliest stage of development, they do not, thereby, imply that later experiences do not play a role in precipitating the psychosis and in determining its particular symptomatology. Unfortunately, there has, as yet, been no clear identification of the particular patterns of early infantile experience nor of the constitutional defects which predispose and individual to develop psychosis.

2. *Anal Stage.* This stage is divided into the "anal-sadistic" and "anal-erotic" periods.

(1) The anal-sadistic period lasts from about eight to twenty-four months; the anus, buttocks, and musculature system are eroticized; the *mode* of obtaining pleasure is eliminative and

is expressed through such activities as defecating, expelling, or destroying; *object cathexis* is primarily autoerotic and narcissistic but is also directed toward the mother. The main *normal frustrations* are the onset of toilet training and other demands for self-control. The characteristic *defense mechanism* is projection; the main *character traits* reflecting this period include bossiness, hostility, disorderliness, irresponsibility, lewdness, dirtiness, restlessness, extravagance, assertiveness.

(2) The anal-erotic period lasts from about one to four years; the anus, the buttocks, sphincter, urethra, and muscular system are eroticized; the *mode* of obtaining pleasure is retentive and is expressed through such activities as retaining and controlling feces and urine; *object cathexis* is primarily narcissistic but also is directed toward the mother and to a lesser extent toward the father. The main, *normal frustrations* are toilet training and other demands for self-control. Characteristic *defense mechanisms* are reaction formation, isolation (isolating the thought from its appropriate affect), undoing, intellectualization, and rationalization. *Social attitudes and character traits* reflecting this period include orderliness, stubbornness, parsimony, punctuality, pedantry, cautiousness, righteousness, tendency to collect things, indecision, possessiveness, submissiveness.

The anal stage presents the child with the *developmental crisis of autonomy versus shame and doubt*. The problem for the child is to acquire, as Erikson (1950) has put it, "self-control without loss of self-esteem." From this achievement comes a lasting sense of autonomy and pride. On the other hand, premature attempts at control or parental overcontrol can lead to a lasting sense of doubt and shame. *Ego development* is reflected in the rapid growth of the child's ability for locomotion, manipulation, and communication. The acquisition of language helps the child to mold perception and thought processes into the logical, socially communicable schemes characteristic of his social environment. It eases the development of his sense of self and his ability to react to himself, and facilitates his development of the superego. As White (1960, p. 118) has stated it: "During the second and third years, then, the child, because of practiced maturing of general coordination and of verbal capacity, reaches a critical juncture in his ability to interact with his social environment." He begins to act more like a self, with a more organized sense of competence. He tries to develop ways of preventing himself from being pushed around by his environment and ways to establish and affirm himself.

In the oral stage, the mother acts as the infant's means of need satisfaction, with the infant having no responsibility for pleasing the mother. In the anal stage, however, the mother and child have reciprocal role responsibilities. The mother's responsibilities involve helping the child to establish both a sense of competence and of self and also a sense of acceptance of rules of conduct determined by adults. The mother, in effect, faces the delicate and often conflictual task of helping the child to recognize and accept the distinction between authority and power over himself and over his environment. The child's dependency and needs for affection established during the oral stage provide a positive basis for maternal authority and for the child's compliance with it. The child's responsibility is to learn to respect and obey parental authority as he requires greater competence and self-awareness. To buttress the maternal authority and to prevent the mother from backsliding into her "oral" role of unconditional acceptance and approval of the child, paternal authority (force and the threat of punishment) remains as the ultimate authority for inducing obedience.

Psychopathologies related to the anal stage include: paranoia (characterized by systematized delusions in which the patient believes himself to be the object of an organized conspiracy to attack, humiliate, or control him); psychopathy (characterized by an indifference to right and wrong and by a lack of guilt when violating moral values); the sado-masochistic disorders (characterized by needs to control or to be controlled, to dominate or to submit, to exploit or to be exploited, to beat or to be beaten); and the obsessive-compulsive disorders (characterized by compulsive symptoms, inability to make decisions, excessive rumination, doubt, guilt).

3. *Phallic Stage.* This stage lasts from the ages of about three to six years; the genitalia become the loci of libidinal energy; the *mode* of obtaining pleasure is intrusive (for boys) and incorporative (for girls) and is expressed in masturbatory activity; the *object* of libidinal energy is primarily the opposite-sexed parent. The major *normal threat* for the boy is the threat of castration from the father; for the girl, on the other hand, the sense of having been castrated leads her to shift her affections from her mother to

her father. Being less vulnerable to the threat of castration than the boy, she will have less motive to dissolve her Oedipus complex, her attachment to the opposite-sexed parent. The *characteristic defense mechanisms* are repression, displacement, and conversion. *Social attitudes* and *character traits* reflecting this stage include impulsiveness, naïveness, fickleness, conformism, shallowness, opportunism, haughtiness, assertiveness, arrogance.

Erikson indicates that the developmental problem confronting the child in this period is that of *initiative versus guilt:* the task of "growing together" so that he can aim his efforts toward future adult roles with the sense of personal worth and with the sense that he will not injure nor be injured in the process. "It is at this stage that the great governor of initiative, namely, conscience, becomes firmly established" (Erikson, 1959, p. 80). The problem at this stage is to develop a conscience which will foster dependable initiative rather than impair it.

Ego development is characterized by rapid developments in locomotion, language, and imagination. White (1960, pp. 122 f.) writes:

> Locomotion reaches the point of being a serviceable tool rather than a difficult stunt. . . . The emergence of these seemingly adult motor patterns makes it possible for him to compare himself with grown-ups, yet to wonder about the difference in size. . . . Language likewise reaches a stage of development at which it can support wider understanding and social exchange . . . linguistic competence now opens ready channels for finding about the world. . . . Imagination is the third sphere of competence in which a marked development takes place during the fourth and fifth years. . . . It is the time when he can begin to dramatize himself in different adult roles . . . when he begins to have frightening dreams involving injury and pursuit by wolves.

With the rapid expansion of the child's awareness of his social environment, he begins to grasp the nature of sex roles and aspires to the role of his like-sexed parent. This aspiration places him in conflict with the existing occupant of the role, resulting in Oedipal crises. The superego is fully formed only with the satisfactory resolution of the Oedipal crisis by the child's renunciation of the choice of the opposite-sexed parent as his sex role-mate and by his internalization of the key values governing his sex's adult and sex roles.

On the level of the *social system,* the phallic period involves the transition of the child from a parent-child system differentiated only in terms of power into a system which involves two axes of role differentiation: sex (male-female) and power (adult-child). The prephallic (more often referred to as pregenital) child is "sexless," as are the child's pregenital versions of "mother" and "father." Parsons (Parsons & Bales, 1955, p. 101) suggests: "The most fundamental difference between the sexes in personality types is that . . . the masculine personality tends more to the predominance of instrumental interests, needs, and functions . . . while the female personality tends more to the primacy of expressive interests, needs and functions." By "instrumental," Parsons refers to the tendency to be oriented toward accomplishing tasks, solving problems, overcoming difficulties in the external environment; by "expressive," Parsons refers to the tendency to be oriented toward establishing harmonious, supportive interpersonal relationships, toward reducing tension and providing comfort.

The transformation of the pregenital child into "boy" or "girl" requires that the father's role be distinguished from the mother's role. While the child is in the anal stage, the mother is the primary source both of love and of demands for self-control. When the child reaches the phallic stage, the father becomes the primary source of the new demands for conformity and performance, whereas the mother remains the primary source of acceptance or love. The new demands are differentiated by sex and consist of demands for behavior appropriate to a "boy" or "girl"—demands that the child identify itself simultaneously with the "we-ness" of the family as a group, with the "we-ness" of being a child rather than an adult, and with the "we-ness" of being male like the father (or of being female like the mother). These demands conflict, on the one hand, with the mother-child relationship characteristic of earlier stages and, on the other hand, with precocious strivings for adulthood. The mother and father, by functioning as a differentiated team of socializing agents, help the child to overcome these conflicts. The mother's responsibility at this stage is gradually to withhold infantile care from the child, to support the father's demands for increased performance of the role of "boy" or "girl," to be permissive and understanding with regard to the child's symbolic expressions of frustration, dependency, and aggression, and to be accepting and approving of the child in its role as "boy" or "girl." The father's responsibility is to provide support for the mother as she withholds care, to articulate the new demands on the child that will prepare him to perform appropriately in non-family settings, and to provide approval for the child's satisfactory performances. The child's responsibility is to give up its pre-Oedipal attachment to the mother and to achieve a sex-role identification with its like-sexed parent—to become a "boy" or a "girl."

Psychopathologies reflecting this stage include conversion hysteria (characterized by symptoms which imitate a physical ailment; an hysterical paralysis is an example) amnesia or loss of memory due to repression, anxiety states, and phobias.

4. *Latency Stage.* This stage lasts from the ages of about five to twelve, during which libidinal energy is desexualized and redirected outside the family to parental surrogates such as teachers and to friends of the same sex. The major *normal threats* are inferiority in achievement and social rejection by peers. The characteristic *defense mechanisms* include identification with the aggressor and reaction formation, which are often manifested in an unquestioning loyalty to the leader and to the group. *Social attitudes and character traits* reflecting this stage include industry, inferiority, sociability, competition, cooperation, loyalty, altruism, moralism, compulsive masculinity.

During the latency period, the child becomes part of the world outside the immediate family: the discriminations between "mother" and "woman," "father" and "man," "sister" and "girl" are made. He begins to understand what is "particular" to his relations in his family and what is "universal" for boys or for pupils in his category. This distinction between the particular and the universal facilitates the development of logical thought. He begins to acquire the attitudes and skills necessary to the fulfillment of his expected role in the adult community. The school inculcates community values and provides a transition from the personal and particularistic orientations of the family world to the impersonal and universalistic orientations of the broader community. The peer group provides the possibility of the development of relations based on equality of status and permits the choice or rejection of others as friends.

The earlier and more traditional psychoanalysts did not conceive of the latency period as giving rise to any particular forms of psychopathology, but, to the contrary, believed that problems during the latency period simply reflect inadequate resolution of earlier conflicts. More recently, psychoanalysts have recognized that developmental problems exist throughout life. Thus, Erikson (1950) has been concerned with the "eight stages of man," from the earliest infancy to adult maturity. He identifies the specific danger of the latency period as lying in the development of a sense of inadequacy and inferiority.

Sullivan (1953), who more than most analysts was concerned with the detailed clinical investigation of developmental experiences extending into late adolescence, discussed the "latency period" under the term "the juvenile era." He referred to people who were fixated in the juvenile era as "chronic juveniles": people who constantly have to impress their peers with how accomplished or successful they are. In chronically juvenile people, "one sees a competitive way of life in which nearly everything that has real importance is part of a process of getting ahead of the other fellow" (Sullivan, 1953, p. 232). More generally, Sullivan suggests that the "warps" reflecting the juvenile era express the fact that the youngster did not successfully establish himself in his peer group: his preoccupation with "competition," "compromise," "popularity," "ostracism," "disparagement" reflect this failure.

5. *Puberty and Adolescence.* In the classical psychoanalytic literature, puberty and adolescence are seen as being initiated by the biological process of sexual maturation, which brings with it a return of the instinctual sexual impulses repressed during the latency period. Blos, one of the few "orthodox" psychoanalysts who have attempted to extend and apply psychoanalytic conceptions systematically to adolescence, writes (1962, pp. 11 f.):

> Adolescence is here viewed as the sum total of all attempts at adjustment to the stage of puberty, to the new set of inner and outer —endogenous and exogenous—conditions which confront the individual. The urgent necessity to cope with the novel condition of puberty evokes all the modes of excitation, tension, gratification, and defense that ever played a role in previous years—that is, during the psychosexual development of infancy and early childhood. This infantile admixture is responsible for the bizarreness and the regressive character of adolescent behavior; it is the typical expression of the adolescent struggle to regain or to retain a psychic equilibrium which has been jolted by the crisis of puberty. The significant emotional needs and conflicts of early childhood must be recapitulated before

new solutions with qualitatively different instinctual aims and ego interests can be found. . . . The gradual advancement during adolescence toward the genital position and heterosexual orientation is only the continuation of a development which temporarily came to a standstill at the decline of the Oedipal phase.

In other words, the sexually awakened adolescent is faced with the developmental task of converting his incestuous feelings into heterosexual activities directed toward age-peers of the opposite sex outside of his family. Paralleling this task is the associated developmental task of establishing an identity which enables oneself and others in the community to know who one is. Such an identity is exemplified in the values, roles, and groups one is committed to and aspiring to. In a neat formulation, Erikson has pointed out that adolescence is a period when the "psychosexual moratorium" of the latency period has been lifted and is replaced by a "psychosocial moratorium." He writes (1959, p. 111) that adolescence

can be viewed as a *psychosocial moratorium* during which the individual through free role experimentation may find a niche in some section of his society, a niche which is firmly defined and yet seems to be uniquely made for him. In finding it the young adult gains an assured sense of inner continuity and social sameness which will bridge what he *was* as a child and what he is *about to become*, and will reconcile his *conception of himself* and his *community's* recognition of him.

Erikson points out (1959, pp. 117 f.):

The diffused and vulnerable, aloof and uncommitted, and yet demanding and opinionated personality of the not-too-neurotic adolescent contains many necessary elements of a semideliberate role experimentation of the "I dare you" and "I dare myself" variety. Much of this apparent diffusion thus must be considered *social play* and thus the true genetic successor of childhood play. Similarly, the adolescent's ego development demands and permits playful, if daring, experimentation in fantasy and *introspection*. . . . The same must be said of the adolescent's "fluidity of defenses." . . . Much of this fluidity is anything but pathological; for adolescence is a crisis in which only fluid defense can overcome a sense of victimization by inner and outer demands, and in which only trial and error can lead to the most felicitous avenues of action and self-expression.

Erikson goes on to indicate that adolescent presocieties provide joint support for free experimentation and that whether a given adolescent's newly acquired capacities are drawn back into infantile conflict depends to a significant extent on the quality of the opportunities and rewards available to him in his peer clique.

Parsons (1942) uses the term "youth culture" to refer to the adolescent subcultures. He suggests that the youth culture has important positive functions in easing the transition from the security of childhood to full adulthood as expressed in a commitment to a marital and occupational status. By contrast with the emphasis on responsibility that is characteristic of adult roles, the orientation of the youth culture is more or less specifically irresponsible. (Its "irresponsibility" may be a necessary condition for free experimentation during the psychosocial moratorium.) Parsons points out that one of the dominant notes of the youth culture is "having a good time," with a particular emphasis on social activities in company with the opposite sex. One could suggest that the romanticizing of self and the glamorizing of the sex roles characteristic of the youth culture may serve the functions of providing some compensatory gratification as the youth moves into the specialized and segmentalized roles of the adult world and, hence, away from the diffuse affectional ties with his family and away from the sense of undifferentiated wholeness characteristic of the role of being a child. The romanticizing of "self" preserves a sense of wholeness as the adolescent attempts to establish an adult identity, whereas the glamorizing of sex facilitates the redirection of sexual feelings away from parental figures toward the "young and glamorous" age-peers.

An increasing sense of identity is experienced as a feeling of "being at home in one's body," a sense of "knowing where one is going," and an inner assuredness of anticipated recognition from those who count. Not all adolescents are able to receive this sense of identity, however: Erikson has coined the term "identity diffusion" to refer to the kind of psychological disturbance that reflects pathological outcomes of the specific developmental tasks of adolescence. Identity diffusion usually manifests itself in psychological disturbance when a youth finds himself exposed to a combination of experiences which demand his simultaneous commitment to an intimate relationship, to decisive occupational choice, to energetic competition, and to psychosocial self-definition. Individuation or self-definition and the need to make enduring commitments bring some of the dearest dreams of childhood to an irrevocable end.

As Blos (1962, p. 12) has put it:

> The realization of the finality of the end of childhood, of the binding nature of commitments, of the definite limitation to existence itself—this realization creates a sense of urgency, fear, and panic. Consequently, many an adolescent tries to remain indefinitely in a transitional phase of development; this condition is called *prolonged adolescence*.

The symptoms of identity diffusion or prolonged adolescence are, of course, as diverse as the "symptoms" of adolescence. They are manifested in ego disturbances (such as a distortion of time perspective, an inability to subordinate fantasy to realistic thinking, or a fluidity of defenses and control processes), in excess or lack of self-awareness, in an inability to make enduring commitments, in the need for continuing crisis and turmoil, in the alternation between intense involvement and boredom, in continuing involvement in the "youth culture," and so on. Exalted self-expectations are often dominant in the lives of these young people as a result of their having been "stars" in their early family life or as a result of parental fantasies of vicarious achievement through the achievement of their children.

For these chronic youths, as Blos (1962, p. 224) points out: "Their great future lies behind them. . . . [Nothing] that reality has to offer can compete with the easy sense of elation and uniqueness which the child experienced when he was showered with maternal admiration and confidence."

6. *Three Stages of Adulthood.* Apart from some remarks by Erikson and some comments by Jung, psychoanalytic theorists have not concerned themselves with adulthood. Erikson (1959), however, points out that the achievement of intimate relations with others is one of the developmental tasks of *young adulthood;* failure to achieve it leaves the individual self-absorbed, isolated, or perpetually seeking intimacy in repeated attempts and repeated failures. The establishment of a true and mutual psychological intimacy with another person requires a sense of identity; thus, it requires successful transit through the prior stages of development. The counterpart of intimacy is "distantiation": the readiness to oppose and to stand against those who are destructive of what one

values. In young adulthood, the capacity to be unambivalently *for* or *against* is strengthened.

The developmental task of the second stage of adulthood Erikson has termed "generativity": the interest in establishing and guiding the next generation. This interest may be expressed directly in the assumption of parental responsibility or indirectly in other forms of altruistic concern and creativity. Erikson notes (1959, p. 97): "Individuals who do not develop generativity often begin to indulge themselves as if they were their own one and only child." Becoming a parent does not necessarily imply generativity; many parents suffer from the retardation of or the inability to develop this stage.

Maturity, the third of Erikson's stages of adulthood, is characterized in terms of the achievement of *integrity* (Erikson, 1959, p. 98):

> [The] acceptance of one's own and only life cycle and of the people who have become significant to it as something that had to be and that, by necessity, permitted of no substitutes. It thus means a new different love of one's parents, free of the wish that they should have been different, and an acceptance of the fact that one's life is one's own responsibility. It is a sense of comradeship with men and women of distant times and of different pursuits, who have created orders and objects and sayings conveying human dignity and love.

Lack of ego integrity is expressed in despair: the feeling that the time is too short for the attempt to start another life and to discover alternative roads to integrity.

Criticism of the Psychoanalytic Theory of Psychosexual Development

An evaluation of the psychoanalytic theory of psychosexual development must acknowledge the revolutionary and stimulating impact of the view that personality evolves as a consequence of the individual's specific experiences in a sequence of developmental stages that derive from biosocial characteristics of the human species. An enormous amount of research into the effects of child-raising practices on personality development has been stimulated by the identification of specific developmental stages and the detailed characterization of each stage in terms of its typical pleasures, frustrations, defense mechanisms, ego resources, developmental functions and pathologies. Much of this research (see

Lindzey, 1954, for a summary) does not, however, support the view that the characteristics of the adult personality are derivatives of specific experiences of pleasure or frustration in a particular developmental stage. For example, the so-called "anal" character—one which is orderly, stingy, and obstinate—apparently does not derive from specific experiences during toilet training, but rather from more enduring experiences throughout the various phases of development.

Other major criticisms have been leveled at the Freudian theory of development.

1. In its original version, the theory assumed that individual development was a recapitulation of phylogenetic patterns and, hence, that the stages of development—including the development of the Oedipus complex—occur in a genetically invariant and predetermined manner. This version of the theory allowed little scope for the effects of social influences upon personality development and could not explain the manifest differences found in different cultures. Even in the more sophisticated version which stresses social influences (the version we have attempted to present), however, the stages of development are largely constructed from the study of individuals in our culture and are not necessarily valid for human nature in general. Clearly, the so-called oral period takes on different characteristics when children are allowed to suckle until they are four years old or older; the "anal period" is different where there are no toilets and no systematic toilet training; the "phallic period" must take on special characteristics in the one-room huts of much of the world, in which parents and children share the same bedding; the "latency period" hardly characterizes the many societies which permit and encourage sexual play between boys and girls.

2. The psychoanalytic account of development is a very partial account. It underemphasizes the importance of cognitive development and the role of language in transforming the child and in developing the child's motivation. More generally, the development of the nonsexual systems (perception, cognition, motoric activity, and the nonsexual motives) are neglected. Yet these also have a developmental course and are much influenced by early experience. Processes of learning, and how they affect and are affected by development, are largely ignored.

3. Personality development is conceived of only in terms of

inner dynamics and structure, and the relationships between personality and social structure and social dynamics are neglected. This conclusion applies in the large (for example, the Freudian neglect of such external factors as social class, poverty, or war in personality development) and also in the small (for example, the tendency to view parent-child relations only in terms of the parent's influence on the child rather than in terms of an interacting system in which the child also influences the parent).

4. The Freudian theory of development is analogous to a geological layering of different epochs of development, in which the earlier strata are covered but not transformed by the later stages. The notions of fixation and regression reflect this view. A "regressed" adult, however, is not like a child; there are marked differences between the thought processes of an infant and those of a schizophrenic.

5. The concretistic imagery of the psychosexual theory of development casts parent-child transactions into overly stereotyped forms. Parental nurturance of an infant is not, for example, exclusively a transaction between a maternal breast and an infant's mouth; nurturance is expressed in many different activities and is expressed in many different organ systems. Nor is it likely that generalized attitudes toward "being cared for" are determined solely by transactions in one interactional mode: the oral.

6. The theory is vague in identifying both the constitutional and the experiential determinants of the course of psychosexual development. In other words, the theory gives little guidance in making predictions about the circumstances which will lead to "fixation" or "regression," the conditions which will determine whether a "fixation" of an infantile trait (such as "anal eroticism") will lead to a "continuation" of the trait ("messiness") or to a "reaction formation" against the trait ("compulsive cleanliness") in later life. Thus, the theory does not provide much specific guidance to parents who want to help their children navigate past the pitfalls of early development. This is not to deny that it has clearly indicated some of the dangers that may result from excessive frustration or indulgence of children as they cope with their major developmental tasks.

Psychoanalytic Contributions to Social Psychology

Freud's influence on social psychology has been pervasive, and the psychoanalytic approach, as outlined in the previous sections, has profoundly influenced the thinking and work of many social psychologists, sociologists, and anthropologists. To be considered in this section are (1) Freud's own writings in the social sciences, (2) psychoanalytic contributions to the study of attitude formation, as illustrated in the work on *The Authoritarian Personality* (Adorno, Frenkel-Brunswik, Levinson, & Sanford, 1950), and (3) psychoanalytic contributions to the study of culture and personality, especially as reflected in the work of Abram Kardiner.

Freud's Work in Social Psychology

Freud wrote five major books in the social sciences: *Totem and Taboo* (1913), *Group Psychology and the Analysis of the Ego* (1921), *The Future of an Illusion* (1928), *Civilization and Its Discontents* (1930), and *Moses and Monotheism* (1939). By any standard, these works are fascinating and imaginative speculations. Nevertheless, by today's standards they are outdated, having drawn on anthropological assumptions and materials that are no longer considered valid. For example, Freud assumed that individual development recapitulates "cultural evolution" and that existing primitive societies were at an earlier "stage" of "cultural evolution." Hence, presumably, in primitive cultures we have a well-preserved early stage of our own cultural development, and in the psychic life of the primitive we have a replica of an early stage of our own psychic development.

In *Totem and Taboo,* Freud presented the view that the taboo systems and totemism observed in primitive societies derive from conflict between the father and sons for the mother, a conflict which early in man's history resulted in the jealous sons' banding together to slay and eat the father. This "original sin" led to remorse, the erection of taboos as defensive measures against the forbidden incestuous feelings, and totemism as a way of strengthening the sons' identification with the father. Freud presented the views that man's Oedipus complex derives from such a primal

patricide and that animal phobias in children are an infantile re-
currence of totemism (the rivalry with the father for the love of
the mother leads the child to displace his fear and hatred onto an
animal). These views presuppose a Lamarckian inheritance of
characteristics required by experience, an assumption for which
there is no scientific support.

In *Group Psychology and the Analysis of the Ego,* Freud
turned to the question of why societies hold together, to the nature of the social binding force. His answer is in terms of two
basic concepts: "desexualized libido" (people are bound together
by friendship, which is considered to be aim-inhibited, desexualized, or sublimated love); and "identification" (people are bound
together into a primary group because they have taken the same
leader for their ego ideal, have identified with him, and have
consequently identified themselves with one another). Identification does not presuppose unambivalent positive feelings toward
the leader; to the contrary, Freud viewed identification with the
leader as, in part, a mechanism of defense against hostile feelings
toward the superior (the father) and as an indirect means of "becoming" the leader by identifying with him. Thus, according to
Freud, social feeling is based, to some extent, on a reversal of
what initially was a hostile feeling.

In *The Future of an Illusion,* Freud pointed out that as the
price for its protection, society demands that the individual control or renounce certain instinctual gratifications. These demands
provoke hostility, which is countermanded by identification with
the forbidding authority and internalization of it. Freud maintained that God serves much the same functions for the adult as
does the parent for the helpless child. Belief in God helps man
to overcome his feelings of helplessness against the forces of nature and, as a price for this help, man is more willing to control
or renounce instinctual gratifications which might disrupt society. Here Freud hinted at an idea which Kardiner was later to
expand—that cultural systems for structuring the outer world and
man's relations to it are much influenced by the child's experiences with his parents and often directly reflect them.

In *Civilization and Its Discontents,* Freud again presented the
view that the aims of the individual and of society do not coincide.
He postulated here an innate aggressiveness or destructiveness in
man which he viewed as one of the chief disintegrating forces in

society. Society controls the aggressive instincts by internalizing them in the form of the superego and directing them against the ego. Under the influence of the sadistic superego, the ego may become masochistic or self-destructive. Freud was, in effect, assuming that there is a basic destructiveness in man which will be expressed against others (sadistically) or against himself (masochistically). The notion that sadism and masochism are alternative expressions of the same motivational structure is a view that underlies much of *The Authoritarian Personality,* to which we now turn.

The Authoritarian Personality

The psychoanalytic point of view contained, in its early years, a radical critique of the social values of Western society. It was an unmasking psychology which exposed the discrepancies between social appearances and underlying psychological realities; it revealed the difficulties that men and women were experiencing in their most intimate relations; it indicated how the authority of parents was utilized to alienate the child from his basic impulses; and so forth. Its criticisms of society attracted the attention of many liberal social scientists who were interested in the relations between culture and personality.

During the period between the two World Wars, this interest was reflected in the initiation of psychoanalytically oriented investigations of the relations between culture and personality, and in psychoanalytically inspired studies of authoritarianism. These latter studies were stimulated by the emergence of Fascism and Nazism; the authoritarian character of Stalinism was generally overlooked, partly because it was cloaked by the humanistic slogans of Marxism and partly because of the initial illusions of many liberal social scientists.

Lasswell (1930), Fromm (1941), Maslow (1943), Sartre (1946), and Reich (1946) were among the pioneers in the attempt to describe in depth the functions of social attitudes in the personality. Following in the path of some of these earlier works, *The Authoritarian Personality* (Adorno et al., 1950) was aimed at understanding the roots and corollaries of prejudice. Its approach fused the theoretical orientation of psychoanalysis with the methodologies of social and clinical psychology.

Although the theory underlying *The Authoritarian Personality* was never presented by its authors in a concise or systematic form, it may be summarized as follows: The "authoritarian personality" is produced by parents who use harsh and rigid forms of discipline on the child, who make their love and approval conditional on unquestioning obedience from the child, who emphasize duties and obligations rather than the exchange of affection in family relations, who are overly conscious of distinctions of status in their interpersonal relations and are contemptuous or exploitative toward those of lower status. As a result of being forced to submit to a harsh, arbitrary parental authority, the child develops hostility which is too dangerous to express toward the frustrating but feared parents. Having submitted, he also develops a view of himself that makes him feel more dependent on his parents, and thus less able to defy or even question them.

The child's need to repress rigidly all hostility toward the parents leads to an identification with authority and an idealization of it, with a concomitant displacement of the hostility onto out-groups, who usually are of lower status. Accompanying the displacement of his hostility is a projection onto out-groups of those of the authoritarian's own impulses which were frustrated and repressed because of their unacceptability within his family. The fear of his own impulses and the need to repress them rigidly leads to a rigid personality organization, to stereotyped thinking, to an avoidance of introspective awareness, and to a moralistic condemnation and punitive attitude toward unconventional values and practices. Personal relations are perceived in terms of power and status; "strength" and "toughness" are idealized, whereas "weakness" and "tenderness" are associated with each other and viewed with contempt.

In brief, the distinctive characteristics of the authoritarian personality presumably reflect defenses against the expression of repressed hostility toward authority; the major defenses are the projection of the unacceptable, frustrated impulses onto out-groups, the displacement of hostility onto the same out-groups, and the identification with the frustrating authority.

The theory has many interesting implications—more than can be indicated here. First of all, it leads one to expect that authoritarians will be dominating and exploitative toward the weak or toward subordinates and submissive and ingratiating toward the strong or toward superiors. This is an apt characterization of the behavior of many Nazis: arrogant in power and submissively ingratiating in defeat. Secondly, it leads one to expect that such authoritarians would be prejudiced, not only toward Jews, but also toward Negroes and other minority groups. Moreover, if one assumes that most prejudice and ethnocentrism are based on underlying personality characteristics, one would expect that they would be correlated with other manifestly different attitudes—political-economic attitudes, attitudes toward power, obedience, sex, and so forth. Thirdly, if most prejudice is rooted in an "authoritarian personality" then prejudice would be difficult to change or overcome unless those in authority took forceful and unequivocal stands against prejudice and discrimination. Even if they did, the authoritarian personality would still be left with the problem of how to find an alternative displacement for his repressed hostility, or how otherwise to manage his repressed hostility toward those in authority.

The authors of *The Authoritarian Personality* began their study of the roots of prejudice in personality by investigating the organization of anti-Semitic attitudes. They constructed five scales to measure beliefs about Jews: (1) their "offensiveness"; (2) their "threatening" character; (3) their "seclusiveness"; (4) their "intrusiveness"; and (5) the desirability of segregating Jews. Despite the surface inconsistency of some of the scales ("intrusiveness" and "seclusiveness"), the intercorrelations among the scales were relatively high (between .74 and .83), indicating that beliefs about Jews constitute a fairly unified system of attitudes.

Adorno and his associates next investigated whether anti-Semitism is part of a more inclusive general attitude of rejection of minority groups. To do so, they constructed an "ethnocentrism" scale consisting of three subscales measuring attitudes toward Negroes, attitudes toward minority groups other than Jews and Negroes, and attitudes toward the United States as an in-group as contrasted with other nations as out-groups. The intercorrelations of the three subscales were relatively high, as were their correlations with the measure of anti-Semitism. These results supported the view that ethnocentrism and prejudiced attitudes form a broad and coherent pattern.

The next step was to develop an instrument that would measure implicit antidemocratic tendencies, making possible the indirect measurement of prejudice. Items with no direct reference to ethnocentrism were constructed around the conception of the authoritarian personality. After much trial and error, the "F-scale" (so called because presumably it measures the predisposition to Fascism) emerged, a thirty-item scale which includes such items as:

- Obedience and respect for authority are the most important virtues children should learn.
- People can be divided into two distinct classes, the weak and the strong.
- Nowadays more and more people are prying into matters that should remain personal and private.
- Homosexuals are hardly better than criminals and ought to be severely punished.
- Familiarity breeds contempt.

Correlations between the F-scale and the ethnocentrism scale ranged from .59 to .87 for various groups and different forms of the scales, providing evidence in support of the authors' conception of prejudice as being rooted in central personality predispositions. Intensive clinical interviews were also conducted with people who scored high or low on ethnocentrism, and the data from the interviews, as well as from projective tests, were consistent with the authors' conception.

Serious criticisms can be and have been made of the methodology of *The Authoritarian Personality* (see various chapters in Christie & Jahoda, 1954). The major valid criticisms of *The Authoritarian Personality* are:

1. The data collected to test the theory were themselves molded by the theory and therefore cannot be considered as an unbiased, independent test of the authors' conception (for example, the interviewers knew the attitude-scale scores of the subjects before the interview and thus may have inadvertently biased the interview data).

2. The questionnaires have various methodological flaws; for example, "agreement responses" lead to high scores on prejudice and authoritarianism, and thus people who tend to be "disagreers" will end up with low scores on prejudice and authoritarianism. Hence the scales also measure the tendency to agree or disagree and not only what they were intended to measure—the scales have no clear dimensionality.

3. The "highs" and "lows" differed systematically in educa-

tion; hence much of the obtained personality difference may reflect differences associated with education and social class.

4. The theory is too content-bound and leads to a neglect of "left-wing authoritarians," whereas the underlying psychoanalytic theory does not necessitate an inevitable link between an individual's personality structure and the content of his ideology.

5. The theory is too culture-bound in its assumption that anti-Semitism, ethnocentrism, and authoritarianism are linked together in underlying personality tendencies without regard to the attitudes prevailing in a given culture.

6. The authors commit the fallacy of implying that the prejudiced are usually authoritarian because their findings suggest that authoritarians are often prejudiced.

Despite the criticisms it evoked, *The Authoritarian Personality* stimulated a great deal of subsequent research, most of which correlated the F-scale with other personality, attitudinal, and behavioral measures. The results of this mass of research are too many and complex to summarize briefly; for extensive surveys see Christie and Cook (1958) and Titus and Hollander (1957). One may note, however, that the F-scale is correlated with a wide range of social and personality variables. Thus, people who score high on authoritarianism are more likely to be lower class, less educated, less intellectually sophisticated, less liberal politically, more prejudiced, less successful as patients in psychotherapy, more religious, and stricter in their child-rearing practices than people who score low on authoritarianism.

The relationships between authoritarianism and other variables are undoubtedly very much influenced by the sociocultural environment. Thus, Pettigrew (1958) demonstrated that South African college students who were extremely prejudiced against Negroes were not more authoritarian than the less prejudiced American college students. Afrikaans-speaking, as compared with English-speaking, South African students were more prejudiced against the black African but less prejudiced against the African Indian.

Many critics have pointed out that authoritarianism is not confined to the political right wing; there are many left-wing authoritarians. Rokeach (1960, p. 6), for example, contends that authoritarianism "cuts across specific context; that is, it is not uniquely restricted to any one particular ideology, or religion, or philosophy, or scientific viewpoint. . . . [It] is not so much what you believe that counts, but how you believe." Rokeach's central thesis (1960, p. 395) is that "we organize the world of ideas, people, and authority basically along the lines of belief congruence," liking those with similar beliefs and disliking those with dissimilar beliefs. There are individual differences among us in the absolute extent to which we are willing to accept or reject others on this basis; these differences reflect the structural "openness" or "closedness" of the belief systems. In Rokeach's terms a system is open to the extent that the person can receive, evaluate, and act on relevant information from the outside on its own intrinsic merits. Rokeach, like the authors of *The Authoritarian Personality,* stresses the role of an enduring state of threat in creating the closed mind; his view of the origins of the closed mind is similar to their view of the origins of the authoritarian personality.

In accordance with this more general conception, Rokeach developed scales to measure "dogmatism" and "opinionation" (unfortunately, as with the F-scale, he allows "agreeing responses" to be confounded with his measures). These scales were aimed at measuring the "closedness" or "openness" of the mind of the believer: authoritarianism was hypothesized to be a reflection of closed-mindedness. Although not conclusive, his investigations indicated that people who were highly opinionated—whether their opinions were "left" or "right"—tended to be dogmatic. People who were highly (right-wing) authoritarian as measured by the F-scale were likely to be highly dogmatic and opinionated. Rokeach has also demonstrated that open-minded students were more able to solve an intellectual puzzle involving the ability to integrate new beliefs into a new cognitive system than equally intelligent closed-minded students. His findings generalize and qualify the conclusions in *The Authoritarian Personality.*

What over all conclusions can be drawn about the relations between personality and attitudes as a result of the research stimulated by *The Authoritarian Personality?* It is evident that personality characteristics can influence attitudinal characteristics—most directly by determining the structure and organization of belief systems, and by determining the individual's particular responsiveness to different types of people, roles, or groups as sources of influence.

Thus, from knowledge of personality characteristics alone, without the additional knowledge of the beliefs held by significant people and groups in the individual's social environment, one cannot predict the particular content of his attitudes and beliefs: an "authoritarian" in the United States is likely to be anticommunist, anti-Semitic, prosegregation, anti-Castro; an "authoritarian" in the Soviet Union is likely to have a different pattern of attitudes. Also, knowing only that a person is "prejudiced" does not enable one to assert that the person has a given personality structure— "authoritarian." As Pettigrew (1958) has demonstrated, prejudice against Negroes is one thing in a South African college student and a rather different thing in an American college student.

On the basis of the available evidence, it seems reasonable to assume that the early experiences of the child in an "authoritarian" family may predispose the child to develop defensively rigid and closed belief systems. It will also predispose him to be sensitized to influence from people in authority who are perceived to have beliefs and values which are either congruent with or opposed to those of parental authority. This statement, as well as the psychoanalytic theory with which it is consistent, are both unsatisfactorily vague. They do not specify the conditions under which rebellion or acquiescence to the values of authority (of the authorities who symbolize parental authority) will occur; nor do they provide any way of knowing which authorities will be symbolic of parental authority. The statement does, however, indicate *how* and, to some extent, *whom* people will believe, even if it does not directly indicate *what* they will believe. With knowledge of the individual's social environment, knowledge of the *how* and the *whom* will help to specify the *what*.

Culture and Personality

Clyde Kluckhohn, a well-known anthropologist, described the attraction of psychoanalysis for anthropologists in these terms (Kluckhohn, 1954, p. 964): "For all of the extravagant dogmatism and *mystique* of much psychoanalytic writing, the anthropologist sensed that here at least he was getting what he had been long demanding in vain from academic psychology: a theory of raw human nature. . . . [Psychoanalysis] provided anthropology with a general theory of psychological process that was susceptible of cross-cultural testing by empirical means and with clues that might be investigated as to the psychological causes of cultural phenomena." The relation between psychoanalysis and cultural anthropology was, however, neither one-sided nor that of uncritical acceptance.

The theory of "raw human nature" provided by Freud, with its emphasis on a genetically based and culturally invariant sequence of psychosexual stages of development, was, of course, difficult for cultural anthropologists to accept. Their professional identities are, after all, based on the understanding of cultural differences. Initially, such anthropologists as Malinowski (1927) and Margaret Mead (1928; 1930; 1935) worked to demonstrate the defects of such psychoanalytic notions as assumed a universal Oedipal complex or a culturally invariant latency stage. The findings of various anthropological studies of simpler, non-Western societies did much to debunk the curious psychoanalytic view that the middleclass Viennese who were Freud's patients were prototypes of mankind. These findings also influenced many psychoanalysts to place more emphasis on the specific social experiences of the child, especially as these experiences were molded by his family's childrearing practices. Various psychoanalytic theorists who reject the libido theory—Harry Stack Sullivan, Karen Horney, Erich Fromm, Erik Erikson, Sandor Rado, David Levy, Abram Kardiner—have been profoundly influenced by the research of cultural anthropologists. Of these theorists, Kardiner has worked most directly with leading anthropologists and has undoubtedly contributed most to the work of anthropologists and utilized theirs most thoroughly.

During the 1930's Kardiner conducted a series of seminars—initially at the New York Psychoanalytic Institute and later at Columbia University—which brought together anthropologists, psychoanalytic theory, and anthropological data. Such noted anthropologists as Ralph Linton, Ruth Benedict, Ruth Bunzel, Cora DuBois, and Margaret Mead at one time or another participated in the seminar. During the seminar, it became evident that existing anthropological data were not adequate for a systematic application of Kardiner's psychodynamic analysis. For this reason a field expedition to the island of Alor (in what was then the Netherlands East Indies) was initiated to obtain the relevant data; the expedition was undertaken by Cora DuBois and financed largely by Kardiner.

The fruits of Kardiner's seminar are described in two major works, *The Individual and His Society* (1939) and *The Psychological Frontiers of Society* (1945). In essence, Kardiner's approach is based on the central Freudian notion that childhood frustrations can affect the course of personality development by mobilizing certain defensive attitudes and by stimulating substitutional or compensatory processes which may be continued into adult life. Kardiner's approach differs from Freud's in that he stresses the specific technique employed in the care and rearing of the child, which he views as being culturally patterned. He rejects the view that childhood frustrations are phylogenetically determined. (Interestingly enough, Kardiner, who was analyzed by Freud, has indicated in conversation that Freud in person was not as "orthodox" a Freudian—either as therapist or as theorist—as his writings or his more orthodox followers would suggest.)

From Kardiner's view that the frustrations of childhood result from child-rearing practices that are culturally patterned, it follows that the members of any given society will have many similar experiences in childhood and will, hence, have many elements of personality in common. Kardiner and Linton have employed the term "basic personality" to refer to the personality configuration that is shared by the bulk of the society's members as a result of the experiences they have in common. The term has often been misunderstood as suggesting that all people in a given society have the same personality, but, on the contrary, Linton (1945, p. viii) has pointed out: "It does not correspond to the total personality of the individual but rather to the projective systems or, in different phraseology, the value-attitude systems. . . . [The] same basic personality type may be reflected in many different forms of behavior and may enter into many different total personality configurations."

The detailed application of Kardiner's views to the understanding of the interaction between personality and society implies: (1) the identification of key situations and primary social institutions which influence personality formation; (2) a psychodynamic theory of how culturally specific experiences of frustration and gratification in such key situations will lead to the development of specific defensive and control structures, giving rise to a "basic personality" in the members of a given society; (3) a sociopsychological theory of how the requirements and characteristics of the "basic personality," deriving from the child's experiences in primary social institutions, will shape and constrain the secondary institutions of the society; and (4) a theory of how the specific problems of adaptation to its physical and social environment, in interaction with the basic personality of its members and with its existing social institutions, will influence the future development of social institutions of the society (including those that affect its child-rearing practices) and also the ability of the society to cope with changing environments.

Kardiner (1945, pp. 26 f.) provides a list of key situations that may influence the formation of personality. His list, based on an intensive study of ten cultures, is long, and is a potpourri referring to various aspects of maternal care, discipline, ascribed and achieved role status, techniques of production, systems of belief, religious practices, value systems, and many more factors. The list is *ad hoc;* it does not grow out of a systematic conception of human and societal requirements. Nevertheless, it is clearly concerned with a broader range of situations than are usually the foci of psychoanalytic attention.

Kardiner's work also illustrates how psychodynamic theory can be used to formulate specific hypotheses about the effects of culturally patterned practices of child care on the development of "basic personality." He also shows that the themes of folklore and religion, as well as the characteristics of social institutions, are congruent with the basic personality. The study of the Alorese produced a very dramatic illustration of the correlation between personality and culture. On the basis of ethnographic material supplied by the anthropologist Cora DuBois, Kardiner developed hypotheses about the kinds of personality which would develop under the described conditions of child care—hypotheses which were supported by an analysis of eight native biographies secured by DuBois. Further support appeared in their essential agreement with the personality descriptions made independently by Emil Oberholzer, based upon Rorschach protocols and children's drawing that were collected by DuBois in Alor.

Kardiner (Kardiner & Preble, 1963, pp. 218 f.) summarizes the results from the study of the Alorese in these terms:

> The over-all treatment of children in Alor can be characterized as one of neglect and inconsistency. From studies in our own society one would suspect that these conditions would produce serious integrative disorders in the individual. The biographies and psychological tests of individual Alorese confirm this suspicion. The Alorese are suspicious, mistrustful, and anxious. They lack confidence and self-

esteem. They are fearful and unaggressive, but prey on their neighbors by means of lies, deceptions, and chicanery. They are unable to sustain a love relationship or a friendship based on voluntary interest. They have a limited capacity to master or enjoy the outer world. The appearance of these traits as the common inheritance of the Alorese does not surprise us, knowing what we do about the early experiences of these people with their parents and the environment. What is more interesting, however, and what constitutes a real addition to our knowledge of cultural processes, is the observation that these traits are reflected throughout the entire social structure of the culture.

In the folklore and religion of Alor we note themes and motifs directly related to the life experiences and character traits of the Alorese. In their folklore the most common motif is parental frustration and hatred. In one tale, for example, a child is told by his mother to fetch some water with a water tube which she has deliberately punctured at the bottom. While the child is vainly attempting to fill the tube the parents abandon him. Years later, at his marriage feast, the parents reappear and are presented with food tubes filled with feces.

In their religion there is no idealization of the deity. The deity has no great power for beneficence and is therefore not placated in the expectation of rewards and benefits. Sacrifices to the deity are offered reluctantly and grudgingly, and then only in emergencies. There is no concept of forgiveness and no storing up of virtue as a form of insurance. The only comforting theme that appears in Alorese religion, myth, and folklore concerns supernatural Good Beings who bestow favors capriciously and without solicitation. They are. significantly enough, always total strangers to those whom they help.

. . .

Once we have reached these central insights into Alor, many seemingly idiosyncratic features in this culture take on meaningful and significant relationships. This applies to individual traits, such as the tendency to collapse and wait for death in the event of any kind of illness, and it applies to social institutions, such as the socioeconomic system which greatly exaggerates the importance of status and wealth. In the first example, we recognize the Alorese conviction that one can expect only the worst from life, and in the second we recognize a frantic and desperate effort to bolster self-esteem.

Note that Kardiner advances the thesis that persistent frustrations produce inner tensions which require the elaboration of what he has termed "projective systems," like religion and folklore, which take their distinctive character in a given culture presumably because the conceptions which develop as a result of experiences in childhood are carried forth or projected onto such systems. Projective systems serve the socially stabilizing function of providing an external influence toward conformity to the social order. For example, although there is no idealization of the deity in Alor, the Alorese act toward the deity as though they are under the coercive threat of punishment (very much as they were forced to be obedient when they were children). In other words, since the child-care institutions of Alor produce a personality that is distrustful and unresponsive to affection, the secondary institutions of this society, such as religion, must, to be effective, act on other motivational systems of the personality—the ones developed as a result of the child-care practices.

The necessity for the elaboration of such projective systems as religion is, in Kardiner's view, largely determined by the extent of traumatic experiences during the process of development. The greater the trauma, the greater the resulting inner tension and hostility and the greater the potential for socially disruptive motives, and hence the greater the need for externalized controls to maintain social stability. As Kardiner points out, however, all societies have empirical reality systems, such as those involved in planting, hunting, and the making of tools, which are consciously taught and learned in addition to the projective systems. It makes a great deal of difference for cultural stability and change whether the social institutions of a society are polarized toward the empirical or the projective systems. The adaptability of a society is much impaired by a culture in which external reality is subordinated to the projective systems and evaluated by them. Kardiner (1945, p. 43) writes: "As long as natural law is only a new manifestation of divine will, then one's security does not depend on manipulating reality and important changes in adaptation will be attempted by way of this projective screen, while the social realities are either ignored or they drift aimlessly."

Kardiner, more than any other psychoanalyst, has attempted to characterize the specific reciprocal relationships between social institutions and personality as they are manifested in a variety of cultures. He has stressed that an adequate characterization of these reciprocal relationships entails the acquisition of three related bodies of knowledge: (1) an understanding of the problems of adaptation that the society has faced; (2) an understanding of the homeostatic processes that operate in the society to keep it functioning as a society; (3) an understanding of the "basic personality" that results from the particular homeostatic patterns of a given society. In recognizing the key issues involved in the study of the relationships between culture and personality, Kardiner laid the foundation for an empirical approach to the understanding of psychosocial integration in different cultures.

As a matter of fact, Kardiner (Kardiner & Preble, 1963, p. 223) offers a pessimistic appraisal of his own influence. "Unfortunately," he says, "this particular approach to culture-personality investigation in anthropology has ground to a halt." Nevertheless, there has been a growing interest in studies of child rearing in different cultures (for example, Whiting, 1963), and certainly much of this work is indebted to Kardiner's stimulus. Just as offspring tend to be influenced more by what parents do than by what they proclaim, so recent work in the study of psychosocial integration places too little emphasis on the study of adult functioning and the social situations of adult life. Although Kardiner wrote of the importance of understanding the complex interactions among "basic personality," social institutions, and the problems of environmental adaptation, still, in practice his work tends to assume a more or less direct continuation into adulthood of the social attitudes formed in childhood. His route from child-rearing practices to the secondary institutions of the society has been too direct, for it does not consider how the secondary institutions interact nor how, as a result of their interaction, the child-rearing practices and the problems of adaptation may change.

Concluding Comment

The human metamorphosis from biological, pleasure-ridden organism at birth to socialized, reasoning adult at maturity is the primary subject matter of psychoanalysis. Any attempt to understand man must take into account the social and biological processes which are instrumental to human development. This is what Freud attempted to do in his image of the biologically rooted instincts of the infant being subdued and transformed under the discipline, guidance, and nurturance of the parents. Freud's genius was to reveal in rich detail how man's adult life is permeated by the residues of the developmental processes. No other theoretical approach has provided so many insights into the development and functioning of the human personality. Nevertheless, as Schachtel (1959, p. 10) has noted:

> The concepts and language used by Freud to describe the great metamorphosis from life in the womb to life in the world abound with images of war, coercion, reluctant compromise, unwelcome necessity, imposed sacrifices, uneasy truce under pressure, enforced detours and roundabout ways to return to the original peaceful state of absence of consciousness and stimulation. . . . Only under the pressure of need, such as hunger or of the fear of loss of love and approval, is reality accepted reluctantly.

Although any parent will recognize the important truths contained in Freud's view of the struggle to subdue and civilize the infantile id, this view is one-sided. It neglects the biological roots of curiosity, of wonder, of interest in the world and openness to it; it also neglects the biological basis of pleasure in activity, in accomplishment, in self-fulfillment, in creativity. It is, of course, true that the social reality of modern society often cripples the individual's capacity to relate productively, with active interest, to his surroundings so that the relations between the individual and his social order resemble that of combatants in guerilla warfare. Perhaps it was Freud's unusual sensitivity to prejudice, oppression, and human suffering that led him to emphasize the struggles and sacrifices rather than the joys of growing up.

6

ROLE THEORY

OF ALL THE THEORIES considered in this volume, role theory is farthest from the ideal scientific theory described in Chapter 1. It consists mainly of a set of constructs, with little in the way of an interrelational calculus or rules of correspondence. Indeed, it is often difficult to find consensus on the nature of the concepts themselves. For example, the term "role" itself is used in at least three distinctly different senses. On the other hand, the constructs of role theory are exceptionally rich in their empirical referents and provide an approach to the analysis of social behavior which is missing from the other theories we have considered.

Basic Concepts of Role Theory

The antecedents of role theory lie in both sociology and psychology (Neiman & Hughes, 1951). Thus it is not surprising that Rommetveit regards the concept of role as "the theoretical point of articulation between psychology and sociology," in the sense that it is "the largest possible research unit within the former discipline and the smallest possible within the latter" (Rommetveit, 1955, p. 31). Probably for this reason, role theory has been enriched by contributions from diverse sources. At the same time, this very diversity has frequently led to a lack of conceptual consistency. A valuable discussion of role and related sociological concepts may be found in Bredemeier and Stephenson (1962, especially Chs. 1–6).

Status and Status Sets

Every person occupies positions within a number of "status systems." A status system may be thought of as a multidimensional map which locates different statuses in relation to one another and shows how they are interconnected. A person's *position* or *status* is represented by his location on such a map. Status is necessarily a relational concept; it characterizes a person in terms of a set of rights and obligations that regulate his interaction with persons of other statuses. For example, in our society the position "father" implies, vis-à-vis his children, certain obligations (to provide food and shelter, for instance) and certain rights (to receive respect and obedience, for instance).

All societies are characterized by a large number of status systems. In some such systems, positions are allocated on the basis of what a person is—in terms of his age, sex, family connections, or religion. These are termed "ascribed statuses." In other systems, positions are allocated on the basis of what he can do. These are termed "achieved statuses." Achieved and ascribed statuses are "ideal types"; in practice the statuses one encounters consist of some mixture of the two kinds. For example, one may regard the presidency of a large corporation as an achieved status, but such ascribed characteristics as sex (male) and race (white) may be virtual prerequisites for the position. By exhaustively enumerating all of a person's statuses it is at least theoretically possible to locate him with respect to the status systems of his society. A man may concurrently occupy the positions of father, son, church member, factory worker, union official, member of a bowling team. Such an enumeration, all of a given person's concurrent statuses, is termed his "status set."

Although in popular usage the term "status" almost always refers to position in a specific type of status system, the socioeconomic, that is just one of many systems a society comprises. In the socioeconomic status system, as well as in many other systems, people occupy positions forming a hierarchy, in such a way that members of the society can judge the "desirability," "power," "authority," or "prestige" of a position on a graded scale. In such a status system, the positions are distinguished in terms of their vertical level or rank. Within a given level, and within some status systems, positions are not differentially evaluated. Within a hospital, for example, doctors usually outrank nurses, whereas ordinarily no distinction in rank is drawn between, say, an orthopedist and a cardiologist. Just as differences between positions of different rank are referred to as differences of *vertical* status, differences between positions of the same rank are referred to in terms of *horizontal* status.

Role and Role Sets

Within a culture each position has associated with it a set of norms or expectations. These expectations specify the behaviors which an occupant of that position may appropriately initiate toward an occupant of some other position and, conversely, those behaviors which an occupant of the other position may appropriately initiate toward the first. The concept of role is related to these expectations. It would be helpful if there were a single, generally acceptable definition for role but, as Rommetveit (1955) has pointed out, the divergent usages of the term would make such a choice highly arbitrary. Instead, we shall employ a classification suggested by the work of Rommetveit (1955) and of Thibaut and Kelley (1959). Current usage of the term reflects at least three rather different conceptualizations:

1. The role consists of the system of expectations which exist in the social world surrounding the occupant of a position—expectations regarding his behavior toward occupants of some other position. This may be termed the *prescribed* role.

2. The role consists of those specific expectations the occupant of a position perceives as applicable to his own behavior when he interacts with the occupants of some other position. This may be termed the *subjective* role.

3. The role consists of the specific overt behaviors of the occupant of a position when he interacts with the occupants of some other position. This may be termed the *enacted* role.

Each of these conceptualizations views the same underlying phenomenon from a slightly different perspective, and certainly there will be close relationships between the three constructs as measured empirically. For example, in a coherent and well-integrated social system, the members correctly perceive the social norms that govern their behavior: their subjective roles are similar to the prescribed roles. Similarly, people's actual behavior tends to correspond to what they believe is "expected of them": the enacted roles and the subjective roles coincide. On the other hand, there are often gross disparities between these aspects of the role. An employee, for example, may be mistaken about the amount of familiarity he may appropriately display toward his boss. Because such disparities occur, and because of their significance in social interaction, these distinctions are worth preserving. In general, however, the dominant convention uses the term "role" to denote the behavioral enactment of that part of the status which "prescribes how the status occupant should act toward one of the persons with whom his status rights and obligations put him in contact" (Bredemeier & Stephenson, 1962, p. 31, italics omitted). Let us, therefore, use "role" to mean *the enactment of the prescribed role.*

Of course, a specific status involves interaction with a great number of others. A factory foreman, for example, may interact with his subordinates and with his superiors, with union officials and with foremen in other departments. With each his status rights and obligations differ. The term "role set" denotes "the complement of role relationships which persons have by virtue of occupying a particular social status" (Merton, 1957, p. 369, italics omitted).

Universalistic and particularistic values. There is a further distinction that may be made. The term "role" usually is applied to situations in which the prescriptions for interaction are culturally defined and are independent of the particular personal relationships which may otherwise exist between persons occupying the positions —as between a judge and a person appearing in court. To use the terminology of Parsons and Shils (1951), such roles are defined in terms of "universalistic" rather than "particularistic" values. Sometimes, however, it is useful to refer to the personal or unique aspects of roles—roles as governed by expectations which derive from distinctly personal relations. For example, the rights and obligations associated with the role of "friend" are defined by the culture in a general way; between any given pair of friends, however, there may exist a particular pattern of rights and obligations which is unique to this friendship. Of course, the prescriptions of a role as universalistically defined may conflict with the obligations of a role that is defined particularistically—a judge may have to rule against a lawyer despite his friendship for him.

Deviance from prescribed roles. Roles may be said to be more or less "structured" or "patterned." Within a culture certain roles become well defined and there is reasonably widespread agreement as to the behavior expected from the incumbents. In contemporary American culture, for example, the role of the physician vis-à-vis his patient is relatively well structured. At the same time, a relatively wide range of variation in role behavior is normally permissible, even for well-structured roles. Two physicians sharing the same practice may employ different "bedside manners" or prescribe different treatments and still remain well within the limits of acceptable role behavior. For this reason it is useful to think of the role as prescribing a *range* of behaviors defined rather broadly. Within this range all role behavior is acceptable, although decreasingly so as one moves away from the norm.

The participants in a social system can dispense positive sanctions (rewards) to those who properly enact prescribed roles and negative sanctions (punishments) to those who fall short of these standards. This ability to dispense sanctions serves as one of the ways in which a social system motivates its members to perform their roles. Thus, a mother who behaves in an "unmotherly" fashion toward her children (whose enacted role deviates grossly from the prescribed role) may become the object of her neighbors' gossip and disapproval. If she departs too markedly from the prescribed role she may find herself ostracized and, in really extreme cases, the community as a whole acting through the legal system may punish her directly.

Role Conflict

Implicit in the fact that one's status set involves a wide variety of role relations and expectations is the possibility that he will find himself occupying positions with incompatible role requirements. Such a situation is termed "role conflict." Role conflict may grow out of the status set in a number of ways. Two positions may jointly demand more of a scarce resource, such as time or energy, than one person is able to give (the student athlete may find that there are not enough hours in the day for both sports and studies). Or, two positions may make conflicting demands on the one's loyalties (the elected official who has business interests may find his vote on a particular bill affected by nonlegislative values). Or, two positions may require the espousal of conflicting values (a doctor may find that his religious principles are in conflict with his medical views on the needs of a patient). Finally, some statuses are incompatible with certain others simply because the culture defines them as incompatible. In most cultures, a man and woman who are born to the position of brother and sister may not later occupy the position of husband and wife. In many cultures certain vocations are reserved for special groups, as when all religious leaders are drawn from a priestly caste.

The role set, as well as the status set, may serve as a source of role conflict. The persons with whom one interacts in the context of a given role set may make demands which are incompatible. A factory foreman may feel pressure from his supervisors to act in an authoritarian fashion, while the men in his work crew desire a more permissive atmosphere.

As Getzels and Guba (1954) point out, role conflicts differ in their severity. Some are nearly innocuous and may be borne for an extended period without causing social censure or psychological disruption. More severe conflicts may, on the other hand, become the source of profound disturbance. Getzels and Guba cite two structural factors that determine the severity of role conflict. First, roles vary in the *relative incompatibility* of their prescriptions. The greater the number of prescriptions two roles have in common, the less conflict will they engender. Secondly, roles vary in the *rigor* with which their prescriptions are enforced. Rigor here refers to the amount of deviation that is permitted from the roles' prescriptions. The more rigorously roles are defined, the more stringently are their prescriptions enforced, and, the more difficult it is for a person to resolve the conflict by deviating from them.

All this is not to imply that pressures deriving from multiple roles keep most people in a constant state of conflict. On the contrary, most people seem to manage quite well. As Newcomb remarks (1950, p. 449), "It is rather remarkable how many different roles most of us manage to take with a minimum of conflict." In large part, this is so because potentially conflicting roles are "nonoverlapping," that is to say, they are discharged at different times or in different contexts.

Under unusual circumstances, however, these potential conflicts may be exacerbated. Killian (1952, p. 310), in a study of the reactions of persons in four Southwestern communities to physical disasters like explosions and tornadoes, found that "conflicting group loyalties and contradictory rules . . . were significant factors affecting individual behavior in critical situations." A worker in an oil refinery, faced with the choice of aiding an injured friend or saving the plant, might be torn between the obligations of his friendship and his occupation. Such conflicts generally tended to be resolved in favor of one's primary group. Nevertheless, Killian points to some exceptional cases, such as a state policeman who had to ignore calls for assistance from his friends and neighbors in order to drive out of the community and summon help from surrounding towns. Killian concludes that people's actions in disasters involve the resolution of conflicts deriving from the prescriptions of roles that, under ordinary circumstances, have not been realized as potentially incompatible.

Personality and Role Performance

We have thus far taken up a number of terms centering about the concepts of status and role. Up to this point, to the extent that we have considered him at all, we have treated the individual as being at the intersection of a set of roles which devolve upon him in consequence of the positions he occupies in a variety of status systems. Such a characterization is, however, incomplete, for a person is an integrated and coherent whole rather than merely the sum of a set of compartmentalized roles. Furthermore, people vary in the ways they enact the same roles, and the behavior of a given person will show a certain degree of consistency across different roles. Clearly, then, what is needed is a concept to denote the unique properties of an individual, analytically separable from his role behavior.

One approach to such a conceptualization is contained in the notion of personality. Whereas "role" refers to uniformities in the behavior of different individuals occupying the same status, "personality," in the most general sense, refers to uniformities within the behavior of one individual. As with the concept of role, there is little agreement on the definition of personality. Allport (1937) was able to find nearly fifty different definitions of the term, and since the publication of his book more have doubtless been added. As Hall and Lindzey (1957) point out in their excellent survey of theories of personality, it makes little sense at present to define personality apart from a specific theory of personality; Allport defines personality as "the dynamic organization within the individual of those psychophysical systems that determine his unique adjustments to his environment" (Allport, 1937, p. 48), a characterization of the concept which is adequate here.

The relationship between role and personality is reciprocal. On the one hand, a person may be predisposed by virtue of his personality to occupy certain statuses. Or, put another way, the roles associated with specific positions may serve as a vehicle for the gratification of important personal needs. For example, it has often been pointed out that some persons may be attracted to military service because they perceive it as an outlet for their aggressive and affiliative needs. On the other hand, the values and attitudes associated with particular statuses may themselves be incorporated into the structure of an individual's personality and thus exert a pervasive influence across the totality of his social interaction. For example, Merton (1957, p. 198), in his analysis of the social structure of bureaucracy, points out that "the bureaucratic social structure exerts a constant pressure upon the individual to be methodical, prudent, disciplined." One result of these stresses is that "discipline, readily interpreted as conformance with regulations, whatever the situation, is seen not as a measure designed for specific purposes but becomes an immediate value in the life-organization of the bureaucrat . . . develop[ing] into rigidities and an inability to adjust readily" (p. 199). Thus, orientations learned as components of a specific role set may become a general attribute of one's personality.

The relationship between personality and role suggests a paradox. If personality is a unique configuration of individual characteristics that determines behavior, how is it possible for the same role to be enacted by different persons having rather different personality structures? One answer lies in the fact, already mentioned, that the role prescription specifies a relatively broad range of acceptable behaviors. As Parsons and Shils (1951, p. 24) put it, "This range of freedom makes it possible for actors [individuals] with different personalities to fulfill within considerable limits the expectations associated with roughly the same roles without undue strain."

It should be noted, however, as Getzels and Guba (1954) point out, that one's personality can become a source of role conflict. A person may be unable to fulfill the requirements of a role because the demands are incompatible with his personal needs. A submissive and self-effacing person may find it impossible to assume the status of a Marine drill sergeant. The consequences of such a mismatch between the predispositions of personality and the prescriptions of role are probably exacerbated by such conditions of situational stress as emergencies or military combat, where little deviation can be permitted in the enactment of role prescriptions.

The Self

In the process of interaction with his social environment a person not only takes on characteristics as a consequence of the roles he enacts, he also begins to experience a sense of self. He begins to recognize that others react to him, and he begins to react to his own actions and personal qualities as he expects others to react. This emerging capacity to take the point of view of others and to see oneself as an object gives rise to beliefs and attitudes about oneself—in short, to a "self concept." Role theorists, far more than those of other theoretical persuasions, have developed and employed the concept of the self as a cognitive structure which emerges from the interaction of the human organism and its social environment.

It should be stressed that the self concept is a cognitive structure and as such consists of a set of elements which are organized into a systematic relationship. One way of characterizing this organization is in terms of self-consistency—the elements of the individual's self concept are organized into a structure which is internally consistent. The precise definition of what constitutes consistency often presents something of a problem. In general, a consistent structure has the properties of a "good Gestalt"—it is made up of elements which are perceived as "belonging together." Heider's theory of cognitive balance (see Ch. 2) may be employed to predict the effects of introducing a new inconsistent (imbalanced) element into a consistent self-structure.

William James was one of the earliest theorists to consider the self as a central psychological construct In his *Psychology—Briefer Course* (1892) he distinguished between the "Me" and the "I," the self as known and the self as knower.

Whatever I may be thinking of, I am always at the same time more or less aware of *myself*, of my *personal existence*. At the same time it is *I* who am aware; so that the total self of me . . . must have two aspects discriminated in it, of which for shortness we may call one the *Me* and the other the *I* (p. 176, italics in original).

He goes on to point out that the *I* and *Me* must be termed discriminated aspects and not separate things, "because the identity of *I* and *Me,* even in the very act of their discrimination, is perhaps the most ineradicable dictum of common sense" (p. 176).

Clearly it is the Me (which James also called the "empirical self") that is of greatest concern here. James divided the constituents of the empirical self into three classes: the material me, the spiritual me, and the social me. The material me consists of one's body and the clothes which cover it, one's immediate family, one's home, and, with varying degrees of importance, the objects and property one has amassed. By the spiritual me, James refers to "the entire collection of my states of consciousness, my psychic facilities and dispositions taken concretely" (p. 181).

But it is James's concept of the social me which has had the most important consequences for role theory and the modern version of the concept of the self. The social me, according to James, grows out of the recognition that man receives from other people. He also noted that, since different people respond differently to the same person, there must be not one, but many social selves. He said:

> Properly speaking *a man has as many social selves as there are individuals who recognize him* and carry an image of him in their mind. . . . But as the individuals who carry the images fall naturally into classes, we may practically say that he has as many different social selves as there are distinct *groups* of persons about whose opinion he cares (p. 179, italics in original).

Thus James explicitly links the social self to the structure of social interaction. (It is also worth noting in the above quotation that, with remarkable perceptiveness, James implicitly uses the notion of reference groups, which we discuss later on in this chapter.)

Another important contributor to the development of the concept of self was the University of Michigan's sociologist Charles Horton Cooley. Cooley, who was influenced by the writing of William James, is best known for his concept of the "reflected" or "looking glass" self: "As we see our face, figure, and dress in the glass, and are interested in them because they are ours, and pleased or otherwise with them . . . as in imagination we perceive in another's mind some thought of our appearance, manners, aims, deeds, character, friends, and so on, and are variously affected by it" (Cooley, 1902, p. 184). Thus Cooley, along with James, specified the source of this aspect of the self as the people in one's environment. In addition, however, Cooley specified, in part, the mechanism by which this influence takes place.

What is lacking in both James's and Cooley's theories of the self is a detailed and systematic description of the process whereby the self develops as part of the maturational sequence of the organism. For this we are indebted to George Herbert Mead and his theory of the development of the self.

George Herbert Mead

In a number of ways, George Herbert Mead marks the end of an important period in the development of American psychology. Along with John Dewey, his friend and colleague, he was the last in a tradition of scholars versed in both philosophy and psychology who made contributions to both fields. Mead, in fact, never made a sharp distinction between the two disciplines.

Curiously enough, the works upon which Mead's contemporary reputation as a psychological theorist rests were not published by him. Indeed, for so prominent a scholar Mead published rather little during his career. The main bulk of his psychological theorizing is contained in three papers entitled, "Mind," "Self," and "Society," and one other, "The Point of View of Social Behaviorism," all of which appear in the volume *Mind, Self and Society* (Mead, 1934). These essays are based upon stenographic transcripts of his lectures at the University of Chicago, supplemented by his notes and unpublished manuscripts and the lecture notes of his students. Not surprisingly, they tend to be somewhat discursive and repetitive. These flaws, combined with a vocabulary which is unfamiliar to contemporary students, have made Mead's work appear somewhat formidable. *Mind, Self and Society* was compiled and edited by

C. W. Morris, the noted linguistic philosopher, who also has contributed an excellent essay (Morris, 1934) which serves as a summary of Mead's views.

Influences on Mead

One of the great intellectual revolutions of the nineteenth century was wrought by Charles Darwin's theory of evolution. Its influence was pervasive and long-lasting, especially in the social sciences. To Mead the significance of evolutionary doctrine for social psychology lay in the proposition that the human organism, and especially the mind, its unique characteristic, had to be explained in terms of the interaction of the organism with its environment. That is to say, the mind and the human organism's ability to communicate symbolically (which Mead took to be the *sine qua non* of mind) must be explained as part of an evolutionary process. In addition to this methodological position, Darwin's thinking on the expression of emotion provided Mead with a basis for explaining the development of language.

Mead, along with Dewey and James, was identified with pragmatism, the nineteenth-century American philosophy which held that the meaning (and, therefore, the truth) of a proposition was to be sought in its practical consequences. Most important here is the pragmatic emphasis on the role of reason and rationality. In this respect Mead diverges sharply from MacDougall, who was also strongly influenced by evolutionary doctrine, but whose interpretation of evolution stressed the genetic, automatic, and nonrational determinants of behavior. For Mead, one of the unique characteristics of man is his ability to alter and direct the course of evolution through the exercise of his intellectual powers.

The term "social behaviorism" is often applied to Mead's position to indicate both his agreement and his differences with the behaviorism of J. B. Watson. Mead held that Watson's reduction of the experienced world to the functioning of nerves and muscles was a misleading oversimplification. Especially with regard to social behavior did he find fault with behavioristic reductionism.

> We are not, in social psychology, building up the behavior of the social group in terms of the behavior of the separate individuals composing it; rather, we are starting out with a given social whole of complex group activity, into which we analyze (as elements) the behavior of each of the separate individuals composing it. We at-

tempt, that is, to explain the conduct of the individual in terms of the organized conduct of the social group. . . . The social act is not explained by building it up out of a stimulus plus a response; it must be taken as a dynamic whole—as something going on—no part of which can be considered or understood by itself (Mead, 1934, p. 7).

For Mead, social psychology was behavioristic, not in the sense of ignoring the inner experience of the individual, but in the sense of starting off with observable activity. The human organism's inner experience is to be explained, but always in terms of the externally observable.

The Evolution of Language

The act. Mead conceived of the human organism as an active agent, rather than the passive recipient of stimulation from its environment. The action of the organism determines the relation between the person and the environment. In this view, perception must be considered as an active process; stimuli are responded to selectively as they are encountered in the course of acts. Moreover, these stimuli are interpreted and responded to symbolically. In the course of an act, which may extend over a considerable period of time, the perceived environment changes—new objects are discovered and old ones are redefined. "These new objects and redefinitions are funneled back to the groups and communities to which the individual belongs, for the individual's act and its incorporated perceiving is itself a part of the larger communal action" (Strauss, 1956). Importantly, during the act stimuli will arise which consist of the actions of other persons and these may, in turn, be responses to one's own behavior.

The conversation of gestures. As we have just noted, it was necessary for Mead to demonstrate the evolutionary process which culminated in man's linguistic ability. To do this he had to show the earlier, more primitive form from which a more advanced form had evolved, and the key to this process he found in Darwin's *Expression of the Emotions in Man and Animals* (1872). Darwin pointed out that associated with certain specific emotional states were sets of bodily and, especially, facial expressions. The baring of an animal's teeth denotes an inner state of rage. The adaptive significance of this action is clear for animals that employ their teeth for attacking, but Darwin noted that this manifestation was still observable in man, where it had lost its original value for survival. Therefore, he reasoned, it must have taken on some other adaptive value. Darwin hypothesized that the significance of facial expressions lay in their capacity for revealing something of the inner state of the organism. Mead referred to these expressive states as "attitudes" or "gestures." It is the gesture—an action which forecasts what is to come—which Mead took to be the primitive behavior from which man's communicative ability has evolved.

The gesture as used by animals is, however, automatic and unthinking (or at least Mead saw no reason to regard it otherwise). It is simply part of an act which forecasts what is to come. The animal does not *intend* to communicate his rage by baring his teeth; this is just an early part of the act of attacking. It is a long step from this elementary form to man's complex ability to employ language in a conscious and intentional manner.

Mead demonstrated the communicative or expressive role of the gesture in what he termed the "conversation of gestures." A dogfight provides a good illustration. Two dogs in a fight, circling each other, seeking an opening, are responding one to the other. When one dog makes a move, the other will move to counter it. Each move, then, will be a response to a prior move on the part of the adversary, just as in a conversation each utterance is a response to the previous utterance. In some sense these moves or gestures may be considered symbols, since they "stand for" (or elicit responses appropriate to) the entire act of which they are part. From this same point of view such gestures may be said to have meaning; that is to say, "they mean the later stages of the oncoming act . . . the clenched fist means the blow, the outstretched hand means the object being reached for" (Morris, 1934, p. xx).

The significant gesture. Still, the conversation of gestures is not, in and of itself, communication. Communication, in Mead's terms, involves the use of *significant* gestures or symbols. (The word "significant" is used here to mean "having the qualities of a sign.") In short, the individual must be able to interpret the meaning of his own gesture. As Mead put it, "Gestures become significant symbols when they implicitly arouse in [the] individual making them the same responses they explicitly arouse, or are supposed to arouse, in other individuals" (Mead, 1934, p. 47). It is the human being's ability to anticipate the response his gesture elicits from others, made possible by his highly developed nervous system, which permits him to rise from the level of the conversation of gestures to that of the significant language symbol.

From the significant gesture it is only a step to the verbal gesture, the sound. Mead argues that only through the verbal gesture could man have become self-conscious about his gestures, but it is not clear that this need be so. It is possible, after all, to develop a symbolic system of hand gestures (as in the Indian sign languages) or of written hieroglyphics. We must, however, concede that the vocal gesture is a more convenient and efficient means of communication than either of these.

When Mead refers to the *meaning* of a gesture he is referring to the adjustive response of another toward it; that is to say, the meaning of significant gesture is to be found in the response it elicits in the person to whom it is addressed. Thus, to communicate (to use symbolic gestures or language), one must be able to anticipate the response one's act will elicit from another. One does this, Mead assumed, by *taking the role of the other,* by viewing oneself from the point of view of another person.

The Development of the Self

Man's ability to utilize language also makes it possible for him to develop a self. For Mead, selfhood is distinguished by a man's capacity to be an object to himself and this capacity is inherent in the mechanism of language. To the extent that a person is able to take the role of others, he can respond to himself from *their* perspective and, hence, become an object to himself. Mead viewed the self as a developmental phenomenon; he remarked that "it [the self] is not initially there, at birth, but arises in the process of social experience and activity" (1934, p. 135).

Play and games. Mead delineated two stages in the development of the self: play and games. In play, the child takes on a set of dual roles, his own and that of some other person—teacher, mother, grocer. Such activity affords the child an opportunity to explore the attitudes held by others toward himself. Thus, by taking the role of the other, the child learns to regard himself from an external point of view. At this early stage of development a person's self is constituted by an organization of the particular attitudes held by other persons toward himself and toward one another, in the contexts of those social acts he has explored in his play.

The game is an example of *organized* social activity. In it the child must have the attitudes of all of the others involved in the game. "The attitudes of the other players, which the participant assumes, organize into a sort of unit, and it is that organization which controls the response of the individual. . . . Each one of his own acts is determined by his assumption of the action of the others" (Mead, 1934, p. 155). Thus, in the game the child goes beyond the particular attitudes of specific others. In the game, the "other" is an organization of the attitudes of those engaged in the same process or activity. It should be clear that Mead does not mean to suggest that this second stage of development occurs only through the agency of game-playing. Rather, he uses the game as a model of organized social activities in which the ability of an individual to function depends upon his knowledge of the complex role relationships among the participants.

The generalized other. It is through this process that the child eventually learns the generalized attitudes of the community of which he is part. The organized community or group which gives the individual his unity of self, Mead terms the "generalized other."

In the fullest sense, the development of the self requires that the person also take on the attitudes of the group toward its own organized social activity. In effect, then, in the second stage of development (which Mead terms the "full development of self") he experiences his social group as an organized community of attitudes, norms, values, and goals which regulate his behavior and the behavior of others. The attitudes of the group become incorporated into the structure of the self, just as did the attitudes of particular others. Thus:

> It is in the form of the generalized other that the social process influences the behavior of the individuals involved in it . . . for it is in this form that the social process or community enters as a determining factor into the individual's thinking (Mead, 1934, p. 155).

Although each self is shaped through participation in the social process, it does not follow that all selves will thereby be alike. Mead asserted that each individual self will have "its own peculiar individuality, its own unique pattern" (1934, p. 202) because each has experienced the social process from a slightly different perspective, and each self will therefore reflect this uniqueness. Thus, "the common social origin and constitution of individual selves and their structures does not preclude wide individual difference and variations among them" (1934, p. 202).

Concluding Comment

Mead's great achievement, and indeed the foundation of his theoretical system, was his specification of the relationship between the development of the self and man's intellectual capacities, especially man's ability to communicate through the use of significant symbols. In effect, he held that these uniquely human facets of man are inextricably interrelated—in Morris's words, that "the self, mind, 'consciousness of,' and the significant symbol are, in a sense, precipitated together" (Morris, 1934, p. xxiii).

As Strauss has noted, "Mead's writing offers a clear alternative to psychological theories based upon individualistic assumptions, principally through his insistence that individual acts are part of larger communal acts" (Strauss, 1956, p. xv). Mead's theory, as a *developmental* theory, focuses upon the cognitive development of the child; it is but little concerned with emotional development and maturational change. Such an approach has its contemporary counterpart in the work of the Swiss psychologist, Jean Piaget.

One of the major inadequacies of Mead's theory derives from the fact that it was developed in the absence of systematic empirical evidence. As a result there is in it a lack of specificity about the constructs which makes it difficult to state them in a meaningful concrete form. Because he was not concerned with the systematic empirical testing of his theory, Mead missed the opportunity to restructure his framework in the light of new evidence. For example, as Merton (Merton & Kitt, 1950, pp. 56 f.) has pointed out, Mead stresses the point that the groups to which an individual belongs serve as a significant frame of reference for the formation of his self-image. Still, individuals belong to many groups and frequently these groups have norms which are contradictory. Mead gives us no insight into how such various group influences are reconciled. It is, moreover, clear that a person need not actually be a member of a group for it to serve as a significant frame of reference for him. For example, one who *aspires* to membership in a group may be more strongly affected by the group's norms than are its actual members. These matters are discussed more fully when we turn to the theory of reference groups in the following section.

Mead gave little consideration to the way in which a person's social experience is structured by the organization of society. For him the "social process" remains a rather amorphous notion; although he acknowledged that it is differentiated, he gave the differentiation no systematic form nor did he stress its importance. The sense in which he used the role removed it from the context of an associated status. Hence, role enactment was not related to the performances of others nor to the organized activities of a social system. By removing the concepts of role and self from the structured system of social relationships, the important parallels between a given person's self, his status set, and his social system are by-passed.

Perhaps Mead's place in social psychology is best summed up in Strauss's remark that "Mead offers us not so much specific hypotheses, or even a theory, as a rather abstract frame of reference [which], if taken seriously and consistently, would force questions and suggest lines of investigation that no other competing point of view forces or suggests" (Strauss, 1956, p. xvi).

After having been neglected for many years, Mead's views have recently begun to emerge as a major influence in the texts of sociologically trained social psychologists. Thus Lindesmith and Strauss (1956) and Shibutani (1961) both apply Mead's formulation to the varied subject matter of social psychology. Rose (1962) has edited a volume of theoretical and research papers which attempt to demonstrate that the interactionist position—most fully exemplified in Mead's work—can give rise to propositions which are amenable to empirical verification.

Robert K. Merton

Robert K. Merton ranks among the most productive and influential of American sociologists. His theoretical writings and empirical research have covered a wide variety of topics: bureaucracy, mass communication, the history and sociology of science, anomie, propaganda, and issues of methodology and theory construction, to name but a few. Among his most notable contributions to social psychology are his writings on role theory and reference groups.

The Background of the Theory of Reference Groups

We have already considered the idea that the individual's social self is a product of the attitudes of the significant others in his environment. As Mead put it, "The individual experiences himself as such, not directly, but only indirectly, from the particular standpoints of other individual members of the same group, or from the generalized standpoint of the social group to which he belongs" (Mead, 1934, p. 138). Mead never indicated, however, precisely who these "others" are. Clearly, in the case of a very young child, the significant others will be the members of his immediate family. But the "generalized other" represents the "social group to which he belongs." In contemporary society each community is made up of a large number of groups and any one person belongs to a number of different sorts of groups, organized along lines of ethnic background, or religious affiliation, or cultural interests, or economic class. Because ours is a mobile society, moreover, it is not unusual for individuals to change their group membership rather frequently.

The term "reference group" itself was coined by Hyman (1942), in an investigation of socioeconomic status. He found that one's subjective status (the status to which a person thinks of himself as belonging) could not be predicted directly from such factors as income or education. To a certain extent, it was dependent upon what social groups were used as a framework of judgment. People showed great variability in the groups they selected as frameworks for judgments. Indeed, frequently they used groups of which they were not members. Thus, Hyman found it useful to distinguish between a "membership group" (the group to which someone actually belongs) and a "reference group" (the group which someone employs as a basis of comparison for self-appraisal). In some cases, the reference group is a membership group; in other cases, it is not.

A similar sort of conceptualization was developed by Newcomb (1943), who studied the change in values and attitudes of students at a liberal women's college. A good many of the students, who tended to come from politically conservative families, took on increasingly more liberal attitudes and values over the course of their college careers. Moreover, the sort of development observed was related to the girl's matrix of social relationships within the college. Specifically, Newcomb found that the structure of a subject's attitudes depended on whether she used the college community or her family community as a significant frame of reference.

Writing later of this study, Newcomb (1948) summarized his findings as follows:

> In this community, as presumably in most others, all individuals belong to the total membership group, but such membership is not necessarily a point of reference for every form of social adaptation, e.g., for acquiring attitudes toward public issues. *Such attitudes, however, are not acquired in a social vacuum. Their acquisition is a function of relating oneself to some group or groups, positively or negatively* (p. 154, italics in original). . . . [The] Bennington findings seem to support the thesis that, in a community characterized by certain approved attitudes, the individual's attitude development is a function of the way in which he relates himself both to the total membership group and to reference group or groups (p. 155, italics in original).

Up until this point, the concept of the reference group nevertheless lacked any systematic formulation linking it to the growing body of social psychological and sociological theory. Indeed, in its application, the notion of reference groups seemed to raise more questions than it answered, and the questions it raised were rather complex: "What precisely is a group?" "How should group membership be defined?" Merton's contribution to this area was his clarification and systematization of the conceptual underpinnings of the theory of reference groups in two essays, one published in 1950 (with Alice S. Kitt) and the other in 1957.

The first of these essays (Merton & Kitt, 1950), was stimulated by the publication of *The American Soldier,* a two-volume work (Stouffer, Suchman, DeVinney, Star, & Williams, 1949; Stouffer, Lumsdaine, Lumsdaine, Williams, Smith, Janis, Star, & Cottrell, 1949) reporting the substance of the research done by the Research Branch, Information and Education Division of the War Department during World War II. These studies, investigating the attitudes, sentiments, and behaviors of large numbers of servicemen, represented the greatest single unified undertaking in the social sciences up to that time—and probably since, as well. It is not surprising that such a massive effort made important contributions both to theory and to methodology. It was the purpose of the symposium of which the essay by Merton and Kitt was a part to examine and evaluate these contributions, in order to expedite their assimilation into the mainstream of social research.

One of the significant generalizations which emerged from a number of studies in the *The American Soldier* concerned people's attitudes toward, or judgment of, the deprivation that they were undergoing as a result of military service. Briefly, it was found that a person's attitude toward deprivation was attributable less to the actual degree of deprivation than to the standard he used in evaluating his own condition. For example, it was found that Southern Negroes evaluated their Army experience more favorably than did Northern Negroes; also, that the smaller the opportunity for promotion in a unit actually was, the more favorable the opinions about the opportunity for promotion tended to be. These paradoxical findings, and a number of similar ones, were explained by invoking the notion of "relative deprivation." Thus, the Southern Negro soldier felt less deprived by Army life because he was evaluating his condition relative to that of the Southern Negro civilian, whereas the Northern Negro soldier used the somewhat better-off Northern Negro civilian as a standard. Similarly, the negative correlation between the opportunity for promotion and favorable opinions toward it was explained by supposing that, when the rate of promotion is high, the person who remains in the same position will compare himself to those who have been promoted and as a result will feel frustrated and deprived. Merton and Kitt point out that relative deprivation is a special case (although a very important one) of reference group behavior. The underlying problem, then, concerns the process whereby a person orients himself to groups and to other individuals and uses them as significant frames of reference for his own behavior, attitudes, or feelings.

The Theory of Reference-Group Behavior

Kelley (1952) distinguishes between two functional types of reference group, the normative and the comparative. The normative type sets and maintains standards for the individual (it serves as a source of the values which he assimilates); the comparative serves as a standard of comparison relative to which the individual evaluates himself and others (it enables him to evaluate his position relative to that of others). Both types of reference group must be distinguished from "interaction groups," which "are simply a part of the social environment of the individual. . . . He must take them into account in working toward his purposes but they are not of normative or comparative significance to him" (Merton, 1957, p. 284).

To talk sensibly about a reference group, it is necessary to have an adequate definition of what a "group" is. Merton characterizes a group in terms of three criteria: (1) it comprises a number of individuals who interact with one another on the basis of established patterns; (2) the persons who interact define themselves as group members; and (3) these persons are defined by others (both fellow members and nonmembers) as members of the group.

Such a definition permits us to differentiate groups from the larger class of social aggregates called "collectivities"—"people who have a sense of solidarity by virtue of sharing common values and who have acquired an attendant sense of moral obligation to fulfill role expectations" (Merton, 1957, p. 299). Groups are, of course, a subclass of collectivities; they differ in that interaction among members is not a necessary criterion for the latter. Different from both groups and collectivities are "social categories." They are "aggregates of social statuses, the occupants of which are not in social interaction" (Merton, 1957, p. 299). The individuals in a social category have similar social characteristics, like sex, age, or income, but they are not oriented toward a unique and common body of norms.

It will be seen, then, that the general notion of a "reference group" encompasses a diverse range of social aggregates not all of which are "groups" as defined by Merton. Thus, when the Southern Negro soldier evaluates his own state relative to that of a Southern Negro civilian, he is using a social category as his reference "group." In addition to reference *groups,* we must also bear in mind that *individuals* may form a person's frame of reference. Although work in this area has stressed the reference group and neglected the reference individual, Merton notes that the selection of individuals for reference purposes is no more arbitrary than is the selection of groups. He differentiates between a reference individual and a "role model." A person identifying himself with a reference individual seeks to "approximate the behavior and values of that individual in his several roles" (Merton, 1957, p. 302). The notion of a role model implies a more limited identification, implying only one (or perhaps a few) of the role model's roles.

A group may serve as a *positive* or a *negative* reference group. A positive reference group is one whose norms or standards are adopted as a frame of reference; a negative reference group is one whose norms are rejected in favor of counternorms. Research in this area has focused on the positive reference group, but the notion of a negative reference group offers an analytically useful tool. For example, Newcomb (1943) observes that "adolescent rebellion" may be regarded as a form of reference-group behavior in which parents serve as a negative reference group.

Two of the central problems of the theory of reference groups concern (1) what determines whether a given individual will select a reference group from among membership or nonmembership groups, and (2) what determines which one of several relevant groups will be selected as a reference group in any given instance.

To answer the former question, Merton points to four factors, on the level of the group, the individual, and the social system. (1) The greater the ability of the nonmembership groups to confer prestige upon the individual (relative to the ability of his membership groups), the more likely will he be to employ them as a frame of reference. (2) The less centrally the individual is located relative to his membership groups (the more he tends to be an "isolate"), the greater is the likelihood that he will choose a nonmembership group as his frame of reference. (3) There is some evidence to support the proposition that social systems which have relatively high rates of social mobility (changes of social status) function so as to promote the adoption of nonmembership groups as reference groups. This is true at least partly because in societies with high mobility rates, the assimilation of the new group's attitudes and values often begins before individual changes of status actually take place. Indeed, often such "anticipatory socialization" is a precondition to change of status. (4) Finally, it seems reasonable to suppose that individual personality characteristics also play a role here; unfortunately, empirical work in this area has been too meager to permit anything more than vague speculation.

To a great extent, much of the work done in the area of reference groups has been concerned with reference groups which are nonmembership groups. Merton notes that such an emphasis is unfortunate, since it implies that only nonmembership groups are of any consequence for reference group behavior—a notion which clearly is mistaken.

A good deal less is known about what determines the specific groups a given person will select as reference groups. Merton suggests that the answer here lies in a set of properties which distinguish groups from one another. He presents a list of twenty-six properties, including such attributes as the clarity or vagueness of definitions of social membership in the group, the duration of membership, the degree of differentiation of members, and the degree of expected conformity to group norms. This sort of approach presents two major difficulties. The first has to do with the problem of developing valid and reliable standardized measures for these sorts of attributes, for only with such measures can sensible comparisons among groups be made. Even with such measures, however, it is not clear what Merton's list of properties has told us. For there is, as yet, no way of knowing which of the twenty-six properties are relevant to reference-group behavior. At present one must conclude that rather little is understood about the process of selection of reference groups, and this fact must be regarded as a significant weakness of the theory.

There is a good deal of variation in the degree of generality with which groups may serve as frames of reference. Just as with a role model (the extreme case, where there is identification with a reference individual in only one of his roles), reference groups may operate in terms of fairly specific sorts of evaluation and behavior. Some reference groups affect an individual only in a very narrow context, whereas others have a more pervasive influence. Little is known about the determinants of the generality with which a group serves as a frame of reference, nor why one group rather than another is selected as a reference group in connection with specified kinds of behavior and evaluation. What is known suggests that the "common sense" supposition, that the available group which is substantively or functionally most pertinent is invariably selected as the reference group, is incorrect. For example, it is not always the case that a member of a labor union will use the union as a frame of reference for his views on economic affairs. Such data as are available in this area, based largely on the study of reference individuals rather than of reference groups, suggests that influence is more typically specific than general (see, for example, Eisenstadt, 1954; Rosen, 1955).

Thus, it seems likely that a person will employ a variety of reference groups or individuals at different times, and the particular group or individual employed at any specific time will depend upon complex factors, one of which is the particular facet of oneself which is being evaluated.

One area of the theory of reference groups which has been illuminated by empirical findings concerns the selection of reference groups among status categories versus subgroups with which the individual has sustained interaction. For the most part such studies have been concerned with voting behavior (for example, Berelson, Lazarsfeld, & McPhee, 1954). Though the findings are lengthy and complex, in general they indicate that one's direct associates tend to mediate the influence of the larger social environment; that is to say, the norms of the social category tend to be viewed through the "filter" of those with whom one interacts directly. When there is a lack of consensus among one's direct associates, the normative orientation of the social category takes on a greater importance. These results suggest that, at least for the sorts of behaviors studied, reference *groups* or *individuals* (as opposed to categories or collectivities) seem to have the greater impact on the individual.

It is instructive to contrast the theory of reference groups with Festinger's theory of social comparison (see Ch. 3). Both deal with aspects of a common subject matter—the conditions under which others serve as a significant frame of reference for self-evaluation. As initially formulated, Festinger's theory dealt with the appraisal of abilities, although, as Schachter (1959) has shown, it may be extended to other areas, such as emotional states. It is clear from even a superficial examination that the theory of reference groups is a sociological theory and the theory of social comparison is a psychological theory. Merton is concerned with the *structural* factors which determine reference-group processes, whereas Festinger attempts to establish the *motivational* conditions that predispose the individual to seek out a comparison. Merton attempts to explain an individual's behavior by reference to his position in a social structure; Festinger attempts to derive at least certain aspects of the social structure from the social comparison process.

Social Structure and Anomie

Thus far in the discussion the structure of social systems and the functioning of individuals within social systems have resembled a smoothly running clock. All elements mesh precisely and discharge their functions efficiently, without interfering with one another. With the sole exception of role conflict, we have not considered the "pathologies" of social life—the problems raised when the central values of a culture are inconsistent or contradictory, or when an individual's behavior deviates markedly from the norms of his group, or when subgroups within a culture have norms which are in conflict. The "clockwork" model of a social system is useful as an heuristic device, but it obviously is not true to life. Indeed, if it were, cultures would be static, changing little over time, and helpless to cope with such disequilibrating influences as technological advance, war, and contact with other cultures.

Merton has made an important contribution to our understanding of the way in which deviant behavior is produced by specific types of social structure. He regards deviance not as a matter of psychopathology or idiosyncrasy, but rather as something built into the fabric of society and emerging from it. In Merton's words, *"Socially deviant behavior* is just as much a product of social structure as *conformist behavior"* (Merton, 1957, p. 121, italics in original), and again, "Our primary aim is to discover how some *social structures exert a definite pressure upon certain persons in the society to engage in nonconforming rather than conforming conduct* (Merton, 1957, p. 132, italics in original).

Let us consider two aspects of all social and cultural systems. The first consists of the set of "culturally defined goals, purposes and interests, held out as legitimate objectives for all or for diversely located members of the society" (Merton, 1957, p. 132). These are the things that people feel are worth striving for. That they are culturally defined is clear from the fact that what is a highly valued goal in one culture may be negatively valued in another; it may be considered less important to attain a state of material affluence than one of spiritual grace. We may refer to this element as the "cultural goals."

A second important element "defines, regulates and controls the acceptable means of reaching out for these goals" (Merton, 1957, p. 133); that is to say, a given goal may be attainable by a variety of means but only certain of these means are legitimate, in the sense that they are positively sanctioned by the culture. In our culture, affluence is a near-universal goal, but fraud is not a legitimate means of attaining it. This element is called the "institutionalized means."

Cultures vary widely in terms of both elements, but clearly for a culture to be stable and smooth-running it is important that the two be reasonably well integrated. Persons for whom a particular goal is defined as important should have a legitimate means of attaining it. Merton is especially interested in cultures in which there is a strong emphasis upon the value of cultural goals, but relatively little stress upon the institutionally prescribed means of attainment. When the sort of integration is lacking in a culture, a state of norm-lessness or "anomie" results. Anomie is the term used by the distinguished French sociologist Émile Durkheim to refer to a condition of social disorganization or "disregulation." In his classic work, *Suicide* (Durkheim, 1897), he attempted to show how differentials in the suicide rates of different countries could be accounted for by variations in anomie. Merton's interest centers about "the consequences for the behavior of people variously situated in the social structure of a culture in which the emphasis on dominant success-goals has become increasingly separated from an equivalent emphasis on institutionalized procedures for seeking these goals" (Merton, 1957, p. 139). To this end, he has developed a typology of the modes of adaptation the individual may employ when faced with the situation of anomie.

The individual may accept or reject either the cultural goals or the institutionalized means of attaining these goals, or he may reject them both and substitute new goals and means. The types of individual adaptation are displayed in the table below. A "+" signifies acceptance, a "−" signifies rejection, and "±" signifies a rejection of prevailing values and a substitution of new ones.

Mode of Adaptation	Cultural Goals	Institutionalized Means
1. Conformity	+	+
2. Innovation	+	−
3. Ritualism	−	+
4. Retreatism	−	−
5. Rebellion	±	±

1. *Conformity.* To the extent that a culture is well integrated (and anomie is absent), conformity both to cultural goals and to institutionalized means will be the modal form of adaptation. Because Merton is interested in the effects of anomie, he gives but little consideration to this type of adaptation.

2. *Innovation.* When a person accepts the cultural goal but rejects, for any one of many reasons, the institutionalized means of attaining it, he may seek new means. These means may or may not be legitimate in terms of the culture's value system, and frequently they will not be. Merton notes that innovation resulting in deviant behavior is especially likely to occur in a culture which holds out success as a goal for all, but which at the same time systematically withholds from a sector of the population a legitimate means of attaining success. Thus, people who are disadvantaged because of their race or religion—who are prevented from effectively competing for cultural goals—can be expected to seek new means.

3. *Ritualism.* Some individuals will abandon or scale down radically the cultural goals but at the same time will continue to abide by the institutional norms for attaining them. This mode of adaptation essentially consists of "individually seeking a *private* escape from the dangers and frustrations . . . inherent in the competition for major cultural goals by abandoning these goals and clinging all the more closely to the safe routines and institutional norms" (Merton, 1957, p. 151). The ritualistic adapter has given up any chance of success (whatever the cultural definition of success may be); but he finds security in following through the culturally prescribed routines which are designed to lead to success. So the office worker who cannot stand the gaff of competition may abandon all hope of rising to a higher position, but at the same time he may attempt to conform to the outward ritual of the rising office worker. In a way, this sort of adaptation is exemplified by the long-distance runner, hopelessly behind all the others, who insists on dragging himself across the finish line with his last ounce of strength, although his performance can have no effect on the outcome of the race. Merton contends that, whereas innovation is a mode of adaptation typical of the lower class, ritualism is more frequently encountered in the lower-middle class.

4. *Retreatism.* When anyone has rejected both the goals of his culture and the institutional means associated with them, he has in effect withdrawn from society. This, then, is the mode of adapta-

tion of the hobo, the drug addict, the psychotic, the alcoholic— that is to say, "the socially disinherited who if they have none of the rewards held out by society also have few of the frustrations attendant upon continuing to seek these rewards" (Merton, 957, p. 155).

5. *Rebellion.* This mode of adaptation consists of both a rejection of the culture's values and institutions and the substitution of a new set of values and institutions.

An important contribution to the theory of social structure and anomie has been made by Cloward (1959). Cloward is interested in understanding what determines the specific sort of deviant response a given person will make to a situation of anomie. One obvious determinant is values. As Cloward puts it, "Values serve to order the choice of deviant (as well as conforming) adaptations which develop under stress" (Cloward, 1959, p. 167). Thus, as Merton observes, because the value orientation induced by middle-class socialization emphasizes the importance of rules and obedience toward rules, the typical mode of adaptation to anomie is ritualism; in the lower class, where less stress is placed on the importance of rules, the typical mode is innovation.

Cloward notes, however, that just as access to the *institutional* means of attaining culturally valued goals is socially patterned, so too is access to the *illegitimate* means of attainment; that is to say, the motivations for deviance and pressures toward it do not, of themselves, fully account for deviant behavior. As with legitimate means, illegitimate means of goal attainment are both limited in their availability and differentially available, depending upon the person's location in the social structure.

Cloward notes that the term "means" really refers to two sorts of things: *learning structures* ("appropriate learning environments for the acquisition of the values and skills associated with the performance of a particular role," Cloward, 1959, p. 168) and *opportunity structures* (opportunities to perform the role once the skills have been acquired). The criminal seldom "starts from scratch." Even so relatively unskilled a felon as the "jackroller" or "mugger" must learn how to select a victim and learn the techniques of separating him from his valuables. The technical knowledge of the successful confidence man compares quite favorably with the skills of many legitimate vocations (see Maurer, 1940). Such roles are learned, not through trial and error, but in the context of deviant subcultures to which only some members of a society have access.

Concluding Comment

It is clear that the theory of the reference groups deals with matters which are of central importance to social psychology; what is less clear is whether or not it deserves to be called a theory. It contains no unique central notion; nor does it postulate any fundamentally new social processes. Especially regrettable is the fact that it provides little help in predicting individual behavior with respect to reference groups.

Despite this lack, the notion of the reference group should not be underestimated. The concept has served two important functions. First, it has underscored the importance of individual self-evaluative behavior and the role played by groups in relation to it. Second, it has sensitized social psychologists to the fact that the values and norms of nonmembership groups often affect an individual greatly.

The concept of anomie has a similar status. Unquestionably it has contributed to our understanding of deviant behavior. Most important has been the firm establishment of the position that deviance is a "built in" feature of certain sociocultural systems and is not the product of individual pathology or malice. It is well to recognize, however, that pressures toward deviance exist for most people and that even where these pressures are strongest only a minority manifests deviant behavior. Not all slum children become juvenile delinquents. What determines the impact of deviant pressure on a given person is not yet well understood. There is, however, some evidence to indicate that the family may play a critical role in forming a personality structure which is especially susceptible to deviant pressures (see, for example, Chein, Gerard, Lee, & Rosenfeld, 1964).

Be this as it may, the notion of anomie has provided an approach to the study of such deviant processes as juvenile delinquency, criminal behavior, mental illness, alcoholism, and physical illness. In connection with physical illness, Parsons (1951) has provided an important analysis of the role of the sick person as a response to social pressures of the sort we have considered above.

Merton's development of the concept of anomie has emphasized the strains inherent in sociocultural systems to the exclusion of the supportive mechanisms which develop to mitigate them. For example, although success is a nearly universal goal in our culture, precisely what constitutes success is defined differently for different persons. Nor do all persons assimiliate the central values of a culture to the same degree. For some, the culturally defined goals are not objects of intense striving not because they have been rejected, but rather because they have never been accepted. Finally, it should be noted that the culture itself often prescribes alternatives to the cultural goals. Again using our own culture as an example, success and affluence may be central goals, yet an individual may choose to devote his life to religion or to scholarship and still retain the esteem of his peers.

Both the reference group and the concept of anomie have served to stimulate much research of practical and theoretical significance. For that reason their conceptual deficiencies have been overlooked because of their value as intellectual tools. Perhaps, in the present stage of development of the social sciences, this fruitfulness is all that one may yet justifiably demand.

Erving Goffman

Trained as an anthropologically oriented sociologist and possessing keen insight into human affairs, Erving Goffman has developed a framework for the analysis of social interaction based on an analogy to a theatrical performance. His major work, *The Presentation of Self in Everyday Life* (Goffman, 1959), develops this theoretical model in some detail and applies it to a wide variety of situations. Our discussion of Goffman's work will draw mainly from this source and, unless otherwise noted, all references in this section will be to it.

Both by training and by personal inclination, Goffman tends to concern himself more with wide-ranging social perspectives than with matters of precision and scientific rigor. The evidence he adduces for his theory is based largely upon observations of social interaction in this and in other cultures, made both by himself and by other social scientists. Goffman does not hesitate to draw from fiction, autobiography and memoirs, newspaper and magazine reports, and information gleaned from personal conversations. Like many sociologists and anthropolgists he is neither troubled by the methodological problems which the observational method imposes nor is he excessively bothered by the "looseness" of his theory. To a large extent, the persuasiveness of his theoretical framework is based on how well it throws light upon the examples and illustrations he so freely presents.

Performances

Goffman takes as his point of departure the fact that in order for social interaction to be viable, one needs information about those with whom he interacts. There are many avenues by which such information may be communicated—appearance, previous experience with similar individuals, the social setting in which a person is found. Most important, however, is the information a person communicates about himself through the things he says and does. Goffman focuses on this source of information for two reasons: first, because of its key significance and, second, because such information is to a large extent subject to individual control—that is to say, one can, at least within a certain range, control the "image" which one projects and which others come to accept.

All of this is important because, as Goffman (1959, p. 1) puts it, "Information about the individual helps to define the situation, enabling others to know in advance what he [the individual] will expect of them and what they may expect of him." Goffman is interested in the techniques people employ to "present themselves" to others and the conditions under which these techniques tend to be employed.

A central construct in Goffman's theory is the "performance," defined as "all the activity of a given participant on a given occasion which serves to influence in any way any of the other participants" (p. 15). During a performance, the "actor" (the person whose behavior we are examining) may enact a "part" or "routine"—a "pre-established pattern of action which is unfolded during a performance and which may be presented or played through on other occasions" (p. 16).

The connection between Goffman's ideas and the concepts of role theory is apparent. A person who enacts the same routine to the same audience on different occasions will probably develop a standardized relationship with them. "Defining social role as the enactment of rights and duties attached to a given status, we can say that a social role will involve one or more parts and that each of these different parts may be presented by the performer on a series of occasions to the same kinds of audience or to an audience of the same persons" (p. 16).

Goffman defines the "front" as "that part of the individual's performance which regularly functions in a general and fixed fashion to define the situation for those who observe the performance. Front, then, is the expressive equipment of a standard kind intentionally or unwittingly employed by the individual during his performance" (p. 22). The front may consist of a number of elements. One such element is the "setting"—the physical environment in which the performance takes place, including furniture, decor, and physical layout. The other important element of front is what Goffman terms "personal front"—insignia of office, clothing, age, sex, posture, speech patterns, facial expressions, and so forth.

Another way of dichotomizing the stimuli which comprise front is into "appearance" and "manner." Appearance refers to "those stimuli which function at the time to tell us of the performer's social status" (p. 24). Manner refers to "those stimuli which function at the time to warn us of the interaction role the performer will expect to play in the oncoming situation" (p. 24). Thus, the performer may, by a meek and self-effacing manner, indicate that he intends to play a submissive role in the oncoming situation; or, by an arrogant, aggressive manner, he may indicate the opposite. Goffman shows that we tend to expect a consistency among setting, appearance, and manner; the person whose appearance and manner denote high social rank is expected to present himself in an appropriate setting. For this reason our sensibilities may be somewhat disturbed when we read of a millionaire who chooses to live in a shoddy house or who buys his socks in the five-and-ten-cent store.

To a certain extent, social fronts have a tendency to become institutionalized in terms of a set of expectations of the actor held by the audience. The front thus "tends to take on a meaning and stability apart from the specific tasks which happen at the time to be performed in its name. The front becomes a 'collective representation' and a fact in its own right" (p. 27). Thus, when an individual assumes an interaction role that is well established, he is likely to find that a specified and well-defined front goes along with it.

One of the important problems the actor faces is that of dramatizing his work so that his audience is aware of precisely what it is he is doing. To do so he must frequently perform in a way which is neither personally congenial nor optimally efficient for the task at hand. Goffman gives the example of the baseball umpire who must make his decisions instantaneously, without a trace of hesitation (so as to avoid giving the impression of uncertainty), and in so doing forgoes the moment of thought which might enable him to be certain of his judgment. Goffman points out the paradox that the "work that is done to fill certain statuses is often so poorly designed as an expression of a desired meaning, that if the incumbent would dramatize the character of his role, he must divert an appreciable amount of his energy to do so" (p. 32). Thus, to give a speech which strikes the listener as genuinely informal and spontaneous may require many hours of painstaking care, which the speaker must take pains to conceal from his audience in order that the illusion of spontaneity may be preserved.

Just as performances are dramatized, they also tend to be *idealized*. By idealization we refer to the tendency for a performance to be cast in terms of the "ideal form" of the relevant role. "Thus, when the individual presents himself before others, his performance will tend to incorporate and exemplify the officially accredited values of the society, more so, in fact, than does his behavior as a whole" (p. 35). For example, the religious leader may present himself as a more pious person than he really believes himself to be. On the other hand, there are frequent occasions on which an idealized performance compels the individual to present himself as possessing less of a culturally desirable attribute than he actually possesses. Consider the stereotype of the "Uncle Tom"—obsequious, shiftless, ignorant—to which even a well-educated Southern Negro may occasionally find it expedient to conform. Similarly, a girl may often pretend to be less intelligent or less athletic than she really is in order to avoid embarrassing the men she meets.

Goffman points out that Anglo-American culture tends to differentiate sharply between performances which are "real," "sincere," or "honest," and those which are "false" or "contrived." The former are viewed as the individual's unself-conscious reaction to the reality of his situation; the latter must be built up "out of the whole cloth," since there is no reality for it to reflect. But Goffman argues that the relation between appearance and reality is statistical rather than necessary or intrinsic. It is perfectly possible for an insincere or dishonest performer to give a completely convincing performance (the confidence man is a good illustration) and for a sincere performer (one whose performance is an unself-conscious reaction), through inadvertence, to leave his audience unconvinced.

Performance Teams

Although we have up to this point discussed the performance as though it were simply an extension of the character of the performer, its actual function in social interaction is more pervasive and of broader significance. Most importantly, the performance of any given individual interlocks with that of one or more others and, taken together, these project a definition of a situation which is common to the cooperating players. Goffman uses the term "performance team" or simply "team" to denote "any set of individuals who cooperate in staging a single routine" (p. 79).

The persons who perform on the same team stand in an important relation to one another—one which has two components. First, the fact that any member of the team has the power to "give the show away" makes all members, in Deutsch's (1949a) term, promotively interdependent, which is to say, the ability of any member of the team to achieve his goal is dependent upon the other members reaching their goals. Secondly, because the members of a performance team must cooperate to create a specific definition of the situation, it is difficult for them to maintain the same impression with one another. "Teammates, then, in a proportion to the frequency with which they act as a team and the number of matters that fall within impressional protectiveness, tend to be bound by rights of what might be called 'familiarity' " (p. 83).

Goffman takes pains to distinguish between a team and an informal group or clique. A team is a grouping not in relation to a social structure or organization, but rather in relation to an interaction in which the relevant definition of the situation is maintained.

> In large social establishments, individuals within a given status level are thrown together by virtue of the fact that they must cooperate in maintaining a definition of the situation toward those above and below them. Thus, a set of individuals who might be dissimilar in important respects, and hence desirous of maintaining social distance from one another, find they are in a relation of enforced

familiarity characteristic of teammates engaged in staging a show. Often it seems that small cliques form not to further the interests of those with whom the individual stages a show but rather to protect him from an unwanted identification with them (p. 84).

A single individual can, through his performance, define a given situation as he sees fit, within a wide range of alternatives. In a sense, Goffman asserts, this definition of the situation represents the individual's claim to what reality is. In a team performance, however, the definition of the situation, and hence, reality itself, is defined by the line taken by the team.

Goffman also introduces the notion of regions and region behavior. Region here does not carry the same meaning as in the terminology of Lewin's field theory (see Ch. 3). Rather, in Goffman's terms a region generally refers to a physical (as opposed to a psychological or conceptual) area. In reference to a specific performance, the "front region" is the place where the performance is given. In a restaurant, for example, it is the area to which diners have access. The "back region" is the area in which activities relevant to the performance take place, but to which the audience does not have perceptual access. Thus, in the back region a performer does not feel compelled to maintain his front. In a restaurant, the back region would correspond to the kitchen and the other areas which the diner is not permitted to enter. A waiter (a member of the team which the restaurant staff constitutes) may have to maintain an air of civility, alertness, and fastidiousness while in the front region. In the back region, he may show his fatigue and behave in a sullen and slovenly manner.

The performer's behavior in the front region may be viewed as embodying two types of standard, which Goffman terms "politeness" and "decorum." Politeness refers to the performer's manner in relation to the audience—how he treats them when interacting with them. Decorum refers to the performer's comportment in relation not to the audience but to his surroundings.

Thus far we have presented a set of interrelated constructs, constituting a perspective from which social life may be viewed. These form a bare outline of Goffman's framework. Goffman is quick to point out that this perspective is only one of several from which social life, and more particularly what he calls "social establishments," may be viewed. The four most prevalent analytic perspectives, he suggests, are: (1) *technical* (relating to the efficiency or inefficiency of the social establishment as an instrument for achieving certain predefined goals); (2) *political* (relating to the power which specific individuals or classes of individuals may exercise over others, the sorts of rewards and punishments of which this power consists, and the social controls which designate how power shall be employed); (3) *structural* (relating to status divisions within the social establishment and the relations among differentiated groups); and (4) *cultural* (relating to the values and norms which serve as standards of behavior within the establishment).

Goffman notes that each of these perspectives provides valuable insights into the functioning of social establishments and suggests that his approach forms a fifth and equally useful perspective, that is to say, one may be interested in studying a social establishment from the point of view of the formation of impressions per se. Thus, one would be led to "describe the techniques of impression management employed in a given establishment, the principal problems of impression management in the establishment, and the identity and interrelationships of the several performance teams which operate in the establishment" (p. 240). Goffman notes, moreover, that the phenomena of impression management are also relevant to the other perspectives. He suggests it is therefore useful to examine the intersection of the "dramaturgical" perspective with the other perspectives. For example,

> The cultural and dramaturgical perspectives intersect most clearly with regard to the maintenance of moral standards. The cultural values of an establishment will determine in detail how the participants are to feel about many matters and at the same time establish a framework of appearances that must be maintained, whether or not there is feeling behind the appearances (pp. 241 f.).

Goffman points to the important relation between the structure of the self and the sort of performances one gives in his interaction with others. Such a relation is of particular importance in cultures such as ours which stress that a person should "really be" what he "appears to be." It is clear, however, that the "performed self" is in each case a resultant of the interaction of a performance with a specific audience—as Goffman states it, "a correctly staged and performed scene leads the audience to impute a self to a performed character, but this imputation—this self—is a *product* of a scene that comes off, it is not a *cause* of it" (p. 252, italics in original).

Concluding Comment

Although Goffman does not for the most part employ the terminology characteristically associated with role theory, it is clear that his work is in the same intellectual tradition. One may, for example, draw a parallel between the concept of a routine and the normatively determined expectations of the holder of a given role. Nevertheless, Goffman makes an important contribution to our understanding of role relations by his emphasis on the fact that, to a great extent, the assessment of "proper" role behavior is based, not on discharge of the role's functional requisites, nor even by conscientious enactment of the role's requirements, but rather, a person in a given role must give *the appearance* of discharging the role's requirements. From this conclusion flow a number of important ramifications.

It is unfortunate that much of the richness and intuitive appeal of Goffman's formulation is lost in a skeletonized presentation such as this one. Goffman is careful at many points to note that his view is but one of several perspectives in which social life may be seen; nor does he insist that the "dramaturgical" perspective has greater validity than any of the others.

To a considerable degree, the shortcomings of the model derive from Goffman's approach to the construction of a theory and the nature of the evidence he evinces as support for it. The model may be regarded as analogic, in the sense that it relies upon the parallel between a dramatic presentation and the management of impression formation in social interaction. Goffman is certainly aware of the limitations of "extension by analogy," for he remarks "this attempt to press a mere analogy so far was in part a rhetoric and a maneuver" (p. 254). Still, we may ask, how far can such an analogy carry us? For example, does a professional actor tend to take on the values and attitudes of the character he portrays? Probably not, one would guess. Yet there is evidence that role playing does affect the attitudes and values of subjects in psychological experiments (Janis & King, 1954; King & Janis, 1956).

This observation leads to another point. Although Goffman touches on the importance of the relationship between the "performed self" and the "phenomenal self" (the self one experiences), it is probable that he makes too little of it. The need to maintain consistency between these two facets may be viewed as a highly pervasive and deep-rooted source of motivation, at least in cultures similar to our own. The discussion of the theory of dissonance (see Ch. 3) suggested that it is largely understandable as an attempt to maintain consistency between one's self concept and one's behavior. Thus, some experimental support was obtained for "the hypothesis that a chooser will experience post-decisional dissonance only when he perceives his choice in a given situation to be *inconsistent with the conception of some aspect of himself which he tries to maintain (for himself and others) in that situation*" (Deutsch, Krauss & Rosenau, 1962, p. 18, italics added). This statement implies that the cool, calculating "manager of impressions" envisioned by Goffman is something of a psychological anomaly. Certainly many of us, in fact probably most of us, at times make an effort to foster an impression which is at variance with our true feelings—we may feign interest in a lecture we find dull or try to appear more knowledgeable about modern art than we really are—yet we may well question the pervasiveness and significance of such behavior.

Finally, we need no more than note that illustrations and examples, while serving as useful aids in communicating a theory, can by their very nature provide little in the way of confirmation. The selectivity with which they are obtained opens to question their representativeness as relevant phenomena. Moreover, theories which rely mainly on illustrations for confirmation are highly susceptible to refutation by counterexample.

7

TRENDS IN
SOCIAL
PSYCHOLOGY

ALTHOUGH ITS ANCESTRY in social philosophy can be traced back
to ancient times, modern social psychology was born in the first
decades of the twentieth century. It is a child of psychology and
sociology, having been conceived in the ambivalent mood of optimism and despair which has characterized the Scientific Age.
The rapidly expanding knowledge, the increasing confidence in
scientific methods, the ever quickening technological change with
its resulting opportunities and social problems, the development
of new social organizations and of social planning, the social turmoil, the repeated disruption of communities and social traditions—
all of these helped to create both the need for social psychology
and the awareness of the possibility that scientific methods might
be applied to the understanding of social behavior.

Darwin's theory of evolution dominated the intellectual atmosphere of the time, and it became a model for theorists in social
psychology, who also set as their goal the achievement of a broad,
encompassing theory of social behavior. The programmatic statements of the early theorists such as Cooley (1902), Tarde (1903),
McDougall (1908), and Ross (1908) were grandly ambitious
in scope but meager in their detail. Many of the initial explanations
of social behavior were made in terms of such processes as sym-

pathy, imitation, and suggestion, which, in turn, were thought to be instinctually determined. The "herd instinct," "the instinct of submission," the "parental instinct," and a host of other instincts were invoked as innate, evolutionarily derived causes of behavior.

The instinctual doctrines, however, did not last long. By the middle of the 1920's, they were in retreat. The prestige of the empirical methods in the physical sciences, the point of view of social determinism advanced by Karl Marx and various sociological theorists, and the findings of cultural anthropologists, all contributed to their downfall. The two emphases in the rebellion against the instinctivist position, the rejection of the notion of instinctually caused behavior and the methodological stress on empirical procedures still color contemporary social psychology. Empiricism is an inheritance from psychology; environmentalism is a legacy of sociology.

Opposition to the doctrine of instincts and, along with it, the minimization of genetic as compared to environmental influences upon social behavior led to many studies that illustrated the effects of social factors on individual psychological processes. (Bartlett's "Social Factors in Recall," Sherif's "Group Influences upon the Formation of Norms and Attitudes," Piaget's "Social Factors in Moral Judgment" are classic studies of this genre. They are excerpted in Newcomb and Hartley, 1947.) In consonance with the rapid social changes so characteristic of the modern period, investigations by social psychologists challenged long-held views about the fixity of human nature and about the innate superiority or inferiority of any social class, national group, or race. Social psychologists were not initially unsympathetic to J. B. Watson's (1930) extravagant assertion that "there is no such thing as inheritance of capacity, talent, temperament, mental constitution, and characteristics." More recently, there has been recognition that any full explanation of the development of human behavior must take into account the genetically determined biological equipment with which the individual confronts his environment; yet, the view of innate superiority-inferiority and the notion that social behavior is "fixed" by instinct are still rejected by almost all social psychologists.

The rejection of armchair theorizing about social behavior in favor of empirical investigation provided the stimulus for the development of a variety of methods for studying social behavior:

questionnaires of various sorts to measure opinions and attitudes; systematic interviews to obtain information about the motivations underlying behavior; controlled observational procedures to describe and classify behavior in social situations; methods of content analysis to analyze speeches, documents, newspapers; sociometric techniques to study the social preferences and patterns of social interaction within a community; projective instruments for the study of personality patterns; and so forth. These methods have been extensively applied in public opinion polling, consumer research, studies of morale, investigation or prejudice and discrimination, personnel selection, and the like.

This revolt against armchair theorizing led many social psychologists not only to leave their armchairs but also to stop theorizing. Or, perhaps it is more accurate to say that the social psychologists who left their armchairs to engage in empirical research in the 1920's and early 1930's did little to connect their research with theoretical ideas. During this same period, the psychoanalysts and also the early theorists left the comfort of their armchairs mainly for the lecture podium.

Toward the end of the 1930's, under the enthusiastic but gentle leadership of Kurt Lewin, modern experimental social psychology had begun to flourish. Lewin and his students demonstrated that it is possible to create and study groups in the experimental laboratory that have important features in common with real-life groups. In doing so, they stimulated an interest in social psychological experimentation and attracted many experimentalists to work in this area.

Lewin was, however, not only an experimentalist, but also a theorist reared in the Gestalt tradition. As a consequence, his entry into group experimentation was guided by the Gestalt notion that there are properties of the group which are not simply the properties of its members (its "group atmosphere," its "structure," and so forth). Similarly, members of the other "schools" of psychology have conducted their researches in social psychology under the influence of the doctrines dominant in their own schools.

Apart from role theory, which came from sociology, the differing schools reflect points of view developed in individual psychology. During the 1930's and 1940's, there was sharp controversy among the proponents of the several psychological theories, each one claiming that he had the correct perspective for viewing human behavior. Nowadays it is recognized increasingly that human action must be seen from various perspectives if its many facets are to be understood. There is no one sovereign explanation, no single ruling motive, no dominant psychological process which can adequately characterize the doings of men. Appreciation of human complexity has led many psychologists to realize that the theoretical approaches presented in this volume only partially overlap; each focuses on somewhat different aspects of human interaction. Many of their apparent conflicts reflect fixation by some theorist on the outdated and grandiose notion that there can be one general theory which will embrace all social psychological phemomena. This notion is no more than a prejudice. Physics, it should be remembered, has a muddle of theories. There is need in social psychology for a variety of conceptual frames and theories to embrace the richness of human behavior. This is not to say that any formulation, no matter how vague, will do: it must serve a role in carrying inquiry forward.

Currently, the theoretical statements of social psychologists tend to be more narrowly and sharply focused than those of the theorists of a decade ago, and they are less readily identified as belonging to one or another of the major schools. Contemporary theoretical formulations, in general, arise out of and are tested in laboratory experiments: innoculation against attitude change (McGuire, 1964), leadership effectiveness (Fiedler, 1964), cooperation and trust (Deutsch, 1962), coalition formation (Gamson, 1964), emotional experience (Schachter, 1964), bargaining behavior (Fouraker & Siegel, 1963). In the garb of the lab coat, social psychology is becoming more and more "scientifically respectable" and less and less viewed as the domain for soft-headed "do-gooders."

The desire for respectability often has the wholesome effect of reducing shoddy work, wishful thinking, and undisciplined generalization. Research in social psychology conforms to higher standards and to a more sophisticated methodology than formerly; of this there can be little doubt. There are, however, dangers in the need to be proper. Sometimes propriety leads to an undue emphasis on the form of conduct with a neglect of its substance. This danger is beginning to threaten social psychology.

More and more social psychologists, in the past decade, have turned their attention to carefully controlled laboratory studies, neglecting investigations of social behavior in natural settings. That neglect results from the fact that circumstances beyond the investigator's control often make it difficult for him to execute well-designed, rigorous research in natural settings. Often the light is brighter and vision is clearer in the laboratory; yet, the remarkable things that people do as participants in laboratory experiments, to be seen in perspective, must be viewed from the outside. Knowledge must be sought even where the obstacles are considerable and the light is dim, if social psychologists are to contribute to an understanding of the human problems of their time.

REFERENCES

Abelson, R. P., and M. J. Rosenberg (1958). Symbolic psycho-logic: a model of attitudinal cognition. *Behavioral Science,* 3, 1–13.

Adler, D. L., and J. S. Kounin (1939). Some factors operating at the moment of resumption of interrupted tasks. *Journal of Psychology,* 7, 255–267.

Adorno, T. W., Else Frenkel-Brunswik, D. J. Levinson, and R. N. Sanford (1950). *The Authoritarian Personality.* New York: Harper & Brothers.

Allport, G. W. (1937). *Personality: A Psychological Interpretation.* New York: Henry Holt.

Allport, G. W. (1954). The historical background of modern social psychology. In Gardner Lindzey, ed., *Handbook of Social Psychology,* Vol. 1. Cambridge, Mass.: Addison-Wesley Publishing Company. Pp. 3–56.

Anderson, H. H., and H. F. Brandt (1939). A study of motivation involving self-announced goals of fifth grade children and the concept of level of aspiration. *Journal of Social Psychology,* 10, 209–232.

Arsenian, Jean M. (1943). Young children in an insecure situation. *Journal of Abnormal and Social Psychology,* 38, 225–249.

Asch, S. E. (1946). Forming impressions of personality. *Journal of Abnormal and Social Psychology,* 41, 258–290.

Asch, S. E. (1948). The doctrine of suggestion, prestige and imitation in social psychology. *Psychological Review,* 55, 250–276.

Asch, S. E. (1952). *Social Psychology.* New York: Prentice-Hall.

Asch, S. E. (1956). Studies of independence and conformity: I. A minority of one against a unanimous majority. *Psychological Monographs,* 70, No. 9 (Whole No. 416).

Atkinson, J. W. (1964). *An Introduction to Motivation.* New York: Van Nostrand.

Atkinson, J. W. (1959). Motivational determinants of risk-taking behavior. *Psychological Review,* 64, 359–372.

Back, K. W. (1951). Influence through social communication. *Journal of Abnormal and Social Psychology,* 46, 9–23.

Bandura, Albert (1962). Social learning through imitation. In M. R. Jones, ed., *Nebraska Symposium on Motivation, 1962.* Lincoln: University of Nebraska Press. Pp. 211–269.

Bandura, Albert (in press). *Behavioristic Psychotherapy.* New York: Holt, Rinehart and Winston.

Bandura, Albert, and R. H. Walters (1959). *Adolescent Aggression.* New York: Ronald Press.

Bandura, Albert, and R. H. Walters (1963). *Social Learning and Personality Development*. New York: Holt, Rinehart and Winston.

Barker, R. G., Beatrice A. Wright, and Mollie R. Gonick (1946). Adjustment to physical handicap and illness: a survey of the social psychology of physique and disability. *Social Science Research Council Bulletin*, No. 55.

Bavelas, Alex (1951). Communication patterns in task oriented groups. In Daniel Lerner and H. D. Lasswell, eds., *The Policy Sciences*. Stanford, Calif.: Stanford University Press. Pp. 193–202.

Bennett, Edith B. (1952). The relationship of group discussion, decision, commitment and consensus to individual action. Unpublished doctoral dissertation, University of Michigan.

Bentham, Jeremy (1789). *An Introduction to the Principles of Morals and Legislation*. Oxford: Clarendon Press, 1879.

Berelson, B. R., P. F. Lazarsfeld, and W. N. McPhee (1954). *Voting: A Study of Opinion Formation in a Presidential Campaign*. Chicago: University of Chicago Press.

Berkowitz, Leonard (1962). *Aggression: A Social Psychological Analysis*. New York: McGraw-Hill Book Company.

Blos, Peter (1962). *On Adolescence: A Psychoanalytic Interpretation*. New York: Free Press of Glencoe.

Braithwaite, R. B. (1953). *Scientific Explanation*. Cambridge, England: Cambridge University Press.

Bredemeier, H. C., and R. M. Stephenson (1962). *The Analysis of Social Systems*. New York: Holt, Rinehart and Winston.

Brehm, J. W., and A. R. Cohen (1962). *Explorations in Cognitive Dissonance*. New York: John Wiley & Sons.

Buss, A. H. (1961). *The Psychology of Aggression*. New York: John Wiley & Sons.

Campbell, N. R. (1920). *Physics: The Elements*. Cambridge, England: Cambridge University Press.

Cartwright, Dorwin (1950). Emotional dimensions of group life. In M. L. Reymert, ed., *Feelings and Emotions*. New York: McGraw-Hill Book Company. Pp. 439–447.

Cartwright, Dorwin (1959). A field theoretical conception of power. In Dorwin Cartwright, ed., *Studies in Social Power*. Ann Arbor, Mich.: Institute for Social Research. Pp. 183–220.

Cartwright, Dorwin, and Frank Harary (1956). Structural balance: a generalization of Heider's theory. *Psychological Review*, 63, 277–293.

Chapanis, Natalia P., and Alphonse Chapanis (1964). Cognitive dissonance: five years later. *Psychological Bulletin*, 61, 1–22.

Chein, Isidor, D. L. Gerard, R. S. Lee, and Eva Rosenfeld (1964). *The Road to H: Narcotics, Delinquency, and Social Policy*. New York: Basic Books.

Chomsky, Noam (1959). Review: "Verbal Behavior" by B. F. Skinner. *Language*, 35, 26–58.

Christie, Richard, and Peggy Cook (1958). A guide to published literature relating to the authoritarian personality through 1956. *Journal of Psychology*, **45**, 171–199.

Christie, Richard, and Marie Jahoda, eds. (1954). *Studies in the Scope and Method of "The Authoritarian Personality."* Glencoe, Ill.: Free Press.

Cloward, R. A. (1959). Illegitimate means, anomie, and deviant behavior. *American Sociological Review*, **24**, 164–176.

Coch, Lester, and J. R. P. French, Jr. (1948). Overcoming resistance to change. *Human Relations*, **1**, 512–532.

Cohen, A. R. (1964). *Attitude Change and Social Influence.* New York: Basic Books.

Cooley, C. H. (1902). *Human Nature and the Social Order.* Glencoe, Ill.: Free Press, 1956.

Darwin, Charles (1872). *The Expression of the Emotions in Man and Animals.* New York: D. Appleton, 1896.

Dembo, Tamara (1931). Der Aerger als dynamisches Problem. *Psychologische Forschung*, **15**, 1–144.

Deutsch, Morton (1949a). A theory of co-operation and competition. *Human Relations*, **2**, 129–152.

Deutsch, Morton (1949b). An experimental study of the effects of co-operation and competition upon group process. *Human Relations*, **2**, 199–232.

Deutsch, Morton (1958). Trust and suspicion. *Journal of Conflict Resolution*, **2**, 265–279.

Deutsch, Morton (1961). The face of bargaining. *Operations Research*, **9**, 886–897.

Deutsch, Morton (1962). Cooperation and trust: some theoretical notes. In M. R. Jones, ed., *Nebraska Symposium on Motivation, 1962.* Lincoln: University of Nebraska Press. Pp. 275–318.

Deutsch, Morton, and H. B. Gerard (1955). A study of normative and informational social influences upon individual judgment. *Journal of Abnormal and Social Psychology*, **51**, 629–636.

Deutsch, Morton, R. M. Krauss, and Norah Rosenau (1962). Dissonance or defensiveness? *Journal of Personality*, **30**, 16–28.

Dollard, John, and N. E. Miller (1950). *Personality and Psychotherapy.* New York: McGraw-Hill Book Company.

Dollard, John, N. E. Miller, L. W. Doob, O. H. Mowrer, and R. H. Sears (1939). *Frustration and Aggression.* New Haven, Conn.: Yale University Press.

Dulany, D. E., Jr. (1962). The place of hypotheses and intentions: an analysis of verbal control in verbal conditioning. *Journal of Personality*, **30**, 102–129.

Durkheim, Émile (1897). *Suicide.* Glencoe, Ill.: Free Press, 1951.

Eisenstadt, S. N. (1954). Studies in reference group behavior: I. Reference norms and the social structure. *Human Relations*, **7**, 191–216.

Erikson, E. H. (1950). *Childhood and Society.* New York: W. W. Norton.

Erikson, E. H. (1959). Identity and the life cycle. *Psychological Issues*, **1**, No. 1.

Erikson, E. H. (1963). *Childhood and Society*. (2nd ed.) New York: W. W. Norton.

Fajans, Sara (1933a). Die Bedeutung der Entfernung für die Stärke eines Aufforderungscharakters beim Säugling und Kleinkind. *Psychologische Forschung, 17,* 215–267.

Fajans, Sara (1933b). Erfolg, Ausdauer und Aktivität beim Säugling und Kleinkind. *Psychologische Forschung, 17,* 268–305.

Festinger, Leon (1942a). Wish, expectation, and group standards as factors influencing level of aspiration. *Journal of Abnormal and Social Psychology, 37,* 184–200.

Festinger, Leon (1942b). A theoretical interpretation of shifts in level of aspiration. *Psychological Review, 49,* 235–250.

Festinger, Leon (1950). Informal social communication. *Psychological Review, 57,* 271–282.

Festinger, Leon (1954). A theory of social comparison processes. *Human Relations, 7,* 117–140.

Festinger, Leon (1957). *A Theory of Cognitive Dissonance*. Evanston, Ill.: Row, Peterson (reprinted by Stanford University Press, Stanford, Calif., 1962).

Festinger, Leon (1961). The psychological effects of insufficient reward. *American Psychologist, 16,* 1–11.

Festinger, Leon (1964). *Conflict, Decision, and Dissonance*. Stanford, Calif.: Stanford University Press.

Festinger, Leon, and J. M. Carlsmith (1959). Cognitive consequences of forced compliance. *Journal of Abnormal and Social Psychology, 58,* 203–210.

Festinger, Leon, and John Thibaut (1951). Interpersonal communication in small groups. *Journal of Abnormal and Social Psychology, 46,* 92–99.

Festinger, Leon, Stanley Schachter, and Kurt Back (1950). *Social Pressures in Informal Groups: A Study of Human Factors in Housing*. New York: Harper & Brothers.

Fiedler, F. E. (1964). A contingency model of leadership effectiveness. In Leonard Berkowitz, ed., *Advances in Experimental Social Psychology*, Vol. 1. New York: Academic Press. Pp. 149–190.

Fouraker, L. E., and Sidney Siegel (1963). *Bargaining Behavior*. New York: McGraw-Hill Book Company.

Frank, J. D. (1944). Experimental studies of personal pressure and resistance. *Journal of General Psychology, 30,* 23–64.

French, J. R. P., Jr. (1944). Organized and unorganized groups under fear and frustration. *University of Iowa Studies in Child Welfare, 20,* 299–308.

Freud, Sigmund (1900). *The Interpretation of Dreams*. Standard Edition, Vols. 4 and 5. London: Hogarth Press, 1953.

Freud, Sigmund (1901). Psychopathology of everyday life. In A. A. Brill, ed., *The Basic Writings of Sigmund Freud*. New York: Random House, 1938. Pp. 35–178.

Freud, Sigmund (1905). Wit and its relation to the unconscious. In A. A.

Brill, ed., *The Basic Writings of Sigmund Freud.* New York: Random House, 1938. Pp. 633–803.

Freud, Sigmund (1910). *Leonardo da Vinci: A Study in Psychosexuality.* New York: Random House, 1947.

Freud, Sigmund (1913). Totem and Taboo. In A. A. Brill, ed., *The Basic Writings of Sigmund Freud.* New York: Random House, 1938. Pp. 807–930.

Freud, Sigmund (1915). Instincts and their vicissitudes. In *Sigmund Freud: Collected Papers,* Vol. 4. New York: Basic Books, 1959. Pp. 60–83.

Freud, Sigmund (1921). *Group Psychology and the Analysis of the Ego.* London: Hogarth Press, 1945.

Freud, Sigmund (1928). *The Future of an Illusion.* London: Hogarth Press, 1949.

Freud, Sigmund (1930). *Civilization and Its Discontents.* London: Hogarth Press.

Freud, Sigmund (1939). *Moses and Monotheism.* New York: Alfred A. Knopf.

Fromm, Erich (1941). *Escape from Freedom.* New York: Farrar & Rinehart.

Gamson, W. A. (1964). Experimental studies of coalition formation. In Leonard Berkowitz, ed., *Advances in Experimental Social Psychology,* Vol. 1. New York: Academic Press. Pp. 81–110.

Gerard, H. B. (1953). The effect of different dimensions of disagreement on the communication process in small groups. *Human Relations, 6,* 249–271.

Gerard, H. B. (1954). The anchorage of opinions in face-to-face groups. *Human Relations, 7,* 313–325.

Getzels, J. W., and E. G. Guba (1954). Role, role conflict, and effectiveness. *American Sociological Review, 19,* 164–175.

Goffman, Erving (1959). *The Presentation of Self in Everyday Life.* Garden City, N. Y.: Doubleday Anchor Books.

Grosser, Daniel, Norman Polansky, and Ronald Lippitt (1951). A laboratory study of behavioral contagion. *Human Relations, 4,* 115–142.

Hall, C. S., and Gardner Lindzey (1957). *Theories of Personality.* New York: John Wiley & Sons.

Harlow, H. F. (1953). Mice, monkeys, men, and motives. *Psychological Review, 60,* 23–32.

Hartmann, Heinz (1939). Ego psychology and the problem of adaptation. In David Rapaport, ed., *Organization and Pathology of Thought.* New York: Columbia University Press, 1951. Pp. 362–396.

Heider, Fritz (1927). Ding und Medium. *Symposium, 1,* 109–158.

Heider, Fritz (1946). Attitudes and cognitive organization. *Journal of Psychology, 21,* 107–112.

Heider, Fritz (1958). *The Psychology of Interpersonal Relations.* New York: John Wiley & Sons.

Heider, Fritz (1959). On perception, event structure, and psychological environment. *Psychological Issues, 1,* No. 3.

Helson, Harry (1948). Adaptation-level as a basis for a quantitative theory of frames of reference. *Psychological Review,* **55,** 297–313.

Helson, Harry (1964). *Adaptation-Level Theory.* New York: Harper & Row.

Henle, Mary (1942). An experimental investigation of dynamic and structural determinants of substitution. *Contributions to Psychological Theory,* **2,** No. 3.

Hilgard, E. R., E. M. Sait, and G. Ann Magaret (1940). Level of aspiration as affected by relative standing in an experimental social group. *Journal of Experimental Psychology,* **27,** 411–421.

Hoffman, P. J., Leon Festinger, and Douglas Lawrence (1954). Tendencies toward group comparability in competitive bargaining. *Human Relations,* **7,** 141–159.

Holt, R. R. (1963). Two influences on Freud's scientific thought: a fragment of intellectual biography. In R. W. White, ed., *The Study of Lives.* New York: Atherton Press. Pp. 365–387.

Holt, R. R. (1964). Imagery: the return of the ostracized. *American Psychologist,* **19,** 254–264.

Homans, G. C. (1950). *The Human Group.* New York: Harcourt, Brace.

Homans, G. C. (1961). *Social Behavior: Its Elementary Forms.* New York: Harcourt, Brace and World.

Homans, G. C. (1962). *Sentiments and Activities: Essays in Social Science.* New York: Free Press of Glencoe.

Horwitz, Murray (1954). The recall of interrupted group tasks: an experimental study of individual motivation in relation to group goals. *Human Relations,* **7,** 3–38.

Hovland, C. I., ed. (1957). *The Order of Presentation in Persuasion.* New Haven: Yale University Press.

Hovland, C. I., and I. L. Janis, eds. (1959). *Personality and Persuasibility.* New Haven: Yale University Press.

Hovland, C. I., I. L. Janis, and H. H. Kelley (1953). *Communication and Persuasion.* New Haven: Yale University Press.

Hovland, C. I., A. A. Lumsdaine, and F. D. Sheffield (1949). *Experiments on Mass Communication.* Princeton, N. J.: Princeton University Press.

Hovland, C. I., and M. I. Rosenberg, eds. (1960). *Attitude Organization and Change.* New Haven: Yale University Press.

Hull, C. L. (1943). *Principles of Behavior.* New York: D. Appleton Century.

Hyman, H. H. (1942). The psychology of status. *Archives of Psychology,* No. 269.

James, William (1892). *Psychology: Briefer Course.* New York: Henry Holt.

Janis, I. L., and J. B. Gilmore (1965). The influence of incentive conditions on the success of role playing in modifying attitudes. *Journal of Personality and Social Psychology,* **1,** 17–27.

Janis, I. L., and B. T. King (1954). The influence of role playing on opinion change. *Journal of Abnormal and Social Psychology,* **49,** 211–218.

Jucknat, Margaret (1937). Leistung, Anspruchsniveau und Selbstbewusstsein. *Psychologische Forschung,* **22,** 89–179.

Kaplan, Abraham (1964). *The Conduct of Inquiry: Methodology for Behavioral Science.* San Francisco: Chandler Publishing Company.

Kardiner, Abram (1939). *The Individual and His Society.* New York: Columbia University Press.

Kardiner, Abram, and Edward Preble (1963). *They Studied Man.* New York: New American Library.

Kardiner, Abram, Ralph Linton, Cora DuBois, and James West (1945). *The Psychological Frontiers of Society.* New York: Columbia University Press.

Karpf, Fay B. (1932). *American Social Psychology.* New York: McGraw-Hill Book Company.

Karsten, Anitra (1928). Psychische Sättigung. *Psychologische Forschung,* **10,** 142–254.

Kelley, H. H. (1951). Communication in experimentally created hierarchies. *Human Relations,* **4,** 39–56.

Kelley, H. H. (1952). Two functions of reference groups. In G. E. Swanson, T. M. Newcomb, and E. L. Hartley, eds., *Readings in Social Psychology.* New York: Henry Holt. Pp. 410–414.

Kelley, H. H. (1964a). Interaction process and the attainment of maximum joint profit. In Samuel Messick and A. H. Brayfield, eds., *Decision and Choice: Contributions of Sidney Siegel.* New York: McGraw-Hill Book Company. Pp. 240–250.

Kelley, H. H. (1964b). A classroom study of the dilemmas in interpersonal negotiations. Unpublished paper, University of California, Los Angeles.

Kelley, H. H., J. W. Thibaut, Roland Radloff, and David Mundy (1962). The development of cooperation in the "minimal social situation." *Psychological Monographs,* **76,** No. 19 (Whole No. 538).

Kelly, G. A. (1955). *The Psychology of Personal Constructs.* 2 Vols. New York: W. W. Norton.

Killian, L. M. (1952). The significance of multiple-group membership in disaster. *American Journal of Sociology,* **57,** 309–314.

Kimble, G. A. (1961). *Hilgard and Marquis' Conditioning and Learning.* New York: Appleton-Century-Crofts.

King, B. T., and I. L. Janis (1956). Comparison of the effectiveness of improvised versus non-improvised role-playing in producing opinion changes. *Human Relations,* **9,** 177–186.

Klein, G. S. (1959a). Consciousness in psychoanalytic theory: some implications for current research in perception. *Journal of the American Psychoanalytic Association,* **7,** 5–34.

Klein, G. S. (1959b). On subliminal activation. *Journal of Nervous and Mental Disease,* **128,** 293–301.

Kluckhohn, Clyde (1954). Culture and behavior. In Gardner Lindzey, ed., *Handbook of Social Psychology,* Vol. 2. Cambridge, Mass.: Addison-Wesley Publishing Company. Pp. 921–976.

Köhler, Wolfgang (1929). *Gestalt Psychology.* New York: Liveright.

Koffka, Kurt (1935). *Principles of Gestalt Psychology.* New York: Harcourt, Brace.

Kounin, J. S. (1941a). Experimental studies of rigidity: I. *Character and Personality*, **9**, 251–272.

Kounin, J. S. (1941b). Experimental studies of rigidity: II. *Character and Personality*, **9**, 273–282.

Krasner, Leonard (1958). Studies of the conditioning of verbal behavior. *Psychological Bulletin*, **55**, 148–170.

Krech, David, and R. S. Crutchfield (1948). *Theory and Problems of Social Psychology*. New York: McGraw-Hill Book Company.

Krech, David, and R. S. Crutchfield (1958). *Elements of Psychology*. New York: Alfred A. Knopf.

Lasswell, H. D. (1930). *Psychopathology and Politics*. Chicago: University of Chicago Press.

Leavitt, H. J. (1951). Some effects of certain communication patterns on group performance. *Journal of Abnormal and Social Psychology*, **46**, 38–50.

Lecky, Prescott (1945). *Self-consistency: A Theory of Personality*. New York: Island Press.

Levy, Seymour (1953). Experimental study of group norms: the effects of group cohesiveness upon social conformity. Unpublished doctoral dissertation, New York University.

Lewin, Kurt (1935a). Psycho-sociological problems of a minority group. *Character and Personality*, **3**, 175–187.

Lewin, Kurt (1935b). *A Dynamic Theory of Personality*. New York: McGraw-Hill Book Company.

Lewin, Kurt (1938). The conceptual representation and measurement of psychological forces. *Contributions to Psychological Theory*, **1**, No. 4.

Lewin, Kurt (1939). Field theory and experiment in social psychology: concepts and methods. *American Journal of Sociology*, **44**, 868–896.

Lewin, Kurt (1941). Analysis of the concepts whole, differentiation, and unity. *University of Iowa Studies in Child Welfare*, **18**, No. 1, 226–261.

Lewin, Kurt (1946). Action research and minority problems. *Journal of Social Issues*, **2**, 34–46.

Lewin, Kurt (1947a). Frontiers in group dynamics: I. *Human Relations*, **1**, 5–41.

Lewin, Kurt (1947b). Frontiers in group dynamics: II, *Human Relations*, **1**, 143–153.

Lewin, Kurt (1947c). Group decision and social change. In T. M. Newcomb and E. L. Hartley, eds., *Readings in Social Psychology*. New York: Henry Holt. Pp. 330–344.

Lewin, Kurt (1948). *Resolving Social Conflicts*. New York: Harper & Brothers.

Lewin, Kurt (1951). *Field Theory in Social Science*. New York: Harper & Brothers.

Lewin, Kurt, Ronald Lippitt, and R. K. White (1939). Patterns of aggressive behavior in experimentally created "social climates." *Journal of Social Psychology*, **10**, 271–299.

Lewin, Kurt, Tamara Dembo, Leon Festinger, and Pauline S. Sears (1944).

Level of aspiration. In J. McV. Hunt, ed., *Personality and the Behavior Disorders*. New York: Ronald Press. Pp. 333–378.

Lewis, Helen B. (1944). An experimental study of the role of the ego in work: I. The role of the ego in cooperative work. *Journal of Experimental Psychology,* **34,** 113–126.

Lewis, Helen B., and Muriel Franklin (1944). An experimental study of the role of the ego in work: II. The significance of task-orientation in work. *Journal of Experimental Psychology,* **34,** 195–215.

Lindesmith, A. R., and A. L. Strauss (1956). *Social Psychology.* (Rev. ed.) New York: Dryden Press.

Lindzey, Gardner, ed. (1954). *Handbook of Social Psychology.* 2 Vols. Cambridge, Mass.: Addison-Wesley Publishing Company.

Linton, Ralph (1945). *The Cultural Background of Personality.* New York: Appleton-Century.

Lippitt, Ronald (1940). An experimental study of the effect of democratic and authoritarian group atmospheres. *University of Iowa Studies in Child Welfare,* **16,** No. 3, 44–195.

Lippitt, Ronald, and R. K. White (1943). The "social climate" of children's groups. In R. G. Barker, J. S. Kounin, and H. F. Wright, eds., *Child Behavior and Development.* New York: McGraw-Hill Book Company. Pp. 485–508.

Lippitt, Ronald, Norman Polansky, and Sidney Rosen (1952). The dynamics of power. *Human Relations,* **5,** 37–64.

Lissner, Kate (1933). Die Entspannung von Bedürfnissen durch Ersatzhandlungen. *Psychologische Forschung,* **18,** 218–250.

Luce, R. D., and Howard Raiffa (1957). *Games and Decisions.* New York: John Wiley & Sons.

Mahler, Wera (1933). Ersatzhandlungen verschiedenen Realitätsgrades. *Psychologische Forschung,* **18,** 27–89.

Malinowski, Bronislaw (1927). *Sex and Repression in Savage Society.* New York: Harcourt, Brace.

Margenau, Henry (1950). *The Nature of Physical Reality.* New York: McGraw-Hill Book Company.

Martindale, Don (1960). *The Nature and Types of Sociological Theory.* Boston: Houghton Mifflin.

Maslow, A. H. (1943). The authoritarian character structure. *Journal of Social Psychology,* **18,** 401–411.

Maslow, A. H. (1954). *Motivation and Personality.* New York: Harper & Brothers.

Maurer, D. W. (1940). *The Big Con.* Indianapolis, Ind.: Bobbs-Merrill.

McDougall, William (1908). *Introduction to Social Psychology.* London: Methuen.

McGregor, Douglas (1944). Conditions of effective leadership in the industrial organization. *Journal of Consulting Psychology,* **8,** 55–63.

McGuire, W. J. (1964). Inducing resistance to persuasion. In Leonard Berkowitz, ed., *Advances in Experimental Social Psychology,* Vol. 1. New York: Academic Press. Pp. 191–229.

Mead, G. H. (1934). *Mind, Self and Society*. Chicago: University of Chicago Press.

Mead, Margaret (1928). *Coming of Age in Samoa*. New York: William Morrow.

Mead, Margaret (1930). *Growing Up in New Guinea*. New York: William Morrow.

Mead, Margaret (1935). *Sex and Temperament in Three Primitive Societies*. New York: William Morrow.

Merton, R. K. (1957). *Social Theory and Social Structure*. (Rev. ed.) Glencoe, Ill.: Free Press.

Merton, R. K., and Alice S. Kitt (1950). Contributions to the theory of reference group behavior. In R. K. Merton and P. F. Lazarsfeld, eds., *Continuities in Social Research: Studies in the Scope and Method of "The American Soldier."* Glencoe, Ill.: Free Press. Pp. 40–105.

Miller, N. E. (1944). Experimental studies of conflict. In J. McV. Hunt, ed., *Personality and the Behavior Disorders*, Vol. 1. New York: Ronald Press. Pp. 431–465.

Miller, N. E., and John Dollard (1941). *Social Learning and Imitation*. New Haven, Conn.: Yale University Press.

Morris, C. W. (1934). Introduction: George H. Mead as social psychologist and social philosopher. In G. H. Mead, *Mind, Self and Society*. Chicago: University of Chicago Press. Pp. ix–xxxv.

Mowrer, O. H. (1960a). *Learning Theory and Behavior*. New York: John Wiley & Sons.

Mowrer, O. H. (1960b). *Learning Theory and the Symbolic Processes*. New York: John Wiley & Sons.

Nagel, Ernest (1961). *The Structure of Science*. New York: Harcourt, Brace and World.

Neiman, L. J., and J. W. Hughes (1951). The problem of the concept of role—a re-survey of the literature. *Social Forces*, **30**, 141–149.

Newcomb, T. M. (1943). *Personality and Social Change: Attitude Formation in a Student Community*. New York: Dryden Press.

Newcomb, T. M. (1948). Attitude development as a function of reference groups: the Bennington Study. In Muzafer Sherif, *An Outline of Social Psychology*. New York: Harper & Brothers. Pp. 139–155.

Newcomb, T. M. (1950). *Social Psychology*. New York: Dryden Press.

Newcomb, T. M. (1953). An approach to the study of communicative acts. *Psychological Review*, **60**, 393–404.

Newcomb, T. M. (1961). *The Acquaintance Process*. New York: Holt, Rinehart and Winston.

Newcomb, T. M., and E. L. Hartley, eds. (1947). *Readings in Social Psychology*. New York: Henry Holt.

Osgood, C. E. (1963). On understanding and creating sentences. *American Psychologist*, **18**, 735–751.

Osgood, C. E., and P. H. Tannenbaum (1955). The principle of congruity in the prediction of attitude change. *Psychological Review*, **62**, 42–55.

Ovsiankina, Maria (1928). Die Wiederaufnahme unterbrochener Handlungen. *Psychologische Forschung*, **11**, 302–379.

Parsons, Talcott (1942). Age and sex in the social structure of the United States. *American Sociological Review,* **7,** 604–616.

Parsons, Talcott (1951). *The Social System.* Glencoe, Ill.: Free Press.

Parsons, Talcott, and R. F. Bales (1955). *Family, Socialization and Interaction Process.* Glencoe, Ill.: Free Press.

Parsons, Talcott, and E. A. Shils, eds. (1951). *Toward a General Theory of Action.* Cambridge, Mass.: Harvard University Press.

Pettigrew, T. F. (1958). Personality and sociocultural factors in intergroup attitudes: a cross-national comparison. *Journal of Conflict Resolution,* **2,** 29–42.

Piaget, Jean (1948). *The Moral Judgment of the Child.* Glencoe, Ill.: Free Press.

Piaget, Jean (1952). *The Origins of Intelligence in Children.* New York: International Universities Press.

Polansky, Norman, Ronald Lippitt, and Fritz Redl (1950a). An investigation of behavioral contagion in groups. *Human Relations,* **3,** 319–348.

Polansky, Norman, Ronald Lippitt, and Fritz Redl (1950b). The use of near-sociometric data in research on group treatment processes. *Sociometry,* **13,** 39–62.

Polansky, Norman, Willa Freeman, Murray Horwitz, Lucietta Irwin, Ned Papania, Dorothy Rapaport, and Francis Whaley (1949). Problems of interpersonal relations in research on groups. *Human Relations,* **2,** 281–291.

Rapaport, David, ed. (1951). *Organization and Pathology of Thought.* New York: Columbia University Press.

Rapaport, David (1959a). Introduction: a historical survey of psychoanalytic ego psychology. In E. H. Erikson, Identity and the life cycle. *Psychological Issues,* **1,** No. 1. Pp. 5–17.

Rapaport, David (1959b). The structure of psychoanalytic theory: a systematizing attempt. In Sigmund Koch, ed., *Psychology: A Study of a Science,* Vol. 3. New York: McGraw-Hill Book Company. Pp. 55–183.

Rapaport, David (1960). On the psychoanalytic theory of motivation. In M. R. Jones, ed., *Nebraska Symposium on Motivation, 1960.* Lincoln: University of Nebraska Press. Pp. 173–247.

Rapoport, Anatol, and Carol Orwant (1962). Experimental games: a review. *Behavioral Science,* **7,** 1–37.

Reich, Wilhelm (1946). *The Mass Psychology of Fascism.* New York: Orgone Institute Press.

Rokeach, Milton (1960). *The Open and Closed Mind.* New York: Basic Books.

Rommetveit, Ragnar (1955). *Social Norms and Roles: Explorations in the Psychology of Enduring Social Pressures.* Minneapolis: University of Minnesota Press.

Rose, A. M., ed. (1962). *Human Behavior and Social Processes.* Boston: Houghton Mifflin.

Rosen, B. C. (1955). The reference group approach to the parental factor in attitude and behavior formation. *Social Forces,* **34,** 137–144.

Rosenberg, M. J. (1965). When dissonance fails: on eliminating evaluation apprehension from attitude measurement. *Journal of Personality and Social Psychology*, **1**, 28–42.

Rosenberg, M. J., and R. P. Abelson (1960). An analysis of cognitive balancing. In C. I. Hovland and M. J. Rosenberg, eds., *Attitude Organization and Change*. New Haven, Conn.: Yale University Press. Pp. 112–163.

Ross, E. A. (1908). *Social Psychology*. New York: Macmillan.

Salzinger, Kurt (1959). Experimental manipulation of verbal behavior: a review. *Journal of General Psychology*, **61**, 65–94.

Sapolsky, Allan (1960). Effect of interpersonal relationships upon verbal conditioning. *Journal of Abnormal and Social Psychology*, **60**, 241–246.

Sartre, J.-P. (1946). Portrait of the antisemite. *Partisan Review*, **13**, 163–178.

Sartre, J.-P. (1964). *The Words*. New York: George Braziller.

Schachtel, E. G. (1959). *Metamorphosis: On the Development of Affect, Perception, Attention, and Memory*. New York: Basic Books.

Schachter, Stanley (1951). Deviation, rejection, and communication. *Journal of Abnormal and Social Psychology*, **46**, 190–207.

Schachter, Stanley (1959). *The Psychology of Affiliation*. Stanford, Calif.: Stanford University Press.

Schachter, Stanley (1964). The interaction of cognitive and physiological determinants of emotional state. In Leonard Berkowitz, ed., *Advances in Experimental Social Psychology*, Vol. 1. New York: Academic Press. Pp. 49–80.

Schachter, Stanley, and J. E. Singer (1962). Cognitive, social, and physiological determinants of emotional state. *Psychological Review*, **69**, 379–399.

Sears, R. R. (1943). Survey of objective studies of psychoanalytic concepts. *Social Science Research Council Bulletin*, No. 51.

Sears, R. R. (1951). Social behavior and personality development. In Talcott Parsons and E. A. Shils, eds., *Toward a General Theory of Action*. Cambridge, Mass.: Harvard University Press. Pp. 465–478.

Shibutani, Tamotsu (1961). *Society and Personality*. Englewood Cliffs, N. J.: Prentice-Hall.

Shubik, Martin, ed. (1964). *Game Theory and Related Approaches to Social Behavior*. New York: John Wiley & Sons.

Silverman, Irwin (1964). In defense of dissonance theory: reply to Chapanis and Chapanis. *Psychological Bulletin*, **62**, 205–209.

Skinner, B. F. (1948). *Walden Two*. New York: Macmillan.

Skinner, B. F. (1953). *Science and Human Behavior*. New York: Macmillan.

Skinner, B. F. (1957). *Verbal Behavior*. New York: Appleton-Century-Crofts.

Skinner, B. F. (1963). Behaviorism at fifty. *Science*, **140**, 951–958.

Sliosberg, Sarah (1934). Zur Dynamik des Ersatzes in Spiel- und Ernstsituationen. *Psychologische Forschung*, **19**, 122–181.

Spielberger, C. D. (1962). The role of awareness in verbal conditioning. *Journal of Personality*, **30**, 73–101.

Spielberger, C. D., S. M. Levin, and Mary C. Shepard (1962). The effects of awareness and attitude toward the reinforcement on the operant conditioning of verbal behavior. *Journal of Personality*, **30**, 106–120.

Stouffer, S. A., E. A. Suchman, L. C. DeVinney, Shirley A. Star, and R. M. Williams, Jr. (1949). *The American Soldier*. Vol. 1: *Adjustment During Army Life*. Princeton, N. J.: Princeton University Press.

Stouffer, S. A., A. A. Lumsdaine, Marion H. Lumsdaine, R. M. Williams, Jr., M. B. Smith, I. L. Janis, Shirley A. Star, and L. S. Cottrell, Jr. (1949). *The American Soldier*. Vol. 2: *Combat and Its Aftermath*. Princeton, N. J.: Princeton University Press.

Strauss, Anselm, ed. (1956). *The Social Psychology of George Herbert Mead*. Chicago: University of Chicago Press.

Sullivan, H. S. (1953). *The Interpersonal Theory of Psychiatry*. New York: W. W. Norton.

Tarde, Gabriel (1903). *The Laws of Imitation*. New York: Henry Holt.

Thibaut, J. W. (1950). An experimental study of the cohesiveness of under-privileged groups. *Human Relations*, **3**, 251–278.

Thibaut, J. W., and John Coules (1952). The role of communication in the reduction of interpersonal hostility. *Journal of Abnormal and Social Psychology*, **47**, 770–777.

Thibaut, J. W., and Claude Faucheux (1965). The development of con-tractual norms in a bargaining situation under two types of stress. *Journal of Experimental Social Psychology*, **1**, 89–102.

Thibaut, J. W., and H. H. Kelley (1959). *The Social Psychology of Groups*. New York: John Wiley & Sons.

Thorndike, E. L. (1898). Animal intelligence: an experimental study of the associative processes in animals. *Psychological Monographs*, **2**, No. 4 (Whole No. 8).

Titus, H. E., and E. P. Hollander (1957). The California F scale in psy-chological research: 1950–1955. *Psychological Bulletin*, **54**, 47–64.

Tolman, E. C. (1951). A psychological model. In Talcott Parsons and E. A. Shils, eds., *Toward a General Theory of Action*. Cambridge, Mass.: Harvard University Press. Pp. 279–361.

Watson, J. B. (1919). *Psychology from the Standpoint of a Behaviorist*. Philadelphia: J. B. Lippincott.

Watson, J. B. (1930). *Behaviorism*. (Rev. ed.) New York: W. W. Norton.

Wertheimer, Max (1923). Untersuchungen zur Lehre von der Gestalt: II. *Psychologische Forschung*, **4**, 301–350.

White, R. W. (1959). Motivation reconsidered: the concept of competence. *Psychological Review*, **66**, 297–333.

White, R. W. (1960). Competence and the psychosexual stages of develop-ment. In M. R. Jones, ed., *Nebraska Symposium on Motivation, 1960*. Lincoln: University of Nebraska Press. Pp. 97–141.

White, R. W. (1963). Ego and reality in psychoanalytic theory. *Psychological Issues*, **3**, No. 11.

Whiting, Beatrice B., ed. (1963). *Six Cultures: Studies of Child Rearing*. New York: John Wiley & Sons.

Wolpe, Joseph (1958). *Psychotherapy by Reciprocal Inhibition*. Stanford, Calif.: Stanford University Press.

Zeigarnik, Bluma (1927). Das Behalten erledigter und unerledigter Hand-
    lungen. *Psychologische Forschung, 9,* 1–85.
Zillig, Maria (1928). Einstellung und Aussage. *Zeitschrift für Psychologie,*
    106, 58–106.

INDEX

Leavitt, H. J., 61
Lecky, Prescott, 68
Lee, R. S., 202
Lenin, Nikolai (Vladimir I. Ulyanov), 19, 26
Leonardo da Vinci (Freud), 127
Levin, S. M., 108
Levinson, D. J., 157
Levy, David, 166
Levy, Seymour, 56
lewdness, 145
Lewin, Kurt, 15, 23, 29, 37-54, 58-62, 70, 116, 214
Lewis, Helen B., 42
libido, desexualized, 158; fixation of, 141; in phallic stage, 146
libido theory, 133, 136-138
life instincts, 134
life space, 30, 37-38; and cognitive structure, 45; direction in, 45
Lindzey, Gardner, 155, 179
linear graphs, theory of, 35
Linton, Ralph, 166-167
Lippitt, Ronald, 49, 51, 60-61
Lissner, Kate, 41
listening, reinforcement in, 104
locomotion, 37-38, 57, 147
logic, of dynamics, 38
looking-glass self, 183
love, versus self-love, 136-168
Luce, R. D., 119
Lumsdaine, A. A., 90, 192
Lumsdaine, Marion H., 192

MacDougall, William, 184, 212
MacGregor, Douglas, 50
McGuire, W. J., 215
McPhee, W. N., 197
Mahler, Wera, 42
Malinowski, Bronislaw, 166
man, dependence of, 4; dual nature of, 4; economic, 79; egocentric, 4; eight stages of, 150; irrational, 4; nature of, 3-4; sociocentric, 4; transformation of in society, 24
mand, in verbal behavior, 104-105
manic-depressive psychosis, 144

manner, appearance and, in presentation of self, 205
Margaret, G. Ann, 52
Margenau, Henry, 6, 9
Martindale, Don, 3
Marx, Karl, 26, 213
Marxism, 159
Maslow, A. H., 12, 159
masochism, 134, 159
Massachusetts Institute of Technology, 15
masturbation, 146
mathematical game theory, 119-123
matrix, of social interaction, 119-123
matrix algebra, 35
maturity, adulthood and, 154
Maurer, D. W., 201
maximum-minimum principle, in Gestalt psychology, 18
maze learning, 89
Mead, George Herbert, 130-131, 183-191
Mead, Margaret, 166
Me–I relationship, 181-182
membership group, 191; *see also* group
mental activity, unconscious, 128
Merton, Robert K., 5, 176, 180, 189-203
Michigan, University of, 15, 51, 182
middle-range theory, 10
Mill, J. S., 31
Miller, Neal E., 10, 48, 86-90
Mind, Self and Society (G. H. Mead), 183
models, in behavior experiments, 95-96
Morris, C. W., 184, 186, 189
Moses and Monotheism (Freud), 127, 157
mother–child relationship, 144, 146-149
mother love, 144
motivation, achievement and, 53-54; Freudian theory of, 132-136; in Gestalt psychology, 22; incen-